Essentials
of
Insight Meditation
Practice

For there is suffering, but none who suffers;
Doing exists although there is no doer;
Extinction is but no extinguished person;
Although there is a path there is no goer.

~ VISUDDHIMAGGA

Essentials of Insight

Meditation Practice

A Pragmatic Approach to Vipassana

Venerable Sujiva

Buddhist Wisdom Centre
Petaling Jaya, Selangor, MALAYSIA
2000

Published by

♉♉♉

BUDDHIST WISDOM CENTRE

5, Jalan 16/3, 46350 Petaling Jaya, Selangor Darul Ehsan, Malaysia

Tel 603 7568019

Email bwc@quantrum.com.my

First published in 1991 under the title Pragmatic Approach to Vipassana.
This revised edition published in 2000.

Perpustakaan Negara Malaysia Cataloguing-in-Publication Data

Sujiva, 1951–
    Essentials of insight meditation practice : a pragmatic
    approach to vipassana / Venerable Sujiva.
    ISBN 983-9245-02-3
    1. Vipasyana (Buddhism). 2. Meditation (Buddhism).
    I. Title.
    294.3443

ISBN 983–9245-02-3

Cover photo: Auckland, New Zealand

Cover design & photography by Jotika
Layout & Design by Sukhi Hotu

Printed for free distribution by
The Corporate Body of the Buddha Educational Foundation
11F., 55 Hang Chow South Road Sec 1, Taipei, Taiwan, R.O.C.
Tel: 886-2-23951198 , Fax 886-2-23913415
Email: overseas@budaedu.org
Website:http://www.budaedu.org
This book is strictly for free distribution, it is not for sale.

Scriptural Foreword

Namo Tassa Bhagavato Arahato Sammasambuddhasa
The Four Foundations of Mindfulness

Thus have I heard.

At one time the Blessed One was living among the Kurus,
at Kammasadamma, a market-town of the Kuru people.

There the Blessed One addressed the monks thus: "Monks," and they
replied to him, "Venerable Sir." And the Blessed One spoke as follows:

*This is the sole way, monks, for the purification of beings, for the overcoming of
sorrow and lamentation, for the destroying of pain and grief, for reaching the right path,
for the realisation of Nibbana,
namely the Four Foundations of Mindfulness.*

What are the four? Herein (in this teaching) a monk dwells practising
body-contemplation on the body, ardent, clearly comprehending and mindful,
having overcome covetousness and grief concerning the world; he dwells
practising feeling-contemplation on feelings, ardent, clearly comprehending and
mindful, having overcome covetousness and grief concerning the world; he
dwells practising mind-contemplation on the mind, ardent, clearly
comprehending and mindful, having ovrecome covetousness and grief
concerning the world; he dwells practising mind-object-contemplation on mind-
objects, ardent, clearly comprehending and mindful, having overcome
covetousness and grief concerning the world.

A Word on Layout

Photographs of trees, plants and "nature" occurring randomly within the context of each chapter serve as a visual and mental rest for the reader. The "nature" pictures convey a feeling of "freedom". The ultimate aim of insight meditation is to "free" one from the unsatisfactoriness of cyclic existence.

Readers may also find numerous quotations of the Buddha's teaching on mindfulness, detachment and liberation throughout the entire book. Those verses act as a source of inspiration and purpose to put *vipassana* into practice—a practice that brings about *insight* into the three universal characteristics of unsatisfactoriness, impermanence and non-self which leads one into *detachment* and ultimate *liberation*.

Contents

Preface

This book is from a collection of talks given in the inaugural retreat I conducted at the Blue Mountains Insight Meditation Centre in Australia in March 1996. As my previous edition, *A Pragmatic Approach to the Practice of Vipassana Meditation*, is no longer in print, this edition will serve a similar purpose in guiding new vipassana yogis in their practice, comprising just the necessary information needed. It has been a long time since the previous edition was published and my teachings have also grown, necessitating the addition of new points.

However, not everything can be said in a ten-day course. There are things mentioned in the previous edition which were not expanded upon, such as details for the balancing of the five controlling faculties . These have now been added into the current edition to make it more comprehensive.

Many thanks to those who made this book available, such as Hor Tuck Loon and Lai Fun, David Llewelyn, Quek Jin Keat, Tan Joo Lan and the many donors.

Sujiva
BUDDHIST WISDOM CENTRE,
Petaling Jaya, Malaysia

Essentials
of
Insight Meditation
Practice

A Pragmatic Approach to Vipassana

I will teach you monks, the Four Foundations of Mindfulness,
the cultivation thereof and the practice leading to
the cultivation of the Four Foundations of Mindfulness.
Do you listen to it.

And what, monks, is a Foundation of Mindfulness?

Herein a monk dwells contemplating the body in the body
feelings in the feelings
consciousness in the consciousness
mind-objects in the mind-objects
ardent, clearly comprehending and mindful
having overcome covetousness and grief in the world.

And of what sort, monks,
is the cultivation of a Foundation of Mindfulness?
Herein a monk dwells contemplating the fall of things in the body.
He so dwells contemplating both the rise and fall of things in the body,
ardent, clearly comprehending and mindful
having overcome covetousness and grief in the world.

And of what sort, monks, is the practice leading to
the cultivation of a Foundation of Mindfulness?
It is just this Noble Eightfold Way,
that is: Right View, Right Thought, Right Speech,
Right Action, Right Livelihood, Right Effort,
Right Mindfulness, Right Concentration.

This, monks, is the practice leading to
the cultivation of the Foundations of Mindfulness.

Satipatthana Vipassana Meditation

In many Buddhist traditions, insight meditation is based on the Four Foundations of Mindfulness as mentioned in the Satipatthana Sutta.

The uniqueness of the Burmese/Mahasi approach lies in the using of the "rising" and "falling" movements of the abdomen (as one breathes) as a main object for the beginner. Later, more of the other objects are used. There is considerable flexibility and variation in the instructions given by different teachers. Therefore, in many instances, the decision on what step to take depends on individual experience and skill.

The Satipatthana or the Four Foundations of Mindfulness have been emphasised as the one and only way for the purification of beings. The discourse describes various meditation objects classified into four groupings. These are to be applied to develop mindfulness of things as they really are. They are:

- *Kayanupassana Satipatthana*
- *Vedananupassana Satipatthana*
- *Cittanupassana Satipatthana*
- *Dhammanupassana Satipatthana*

*When things become manifest
To the ardent meditating one,
All his doubts then vanish since
he has known
The utter destruction of conditions.*
UDANA 1.2

BODY CONTEMPLATION AS FOUNDATION OF MINDFULNESS
(Kayanupassana Satipatthana)

Within this foundation are various chapters:

1 breath
2 postures
3 clear comprehension
4 parts of the body impurities
5 four elements (earth, fire, water, and wind elements)
6-14 cemetery contemplation of corpses at different stages of decay.

It is clear that some of them are initially pure tranquillity meditation exercises but are later switched to insight meditation in the closing verse of Satipatthana Sutta—*He lives contemplating origination-things in the body, or he lives contemplating dissolution-things in the body, or he lives contemplating origination and dissolution-things in the body.*

FEELING CONTEMPLATION AS FOUNDATION OF MINDFULNESS
(Vedananupassana Satipatthana)

There are nine types of feelings here, which serve as objects of mindfulness. The first to the third are: pleasurable, painful, neither pleasurable nor painful.

These three are then further noted with regards to being carnal (fourth to sixth) or spiritual (seventh to ninth).

CONSCIOUSNESS CONTEMPLATION AS FOUNDATION OF
MINDFULNESS (Cittanupassana Satipatthana)

Those consciousness which can be the objects of mindfulness are:

1 consciousness with lust
2 consciousness freed from lust
3 consciousness with anger
4 consciousness freed from anger
5 consciousness with delusion

6 consciousness freed from delusion
7 consciousness that is shrunken
8 consciousness that is distracted
9 consciousness that has grown great/expanded
10 consciousness that has not grown great/expanded
11 consciousness which has some other mental state superior to it
12 consciousness which has no other mental state superior to it
13 consciousness which is quiet/tranquil
14 consciousness which is not quiet/tranquil
15 consciousness which is freed
16 consciousness which is not freed

MENTAL OBJECT CONTEMPLATION AS FOUNDATION OF MINDFULNESS (Dhammanupassana Satipatthana)

1 The five hindrances
2 The five aggregates of clinging
3 The six internal and six external sense-bases
4 The seven factors of enlightenment
5 The four noble truths

The body-contemplations (*Kayanupassana Satipatthana*) are taken as the first main objects to build up mindfulness because they are:

1 gross, therefore easily noticeable
2 present to some degree or most of the time and is practical
3 not painful as in feelings. Thus, can be observed over fairly long periods of time without building up much stress.

As one mindfully observes material processes, one naturally cannot help but also notice the mental phenomena which occur hand in hand. To begin with, strong pain may arise with longer sittings and many habitual defilements and thoughts will also assail the mind.

Later, more subtle objects can also be noticed fairly easily with

*Those who have expelled evil states
And who fare ever mindful,
The awakened ones who have
destroyed the fetters—
They are the brahmins in the world.
UDANA 1.5*

improvement in mindfulness and concentration. In the beginning, the meditation objects met with during a sitting meditation session are:

- "Rising" and "falling" of abdomen
- "Sitting" and "touching" sensations
- Thinking or restlessness
- Sleepiness
- Hearing of sound
- Painful and pleasurable feelings

"Rising" and "falling" of abdomen is first used as the main object but when it becomes fainter and infrequent, "sitting" and "touching" sensations are then used as a substitute. Pain and feelings may then take over during longer sittings. Other less frequent objects are taken note of and after they disappear, one returns to observe the main object.

In walking meditation, the same applies with the walking process as the main object and others (pain, thinking, seeing, hearing and others) as secondary objects.

In this way material and mental phenomena can be mindfully observed as they arise and pass away as processes.

Look at the people in the world, afflicted by ignorance,
Come into being, delighting in being, not freed.
Whatever forms of being exist, in any way, anywhere,
All these forms of being are impermanent,
Subject to suffering, of a nature to change.

On seeing this as it actually is with perfect wisdom
The craving for being is abandoned,
Yet one does not delight in non-being.
Nibbana is total dispassion and cessation
(Attained) with the complete destruction of cravings.

A bhikkhu whose cravings are extinguished
By not grasping has no renewal of being.
Mara is vanquished, the battle is won:
The stable one has passed beyond all forms of being.

UDANA 3.10 (EXTRACT)

Basic Preparatory Instructions

The main aim of Buddhist Meditation is to purify the mind of all negative tendencies—such as greed, anger and delusion, through mind control. When all negative tendencies are removed, the mind will be freed from suffering.

The actual aim is very exalted, as it aims at the complete eradication of suffering. This process does not only happen in or cover one existence, it spans over limitless existences.

TRANQUILLITY AND INSIGHT MEDITATION

Generally, there are two types of meditation—tranquillity meditation and insight meditation. Whichever one you practise, the main factor in mental development is mindfulness.

Tranquillity meditation is the concentration of the tranquil and peaceful mind. It involves the very controlled or mindful action of holding the mind to an object, and does not allow the mind to wander. The mind remains completely still, like a stilled candle, neither flickering nor fluttering. This is the nature of tranquillity meditation. When this happens, the mind becomes very peaceful and powerful, because it is a concentration of pure states of mind.

When a brahmin has gone beyond
In things pertaining to himself,*
Then he has surpassed the reach
Of this goblin and his noisy din.
UDANA 1.7

*The Five Aggregates

Insight meditation is different. It does not just involve holding the mind still. It also involves penetrative observation. This kind of penetrative observation, without any thinking, without any conceptualisation, allows the mind to realise the true nature of things as they really are, things like the nature of our mind and body processes, the nature of the person and the nature of the world. With the realisation of the nature of existence, the mind no longer has conflicts with the nature, the mind becomes together with nature, and the mind realises the true nature of things. Consequently, the mind becomes purified. In the process, the mind transcends everything—it transcends conceptual reality, it transcends conditioned reality and finally it goes into absolute reality, which is the unchanging state. After much practice, it is this that is experienced by the mind.

At the start of our practice, we have to recognise the nature of mindfulness, which we have to develop for as long as we are alive. The presence of mindfulness is what really makes the difference between true happiness and false happiness. It can also make the difference between life and death.

At the start of our practice, we have to recognise the nature of mindfulness.

TRUE HAPPINESS AND FALSE HAPPINESS

True happiness is when we really have peace of mind. False happiness is when greed and excitement overcome the mind—the mind is agitated. This can become a matter of life and death, because sometimes when we are not mindful, we can meet with an accident. Mindfulness can also make the difference between heaven and hell, because in the Buddha's teaching, kamma resultant depends on good and evil actions. This kamma resultant will bring us to heaven, earth, or hell respectively. Finally, mindfulness makes the difference between *Nibbana* and *Samsara*—eternal happiness and eternal suffering. Therefore, no matter how we live, where we live, who we are—this mindfulness when practised will make a significant difference.

Since what we are trying to develop is mindfulness, it will be necessary to have a clear idea on the nature of mindfulness.

THE NATURE OF MINDFULNESS

There are many factors in mindfulness. The first factor is **clarity of the mind**. It is a mind that is clear and pure—clear from all greed, anger, dullness, delusion and hallucination. When there is greed or craving, anger or hatred, delusion or dullness, the mind is not clear. For example, when a person is intoxicated with alcohol, would you say that his mind is clear? His mind is not clear, but muddled. All he wants is to drink more alcohol and drown his sorrows. Another example is when a person is angry, loses his temper, is very sad or depressed. Would you think his mind is clear? No, his mind is not clear. His mind is heavy, dark, agitated, dull, and stupid. So, mindfulness is a state of mind when you are very alert, then the mind is clear and undisturbed—this is called clarity of mind—it is like clear water; it is like the clear sky.

The second factor of the nature of mindfulness is **stability, calmness and peace.** Let us compare the opposites; when a person's mind is experiencing anger—it is agitated, not calm, not stable. It is disturbed like agitated or boiling water. When the mind is experiencing craving, it is excited and disturbed, not calm and steady. When the mind is not calm, peaceful, and steady, it is in a confused state, it is dull. The mind which is calm, peaceful, and steady, is just like when we first come out from a good meditation or a good sleep— we have no worries. It is just like when we are strolling by the beach or when we sit at home with a good book. Our mind then is calm and steady although it is not to the level that we would get in meditation. When we are already in a state of calmness, steadiness, and peacefulness, should someone scold us, we remain calm and not disturbed. When this happens, the state of mindfulness is peaceful, happy and stress free. It is the nature of mindfulness that when clarity of mind, stability, calmness and peace have been achieved, a third factor may come into play.

The third factor is **alertness** of the mind. The mind becomes sensitive, not in a bad way, but sensitive in a good way. Being sensitive in a bad way is when somebody says something that is annoying and we become disturbed. Being sensitive in a good way is like a person

Where neither water nor yet earth
Nor fire nor air gain a foothold,
There gleam no stars,
  no sun sheds light,
There shines no moon, yet there is
  no darkness reigns.
When a sage, a brahmin,
  has come to know this
For himself through his own wisdom,
Then he is freed from form
  and formless.
Freed from pleasure and from pain.
UDANA ' 10

who is very calm, alert and stable but very perceptive about what is going on. One knows exactly in detail and in great clarity what is actually happening. Please bear in mind this quality of mindfulness. Think about how the state of mindfulness is like when you are having it. When we are able to know that this quality is in the mind, we can safely say that we are mindful.

There is another type of mindfulness with similar qualities that are found in insight meditation. This is like a light, like an **awareness** that is concentrated within ourselves, into our own mind and body processes. The main aim of insight meditation is to look within and discover our own natures. Because we do not understand what our own natures are, defilements such as greed, anger, and delusion, and all suffering arise.

There are certain special qualities connected with **mindfulness in insight meditation**. First, it is **not thinking**. We do not think, we just observe. It does not mean that during a retreat, we do not think at all. We still think, but we are mindful of the thinking. However, in the actual meditation exercise, the thinking is put aside, and the mind with concentrated awareness observes without thinking. Secondly, when we are without thinking, the **mind is kept to the present or present occurrences**. We do not go to the past or the future. We keep the mind in the so-called present and know what is happening to our meditation object. When we can do that, then our mindfulness is concentrated precisely on what is happening to our meditation object.

The main aim of insight meditation is to look within and discover our own natures.

In brief, the qualities of mindfulness are:

- The mind is clear, without greed, anger, and delusion. The mind should be clear of all confusion and agitation.
- The mind is stable, calm, undisturbed, and peaceful.
- Having made our mind clear, calm, stable, and undisturbed, we then make the awareness sharp and sensitive. When the awareness is sharp and sensitive, we then direct it precisely at our meditation object. When we can direct our awareness repeatedly at our meditation object, all the while knowing

what is happening at the present moment, then the process of insight development arises.

How will we move about in this world if we are mindful? We move about happily, calmly and efficiently. Here we are developing not only the mindfulness that is operating in the world. We are trying to develop something more than that, although eventually it will also bring about such a state in the world.

MEDITATION RETREAT

During actual meditation, when all our energy and aim is directed to the realisation of what is happening within us, within our mind and body processes, that is the time when we get the most benefit. In a retreat, our life is simplified to a minimum number of activities. It can be divided into three types of activities: walking meditation, sitting meditation and other daily activities. Whether it is walking meditation, sitting meditation or other daily activities, the purpose of the practice is:

- To keep the mind in the present moment.
- To keep mindfulness clear, calm and in the present moment.
- To see what is happening to our meditation object.

In walking meditation, the object of the mindfulness is the walking process. In sitting meditation, the object is the "rising" and "falling" process of the abdomen; and in other daily activities, the object is to know what we are doing.

WALKING PROCESS

The walking process can be generally divided into three types:

- Brisk walking
- Moderate walking
- Slow walking

Blissful is passionlessness in the world,
The overcoming of sensual desires;
But the abolition of the conceit
    "I am"—
That is truly the supreme bliss.
UDANA 2.1

Brisk walking

Brisk walking is a walk that is faster than our normal walk. It can be extended to almost a run. When we perform brisk walking, we just keep our mind on the footstep. To keep our mind on the footstep, we may say mentally "right, left, right, left..." or "stepping, stepping..." Usually walking is done in a straight line, covering a not too long distance. At the end of the walking path, we turn.

In long retreats, brisk walking is sometimes used as an exercise because of the long hours of sitting. Sometimes, if we feel sleepy, brisk walking is used. After doing brisk walking for five or ten minutes, we can then change to the moderate walk.

Moderate walking

During a short retreat, most of the walking is done at a moderate pace. First, we must be aware of our standing posture. The standing posture is a good grounding to bring our mindfulness down at our feet. When we are standing, take a deep breath and relax. Relaxation is one of the first steps to arousing mindfulness. When we are tense, we cannot relax and be mindful. When we know that our body is relaxed, let our mind be clear, without any thinking. Just keep the mind calm, clear and mentally relaxed.

During walking meditation our eyes are downcast but not looking down. Our eyelids are half-closed when we are relaxed. Only when we really want to look at something, do we look straight ahead. Otherwise when we are relaxed, our eyes are downcast.

When the eyes are downcast, the eyes are not looking at what is on the floor. We are not focusing on anything because our awareness is brought to the soles of our feet. When we bring the awareness from the head to the soles of the feet, we will know that the body is standing erect and firm. We can say in our mind "standing, standing..." and at the same time be aware of the whole body. We have to make sure that we have the real awareness which has been described earlier—clear, steady, calm, very alert and sensitive to the sensation of the body standing. Then we bring the awareness to the soles of the feet. The awareness is like a light shining precisely onto the spot. We keep our mind very calm and sensitive, clear and alert, and then we direct the awareness—rightly aimed.

We will feel, with the sole of the feet on the ground, the sensations there—which may be weight, texture, heat, coolness or just clear awareness.

When we find that we can feel a lot of sensations, we will normally take that for granted. We need to focus our awareness on the sensations. All these sensations are basic experiences before the other form of thought processes—the idea of who we are, what we are, what is happening around us—begins. When we know these sensations, we think about them and then the mind creates based on them. Therefore, sensations are a more basic form of experience and existence, the beginning before all complicated things arise.

When we have become aware of the sensations, we then start walking—right step, left step, right step, left step, saying in our minds "right step, left step, right step, left step." Mentally saying "right step, left step" helps us keep our minds on the object; otherwise we will start thinking.

Usually the hands are folded in front of or at the back of the body. The feet should not be lifted too high; otherwise, you will not be stable. The space between our feet should not be too far apart, otherwise your walking will not be stable too. The pace of walking should be moderately slow and you should just take steps which are half the normal distance. When you move more slowly, you will find the feet as if gliding parallel to the ground. You do not have to purposely lift your leg up high. When the body shifts forward, the heel automatically turns up; you do not have to turn your heel to the maximum, only slightly.

Then push the foot forward and step down. The stepping down should be levelled, like a slow natural walk. Make sure that you are mindful, clear, stable, peaceful, and very alert, aiming precisely at what is happening at the footstep. It may seem a very simple process, but the mind is really unruly. It may not be focused at the foot for long but goes somewhere else—thinking, or it becomes dull—there is no more mindfulness.

Whatever bliss in the world is
found in sensual pleasures
And whatever there is of
heavenly bliss,
These are not worth
a sixteenth part
Of the bliss of craving's
destruction.
UDANA 2.2

Sometimes during a stretch of walking, the thinking can arise many times and you may have to stop many times.

Thinking during walking meditation

There are two types of "thinking:"

1 We know that we are thinking. Once we know that we are thinking, the thinking goes away. In this case, we do not have to stop walking.

2 We know that we are thinking but we are unable to stop thinking. In this case, we have to stop and say in our mind "thinking, thinking..." When we are aware of the thinking, it will go off. When the thinking goes off, we are aware again. Then we can bring our mind to the sole of the feet and start once again.

Sometimes during a stretch of walking, the thinking can arise many times and you may have to stop many times. Another thing that can happen is boredom. As we walk, we may start looking around. When we find ourselves looking around, we must say mentally "looking, looking." When we find that we are not doing what we should be doing, we stand and bring the mind back to "standing, standing" and start all over. When the mind is no more mindful, it is as if our motorbike has overturned, or if we are surfing, it is as if the surfboard has overturned in the water and we have to bring ourselves back to balance again. This is "surf walking" and the waves are all the phenomena around. Once we find ourselves losing mindfulness, we should stand and balance ourselves with mindfulness and start all over.

At certain times, the mind tends to be very disturbed. Even when we stop and mentally say "thinking, thinking..." the mind still thinks. In this case, we have to resort to the fast walking "right, left, right, left..." keeping a continuous pace.

Observation in walking meditation

Once we get into the feel of it and there is no more thinking, the mind follows a certain rhythm. When the mind follows a certain rhythm and pace of walking, it is easier to follow the processes. It is just like when we are dancing, we get into the rhythm of the dance.

We will find the mind following our walking at a certain pace—at a certain rhythm—comfortably, and if we keep at it, the awareness and the concentration will build up. Thus, there are three processes here:

1 **Arousing the awareness**—we tell ourselves to relax and clear our mind; to be mindful of what is happening every time we think, whether the mind is dull, or wanders elsewhere. When we think, or when the mind is dull or wanders elsewhere, it means we are not mindful, so we need to bring back the awareness and stabilise ourselves.

2 Once our mindfulness is aroused, we **follow the object** with awareness—the footsteps "right, left, right, left..." Unlike shooting a fixed target, this is more like shooting a moving object—like a video camera following movement.

3 Once we can follow the object over a period of time, we come to the third phase of meditation—the actual phase of insight meditation—**observation**. If we cannot follow the object properly, the observation cannot be done very well.

During this third phase of meditation, observation of the walking must be done at a much slower pace. Here, we are observing the sensations, eg, when we lift our hind foot, there is a feeling of a pulling force. How this is being experienced will depend on how clear and sharp our aim is at that process. At that point when our foot starts lifting, what is the sensation like? To give an example, if we are lifting our bag, how do we feel? When the muscles pull, we can feel the tension of lifting up. If the bag is not so heavy, we do not feel the tension; we just feel the lifting movement. We do not choose what to experience. We just direct our mind onto the object and allow our mind to pick up the experience.

When we lift our leg, we mentally say "lifting, lifting" and we observe the lifting sensations.

When we push, we mentally say "pushing, pushing" and we note the pushing sensation. The pushing sensation is like when we push our cart in the supermarket. How does the pushing feel like? Of course, it might feel a bit heavier after

Discomfort in the guise of pleasure,
The unloved in the guise of love,
Suffering in the guise of bliss
Overpower the heedless one.
UDANA 2.8

a meal, but if our mind feels light then the movement is faster and we feel only the pushing sensations.

When we step, we mentally say "stepping, stepping" and feel the stepping sensations. It is like putting our bag down again. How do we feel? There is a kind of relaxing sensation. Therefore, as we put our foot down, touching the floor, we can feel the sensations of the sole again. We follow each step—the sequence or the series of processes of the sensations—happening from the calf to the sole. It is here that we begin to discover what is happening before the conceptualisation takes place. It is the reality that is happening within us all.

SITTING MEDITATION

Having done walking meditation, we proceed to the sitting posture. As in walking meditation, we should first relax. We take a deep breath to relax. Relaxation is one of the first conditions for mindfulness to arise. Having relaxed ourselves and made the mind clear, we then direct our **awareness to the abdomen**. When we breathe in and out, there is a movement at the abdomen, which comes with the breathing. We call the outward movement or upward movement, the **"rising."** We call the downward or the inward movement, the **"falling."** Beginners may not be so aware of this sensation, so one is advised to put the hand or fold it at the abdomen.

To feel the movement better, take a few deep breaths. When the abdomen rises, we mentally say "rising" and when it falls, we mentally say "falling." When our mind is thinking, sleepy or dull, then we cannot feel the "rising" and "falling" sensations at all. When the "rising" and "falling" sensation is not there, this usually means that we are not mindful. It is the same way as in walking meditation, first be mindful and then follow the object precisely.

Once we can follow the "rising" and "falling" of the abdomen with mindfulness, concentration will be built-up. When the

VARIOUS SITTING POSTURES

Both legs are placed evenly on the ground one in front of the other.

One leg is placed in front whilst the other is curled to the back.

Both feet are placed right up onto the thighs.

Both legs are curled to the back.

One foot is placed on the calf (lower part of the leg while the other is tucked underneath).

concentration is being built-up and we can follow each "rising" and "falling" carefully from beginning to end, we can observe the sensations. It is like observing the waves going up and down. It comes up and down according to conditions. We then follow it more closely and precisely, as if our mind is getting closer and closer to the waves—"rising" and "falling"—moving up and down. Then we observe how it goes up part by part until it stops, and then part by part or moment-to-moment until it goes down in a similar way. Be mindful, follow, and observe the processes.

Of course, we may not be able to follow the object and ride on it so easily. What happens is that after a while, because the mindfulness is not stable—our grounding is not stable—it "flips" over. That means the waves or the thoughts will come and splash us off, and we are lost in thought again. The moment we come to our senses, "Oh! I have been thinking! My mind has wandered!" we should note "thinking, thinking…, aware, aware…" Then when we are aware, the thoughts will go off. If we ride with the thoughts, there is no end to it, and we will most probably spend the whole session thinking. When the thoughts disappear, we stabilise our mindfulness again and look for our object—how it goes up and down.

Another possibility is that instead of thinking, we sink into the water and drown, ie, we fall asleep and do not know what is happening. The moment we come to our

It is like observing the waves going up and down.

senses, we know "Ah! Now I am feeling sleepy, sleepy… Be awake, be awake…" We open our eyes, be awake and start all over again.

In the beginning, there will be countless number of times when we are thinking or sleeping. Each time, as soon as we know that we are thinking or sleeping, we must arouse our awareness and put the awareness back into the "rising" and "falling." With practice, we will be able to be mindful, to follow and observe the waves more closely and precisely.

Distractions during sitting meditation

During sitting meditation, things do happen and there could be complications. Many distractions await us as we sit. One of them is pain. We try not to be bothered by little pains here and there. We keep on noting our "rising" and "falling." At times, the pain can become very intense, particularly, if we are not used to sitting cross-legged on the floor for a long period; or if an itch arises from a mosquito bite. If the pain is very strong, we abandon the main object of "rising" and "falling." We switch to the pain or itch as the main object for the arousing of awareness. The principle is the same, make sure our mind is clear, alert, stable, and mindful, and then observe the pain. The mindfulness is now directed to the pain and is observing it. We watch and feel how the pain behaves—the types of pain, how they come and go—without being affected by it. If we watch the pain long enough, it may go away. Then we return to the "rising" and "falling." If the pain does not go away and we cannot bear with it anymore, we then shift our posture mindfully. We stretch out our legs mindfully before crossing them back into position. The mind will be calm again, and we direct it back to the "rising" and "falling."

Briefly, make sure that the mind is neither thinking nor sleepy. If the mind is thinking or sleepy then we have to bring the awareness back—bring the mind to the meditation object. If "rising" and "falling" is there, stay with it. If pain is much clearer and stronger, we watch the pain until we cannot bear it anymore or until it goes away. Then we return to the awareness of "rising" and "falling." The main thing is to keep clear awareness and mindfulness on your present feeling or sensations.

Sometimes, the "rising" and "falling" of the abdomen is not discernable. "Rising" and "falling" is not always there and not the same all the time. It changes—sometimes fast, sometimes slow, sometimes long, sometimes short, sometimes wave-like or sometimes "tense." It is like a wave that is never the same all the time. Sometimes the wave is high, sometimes it is low; sometimes it is

In whom exist no inner stirrings,
Having passed beyond being this or that,
Free from fear, blissful and sorrowless,
The devas are not capable of seeing him.
UDANA 2.10

very rough, sometimes it is very smooth. Whatever the sensation is, we try to follow it and know it as it is—that is the training in mindfulness.

Sitting and Touching method

When the "rising" and "falling" is not discernable, we go back to the "sitting" and "touching." We are aware of the posterior coming in contact with the cushion or the floor and can feel the sensation there. As we watch, we mentally say "touching, touching..." At first, we may not feel anything but if we really concentrate and hold our mind on the touch point long enough, a series or a wave of sensations will come one after another and this becomes our object of contemplation. In the beginning, we may not have to use a lot of "sitting" and "touching" as "rising" and "falling" is present most of the time. If "rising" and "falling" is not there, we go to "touching" and alternate it with "sitting," ie, watching the tension at the spine; mentally say "touching, touching, sitting, sitting, touching, touching..." while observing. Usually we do not have to watch "sitting" and "touching" that long. When "rising" and "falling" stops for a while, we go to "touching" then come back again to "rising" and "falling." When "rising" and "falling" goes off for a longer period, we observe more touching sensations at the posterior and legs—"touching," "touching," followed by the tension at the spine—"sitting." Then we go back to "rising" and "falling."

Why do you want to do this? The reason is to maintain the continuity of mindfulness, calmness and clear awareness, that is so beneficial for us. Usually, a person is aware only for a short period— he lacks continuity and his mindfulness is not deep. He is not able to bring lasting peace and deep understanding within himself. If we are trained to maintain the continuity of this kind of clear awareness, then the understanding within oneself will last longer and deeper. If one carries on further, the deep understanding will become insight realisation which can purify our mind and bring satisfying happiness.

OTHER DAILY ACTIVITIES

When we have understood how sitting and walking meditation is done, we can apply the method to other daily activities that are very much part of our life, eg, going to the toilet to answer the call of nature. We have to be mindful to follow and **observe all the activities** that happen from the moment we go to the toilet until we have finished answering the call of nature. When we are eating or drinking water, we have to practise awareness as well. For example, when drinking water, we have to be aware of looking at the water, looking at the cup, how we move our hands, how our hand brings the cup of water to our mouth, how we drink the water, how the water goes into our throat, the experience of coolness of the water, the experience of the sensations and how the sensations come and go.

Besides these daily activities, try also to **catch the intention** or **impulse**. Between every action, sitting and walking, walking and standing, etc, there is an intention or impulse. For example, after sitting for a long time, say half an hour, we may want to get up. We do not feel like sitting anymore. The mind will tell us "I do not want to sit anymore. I want to get up." It comes as an urge, it comes as an intention. Sometimes, it comes with reasoning. When this arises, we have to take note of it. Other examples—intention to wake up, to stand up and walk, to sit down. We have to take note of all these intentions because these are part of the mind and body processes and if we want continuous mindfulness, we have to note them.

We must be very aware of all these activities. When we are aware of them, the mind becomes very peaceful, calm, and happy. As we progress further, we realise that all these are natural phenomena. In the deeper aspect of the practice, when the mindfulness is continuous, then the mind can really be concentrated in the correct and pure way, and the mind sinks and merges with each object that comes and goes. Then we can understand the true nature of the object, the reality of which is described as impermanent, suffering and non-self.

That bhikkhu who has crossed the mire,
Crushed the thorn of sensual desire,
And reached the destruction of delusion
Is not perturbed by pleasures and pains.
UDANA 3.2

Whoso has faith and wisdom yoked in harness,
With conscience as the pole, the mind as reins
And mindfulness as watchful charioteer,
Goes in a chariot equipped with virtue,
Its axle meditation, energy its wheels
Mind's equipoise its even shaft,
Desirelessness its drapery, his arms
Are freedom from all malice, harmlessness,
Detachment of the mind; his leather coat
Forbearance.
Furnished thus, the chariot
Rolls on from bondage to security.

Built by oneself alone is it,
This vehicle divine and unsurpassed.
In it the wise are carried from the world,
In it they drive to certain victory.

MAHAVAGGA XLV 4

Practical Aspects of Satipatthana Practice

I n Malaysia, the interest in Vipassana is apparently growing but not many have the opportunity to obtain proper instructions from a meditation teacher. This is only to be expected considering how recent interest in meditation (or even active interest in Buddhism) has been. Furthermore, the training of a Vipassana teacher requires time as personal experience also counts a lot.

Books, however, can be of great help. But, there is a lack of books on meditation. Also, the few good meditation manuals available may be costly and not readily available. Take for example the *Visuddhimagga* (Path of Purification), an authoritative commentary and manual used by meditation masters. It is not on sale in most bookshops and also, not many can afford it.

Instructions given in many books are usually general. Each individual, however, has his own particular tendencies and characteristics. They also react differently in different environments and circumstances. This is where a teacher is needed most. Precise instructions, which only a teacher observing a meditator can give, will make a world of difference. A teacher also helps in many other ways such as inspiring confidence, giving encouragement and correcting one's errors before they go "out of hand."

Just as a mountain made of solid rock
Stands firm and unshakeable,
Even so,
*   when delusion is destroyed,*
A bhikkhu, like a mountain,
*   is not perturbed.*
UDANA 3.4

Another aspect to consider is the "variations" in meditation instructions. We can also expect this because there are more than one way of handling a problem. But, which one is the best? Obviously, only a teacher on hand would be in a better position to judge and decide. The teacher would also have to know all the various ways to solve a problem before he can select the best approach. He would have to use his wisdom and perhaps, some common sense. In this chapter, I will venture to give some suggestions, discuss the more common problems encountered by meditators, clear up some misconceptions and try to put Vipassana in its proper perspective without too many technical jargons.

MINDFULNESS

One may have read about mindfulness many times before and yet sometimes still feel uncertain as to whether one is mindful or not. Mindfulness is a mental state often described as "thoroughness," "alertness" or "awareness."

Mindfulness is actually a type of knowing and should be differentiated from just knowing. A mad man knows things his own way but he is far from mindful. Mindfulness cannot occur when there is greed, anger, or delusion. When one is mindful, there is, at that moment of mindfulness, no greed, anger, or delusion. One who is mindful is in full control (of his mind) and is in a position to handle well any situation he is in.

In meditation, one must not just know an object; one must know it mindfully. A good illustration is the difference between just tolerating the pain and watching it mindfully. Constant drilling of this point in a retreat has been found to be necessary.

Another mistake is, trying too hard to be mindful. A meditator can become so obsessed with trying to be mindful that every moment he is worried about whether he has been mindful or not. When such tension and distraction arise, we can be sure that things are not quite right. Relaxation, or rather, relaxed mindfulness, is the answer.

Sometimes, adopting a "could not be bothered attitude" about it could help to ease the tension. In other words, allow the mindfulness time to gradually and naturally develop.

Yet another common mistake is to put concentration over mindfulness. If one can be mindful for a continuous period of time, one becomes concentrated in mindfulness. On the other hand, if one is concentrating without mindfulness, then it becomes wrong concentration which can make you become "abnormal." The point to be emphasised here is that one should first understand the correct method before pushing oneself in one's meditation. Pushing oneself too much without correct understanding of the method indicates a lack of mindfulness and a compulsive temperament.

Doing more walking meditation is usually recommended to the beginner rather than sittings which are also not allowed to be prolonged. The reason is that it is easier to be mindful when walking because the objects are grosser and easier to watch. On the other hand, there is a tendency to think or be obsessed in trying to get concentration during sittings. The meditator must always remember that mindfulness must be given the foremost priority.

In meditation, one must try not to think. To experience the truth directly one cannot speculate or have ideas about it. It can be realised only through bare attention. If thinking arises, it should be dealt with in the correct way (which I will explain later under Cittanupassana).

When one is mindful without thinking, it also means that one is not to think about the past or future. Mindfulness can only dwell in the present occurrence of a phenomena, which is experienced as a specific characteristic such as hardness, heat, etc.

All this can be summarised in one sentence: "One should be mindful with bare attention on the presently occurring phenomena which appears to the mind as a specific characteristic."

There will be many characteristics (of heat, cold, hardness, softness, and vibrations etc) experienced in the course of an hour's meditation. With increased mindfulness, one will get to see their relationships with one another. This will lead to direct experience of the three general characteristics of existence—Dukkha, Anicca, and

With mindfulness of the body established,
Controlled over contact's sixfold base,
A bhikkhu who is always concentrated
Can know Nibbana for himself.
UDANA 3.5

Anatta (suffering, impermanence, and non-self). The end result is the elimination of defilements and therefore, suffering.

MINDFULNESS OF THE BODY
(Kayanupassana Satipatthana)

Mindfulness with regards to the body is usually practised first before the other three Satipatthana (of feelings, consciousness and mental objects). This is because the objects involved in mindfulness of the body are relatively grosser. It is easier to build up mindfulness on gross objects than subtle ones. Some of the objects contemplated upon— parts of the body, breath and corpses—are basically to do with pure tranquillity exercises. From tranquillity, one later advances to the practice of Vipassana. In the Abhidhamma, this group of body objects is classified under *rupakhanda* (material aggregates). The beginner is also taught to be mindful of the four postures: sitting, walking, standing and lying down.

Sitting

In practice, one notes "sitting" and "touching." What does one actually do or note? Some visualises the body sitting. This is not correct as visual images are not real. The proper way is just to watch and experience phenomena.

What does one watch? Directly, we say we watch the element of wind which may be expressed in tension, firmness, supporting, pulling or vibration. As one watches with just bare attention, it becomes clearly evident that there is no "I" or "being" in this body but just physical processes or forces taking place. With stronger mindfulness, one would see these processes changing in diverse ways. In the midst of noting the sitting posture, ie the tension and stiffness etc, one will also pick up many other sensations such as heat or coolness and mental phenomena like pain or external phenomena such as sound. In other words, when we note "sitting" mentally, we are just using it as a label to help us direct our mind to watching the realities involved

① Rising ② Falling ③ Sitting ④-⑫ Sitting Posture indicating various touching points

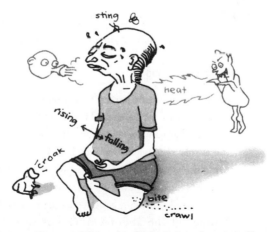

Sitting Posture with some of the many objects that can be noted with mindfulness

in sitting. The labelling can be said to point to a window to which we direct our mindfulness. It helps us hold our mind to the meditation object and thereby, develops the concentration which sees, through mindfulness and bare attention, the realities that occur there. Here, we cannot choose what we see; we only direct our mindfulness to the "window" and observe whatever arises.

Touching

One initially observes the area where the **posterior** and legs are in contact with the seat. A number of touch points can be discerned. One can watch these touch points systematically to increase concentration. The time spent in observing one point varies with the state of mind and clarity of the object. The clearer the object, the longer one can watch it. On the other hand, if it is vague and one is sleepy, one should move more quickly from one object to another. "Touching" is also noted alternately with "sitting." As in watching other objects, we are actually watching the characteristics of the elements arising and passing away when we note "touching." (Refer to diagram on opposite page for the location of touch points given by a manual of Vipassana. The "model" used is, however, not the one in the original drawing).

The clearer the object, the longer one can watch it.

Rising and Falling

When sitting, the beginner is also taught to watch the "rising" and "falling" of the abdomen. The "rising" and "falling" can also be considered as windows through which we see more and more things. One is told that when one watches the rise and fall, one is actually noting the wind element as expressed by movement or motion. But ultimately, one also watches many other things.

One is also initially taught to start by watching the "rising" and "falling" of the abdomen. This is to help us build up our concentration. But, in no way should one be obsessed with the rise and fall to the extent that we try to "hold on" to it or control it (by unnatural breathing). The "rising" or "falling" is also not constant and it may disappear while one is watching it, in which case, one should switch to another "window."

A question often asked is: why should one not watch the breathing at the tip of the nose or lips instead of the abdomen? Watching the breath at the nostrils is well-known to produce concentration. One meditation teacher remarked that *nama-rupa* (mind and matter) can be more easily discerned when one watches the "rising" and "falling" of the abdomen. The breathing (noted) at the abdomen is clearly grosser than that at the nose tip. The three characteristics of suffering, change and non-self are also more clearly manifested. In this way, Right Concentration, which in this case is momentary, aimed at realities and with mindfulness rather than concentration being predominant, is developed. Again, visualisation, counting or controlled breathing are disallowed here (as one is doing Vipassana which basically means watching realities).

Walking

Beginners are usually advised to do more walking than sitting. One teacher had remarked that every sitting should be preceded by walking. He also pointed out that Arahatship can be gained by just walking alone. Meditators have confirmed that after a good walking meditation session, they have a better sitting session. One should not underestimate the importance of walking or take it lightly. To just sit and neglect walking will make one like a lame man, walking on one leg! Walking serves many purposes in Vipassana. Firstly, one is unable to sit all the time and walking very mindfully bridges what would otherwise be termed as wide gaps or periods of non-mindfulness in our meditation. Continuity of mindfulness has always been stressed as otherwise, the concentration needed to develop insight cannot arise.

By itself, walking is also Vipassana *bhavana* (cultivation of insight). Every step is watched in detail. Also, it is the mind that directs the walking. "There is no one that walks..."—this knowledge will come

This world is subject to torment;
Afflicted by contact, it calls a
*   disease "self":*
For however it is conceived
It is ever otherwise than that.*

Becoming something other,
The world is held by being,
Is afflicted by being yet delights
*   in being.*
But what it delights in brings fear,
And what it fears is suffering.
Now this holy life is lived
In order to abandon being.

UDANA 3.10 (EXTRACT)

———
*The perpetual wandering on in the
round of birth and death.

PHASES OF STEPS IN WALKING MEDITATION

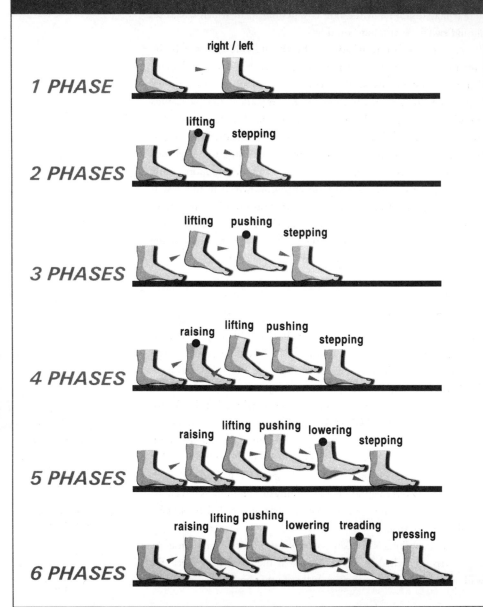

1 PHASE
right / left

2 PHASES
lifting
stepping

3 PHASES
lifting   pushing
stepping

4 PHASES
raising   lifting   pushing
stepping

5 PHASES
raising   lifting   pushing   lowering
stepping

6 PHASES
raising   lifting   pushing   lowering   treading
pressing

● Denotes new phases to note.

naturally by itself as the meditator conscientiously notes the ever-vanishing phenomena of physical and mental processes. Walking has also different characteristics from the sitting practice. Its objects are grosser and varied and so mindfulness can be built up easier. As such, it acts as a powerful balancing factor in that it keeps one's mind inclined towards Vipassana instead of Samatha (tranquillity meditation). In walking, we also note "turning," "seeing," "hearing," "intending," and thus, extend the practice of mindfulness into our daily activities.

The walking meditation is noted in an increasing number of phases in order to step up mindfulness and concentration. One is advised to adopt a pace that one feels most comfortable with. One should be careful in not putting the cart before the horse. Mindfulness is more important than the number of phases being noted. Once mindfulness is built up, the walking is slowed down by observing more phases, or rather, more phenomena. The beginner trying to do very slow walking can end up very tensed because he is trying to watch something he can hardly perceive.

A meditator (both a beginner or "veteran") should start his walking session with brisk steps. Brisk walking will help the mind get "accustomed" to the object. It also exercises the limbs and overcomes lethargy. Then again, there are those who "overdo" it by walking more briskly than is necessary and for too extended a period. They can end up quite distracted and exhausted. "Brisk enough to just arouse mindfulness" should be the attitude.

As one's practice advances, the walking processes are seen as a stream of mind and matter passing away in rapid succession. Walking would then be naturally very slow.

Walking may again be done in a relaxed or intense manner depending on whether energy is excessive or lacking. This is where the balancing of faculties comes in.

Other phenomena that are also watched during walking are sound, pain, intentions, seeing and hearing. One stops walking to note these if they are persistent and predominant. (See pages 33 and 34 for the diagrams on the various phases noted in walking. They are extracted from the same Vipassana manual referred to earlier).

Trivial thoughts, subtle thoughts,
Mental jerkings that follow one
  along:
Not understanding these mental
  thoughts,
One runs back and forth with
  wandering mind.

But having known these mental
  thoughts,
The ardent and mindful one
  restrains them.
An awakened one has entirely
  abandoned them,
These mental jerkings that follow
  one along.

UDANA 4.1

Standing

"Standing" is noted during walking, ie before one starts and as one reaches the end of the walk. In noting "standing" (the upright posture), one can also alternate with "touching" at the soles in contact with the ground. One teacher noted that standing is seldom done for long periods as it demands a lot of energy. Another said that it is not recommended for long periods, especially with women and children, because one may fall when the samadhi (concentration) induces a dream-like state and the knees may turn "soft." The teachers also said there had been reports of the body swaying and the meditator experiencing fears of toppling.

Standing has, however, been noted to be good for those with strong sleepiness. I have personally not met anyone falling down. Standing with feet slightly apart improves stability. We can sweep our mindfulness from head to toe or pick up and stay with whatever sensation is strongest. Sometimes, the "rising" and "falling" return and are noted.

Lying down

This posture is normally not done in serious practice as one will usually end up falling asleep. But, if one is very mindful in this posture, one can actually stay awake and alert, and end up not sleeping at all. But when one intends to sleep, one usually does the lying meditation with more general and superficial mindfulness.

The lying posture recommended is the "lion's posture"—with the body facing the right side. This is preferred to lying on the back or on the left side although both are also not prohibited.

Lying down is done mindfully and one notes "lying," "touching," and when "rising" and "falling" are clear, one notes "rising" and "falling." When pleasure arises, one notes "pleasure," and also with "thinking," "sound" "pain" etc. If one is good, one may actually watch the mind falling into the sleep state or arising from it. The relaxed position induces pleasure and thus, sleep. Energy is usually lacking.

Daily activities

The Satipatthana Sutta mentions some important ones—eating, chewing, answering calls of nature, wearing clothes, talking or remaining silent, looking in front or away.

The mind has to be trained to be mindful, at all times and in all aspects of life; only then will it be powerful, penetrative and useful. "At all times" indicates continuity; "in all aspects" indicates flexibility. There is no time where mindfulness cannot be developed; and insight can arise at any time for such a one.

Failure to apply good mindfulness in daily activities is to greatly limit the usefulness of it as well as obstruct us from integrating and balancing our spiritual and material pursuits.

There are many things to discover in our daily activities. Our failure to do so only shows how insensitive and blind we are to things that occur around us and which affect us. No wonder many lay people find it difficult to concentrate and meditate after work. They often neglect this most important part of their practice.

Details of this aspect are too wide and therefore, not dealt with here. We intend to have essays on this aspect printed later.

As for the mindfulness of the body, a sutta says that it is the one thing that has to be learned. If we perfect it, we shall, it assures us, attain the highest freedom.

MINDFULNESS OF FEELINGS
(Vedananupassana Satipatthana)

Mindfulness of feelings, when developed, overcomes the hallucination of happiness (ie taking what is not happiness for happiness). In order to break this hallucination, we have to see the truth of suffering.

One way in which suffering manifests itself clearly is through pain. Pain is also usually the clearest (though not pleasant) mental phenomenon that appears to a beginner. It offers the meditator something interesting to be mindful of. The danger is in reacting with anger or irritation towards the pain, in which case one is no longer

*Whatever an enemy might do
to an enemy,
Or a hater to those he hates,
A wrong directed mind
Can do even greater harm
than that.*

UDANA 4.3

mindful. If anger arises, a meditator should note it until it vanishes before returning to noting the pain. The idea is to be as relaxed and steady as possible while watching it. If one can do so, one will be able to see pain taking various forms—pulling pain, sharp pain, hot pain, aching pain, etc. If one is not mindful, one will not be able to face the pain. Concentration merely magnifies the intensity of the pain. Merely tolerating the pain with anger is also improper. It may even lead one to hysteria. It you cannot watch the pain, then ignore it. If it cannot be ignored, then change your posture mindfully or get up and do walking meditation (which can help to build up your mindfulness).

If we are able to see pain changing and taking various forms, our perception of change and impermanence (anicca) will become keener. The pain also becomes tolerable. A useful advice given is: "We do not watch the pain to make it go away but to develop our mindfulness and see its true nature." In this way we will become detached from the body as well as feelings.

Sometimes people give up because of fear that they may become paralysed or their health may be impaired. But many meditators have sat for hours and no one has ever become crippled or paralysed. The fear is actually unfounded.

When we watch pleasant feeling, we also do so to see its true nature, which we are told, is suffering or unsatisfactory. It usually arises when pain disappears or when we meet an agreeable object. We have to be mindful of pleasant feeling when it arises; otherwise we will enjoy and be attached to it. Just as anger is inherent in the painful object, attachment is inherent in the pleasant object.

There are some people who "fear" pleasure when it arises because they are afraid they may become attached to it. Pleasant feeling by itself, however, is not harmful. As long as we note it accordingly and are not attached to it, it is harmless. If we are mindful, our concentration will be enhanced. The thing to guard against is complacency which may lead us to wrong concentration or, as a lesser setback, cause us to fall asleep.

It is not very easy to see pleasant feelings change. If we can do so, they will normally pass away to something less pleasant or perhaps neutral. Pleasure also passes away; therefore it is unsatisfactory.

Usually, neutral feeling can only be perceived by the more advanced meditators. According to one teacher, it is noted only at the fifth stage of insight—the knowledge of dissolution. At this knowledge, we begin to abandon concepts and the true meaning of dukkha (suffering) reveals itself. In Buddhism, we sometimes come across the phrase "suffering of formations" (*sankhara dukkha*)—the unsatisfactoriness of incessant change. Words cannot describe the nature of this suffering, for words, after all, are only concepts. The nature of sankhara dukkha must be experienced and understood by each person for themselves. When we can really experience the incessant change, we shall also understand and appreciate the peace that comes from its cessation.

MINDFULNESS OF CONSCIOUSNESS
(Cittanupassana Satipatthana)

As in the other foundations of mindfulness, mindfulness of consciousness has a wide range of objects—from the gross to the subtle ones. Naturally, we develop mindfulness of consciousness with regards to grosser objects first. (Usually, we also note body objects first before proceeding to consciousness).

In developing mindfulness of consciousness, the first object that we should get acquainted with is "thinking." Thinking itself has many forms such as planning, imagining, reflecting, and so on. When we note "thinking," we just note that there is thinking; we do not go into the contents of the thoughts which will only cause us to think even more. Thinking is usually connected with concepts and things of the past and future. We should just note that there is "thinking," "planning," "reflecting," etc and not dwell on the concepts, or the past and future. If the thinking persists, it means that we are not mindful enough. If we are very mindful and exercise just bare

*Whose mind stands like a mountain,
Steady, it is not perturbed,
Unattached to things that arouse attachment,
Unangered by things that provoke anger.
When his mind is cultivated thus
How can suffering come to him?*

UDANA 4.4

attention, the thinking will disappear the moment we note it. In vipassana, we are always observing change, how things arise and pass away. The ordinary person, however, tends to become attached, even to meditation objects. Sometimes, they like concentration, the samatha type of concentration where concentration is fixed on only one object. That is why some people like to learn samatha first. But if we want insight, we have to come back to vipassana and develop our mindfulness regarding the changing nature of phenomena. In vipassana, momentary concentration is sufficient. Momentary concentration is concentration that is not fixed on one object but moves from object to object. But it can be continuous and unbroken; that is why it can develop insight.

When we note thinking, we should also do so calmly as with other objects such as pain. We watch it to see its true nature, not to make it go away. If we maintain this attitude, the thinking will cease naturally. But if we are too wrapped up in wanting it to go away, it is likely to stay longer. If we note mindfully and with detachment, we will be more aware of the three characteristics of suffering, impermanence and non-self. However, if the thinking persists for too long, we should ignore it completely and switch to another meditation object.

The "trick" behind the watching of mental states, according to one teacher, is to be very energetic and continuous in one's noting. The mind runs very fast and we must move equally fast to catch it. The current of defilements is also very powerful, and our mindfulness must be more powerful if we are to overcome it. Thinking, restlessness, etc, usually arise because of our defilements of greed, anger and delusion. Even though the thinking may seem to have stopped, the defilements may still be present. We have to be mindful and note the presence of defilements such as greed (thinking about food?) until they vanish. When we are really mindful of the defilements, we not only know their presence, we also comprehend their true nature of impermanence, unsatisfactoriness and non-self.

So, to be very mindful, we should, for example, also know whether we are slightly sleepy or not at all. Unless the defilements disappear altogether, how can we really note the consciousness without lust, without anger, without ignorance?

"The mind is hard to perceive, extremely subtle, flits wherever it wishes. Let the wise one guard it, a guarded mind is conducive to happiness." It is difficult to watch the mind. Often, people who try to do it end up with a blank sort of dullness or a meaningless wandering mind. The harder they try to watch the mind, the worse they become until they end up seeing stars! Trying to make your mind blank is even worse. The idea here is to be just mindful. If you are mindful, you can be aware of the mindful state of mind. If you are not, then you are mindful of something else—something which is probably clearer, has impinged on your consciousness and demands your attention. In this case, you are also on the right track as you are still mindful of a meditation object.

When we watch the mind, we have to constantly apply mindfulness. Otherwise mindfulness will cease without our knowledge. With progress, we can be mindful of good states of mind and be aware as they change into even subtler states. In the simile of the raft, we are told that even good states of mind have to be abandoned, what more evil states? True, states of mind can be so subtle and blissful that one may actually seem unconscious. Some may even mistake this for enlightenment or true cessation of suffering. Many subtle states of mind occur when one's consciousness is good They may be due to joy, quietude, concentration, and equanimity. So, the Satipatthana says: "One is mindful of consciousness that is tranquil, freed, no states higher than it, grown great, etc."

MINDFULNESS OF MENTAL OBJECTS
(Dhammanupassana Satipatthana)

This foundation of mindfulness is called dhammanupassana. Satipatthana covers a wide field of meditation objects. "Dhamma" itself has been translated as mind object and it includes virtually everything, including Nibbana. Some objects within the other

Diligent, devoted to the higher mind,
A sage trained in wisdom's ways,
There are no sorrows for the stable one
Who is calm and ever mindful.

UDANA 4.7

foundations of mindfulness also come under this foundation, and when thus reckoned, they are classified as mental factors (*cetasika*).

This contemplation of mindfulness helps to eradicate the hallucination of views (of self) by enabling us to see how dhammas are conditioned, and how they arise and fall away.

Contemplation of this mindfulness is divided into five categories: Hindrances, Bases, Aggregates, Factors of Enlightenment and Truths.

Hindrances

The five hindrances are sensual desire, anger, sloth and torpor, restlessness and remorse, and doubts. Under this contemplation, sensual desire refers in particular to the consciousness that is attached to a sensual object or the craving for it. Anger refers to the angry, violent or savage state of the consciousness in relation to the object. Sloth and torpor refer to the consciousness that is sluggish and shrinking away from the object. Restlessness and remorse refer to the consciousness that is agitated and flurried. Doubts refer to the sceptical or perplexed state of consciousness with regards to the Four Noble Truths or the Triple Gem.

Under this contemplation, one notes and knows not only the arising and cessation of these unwholesome mental factors but also the conditions that lead to their origination and dissolution. This is where we come to know when our attention (to an object) is "unwise" and when and how we should apply "wise" attention.

This contemplation of mindfulness is generally more difficult and subtler than the other three foundations. For example, the consciousness with sensual desire and sensual desire itself are not easily separable. Normally, the beginner does not start with this contemplation or dwell exclusively in it. Only when he is well-versed with the contemplation of the other three foundations of mindfulness can he note the subtler mental objects and states of consciousness. According to the commentary, this contemplation is suitable for the very intellectual types.

This contemplation of mindfulness (on mental objects) helps to eradicate the hallucination of views (of self) by enabling us to see how dhammas are conditioned, and how they arise and fall away.

Bases

One observes the six sense-bases (seeing, hearing, smelling, etc) and their objects (eye-object, ear object, etc); how they arise and pass away and the conditions leading to their origination and dissolution.

When we note "seeing, seeing," we only use the word "seeing" as a label to help us observe the process. What we actually see is the colour (of the visual object). The shapes, forms, and other ideas that follow are actually concepts which the mind formulates. By just noting "seeing, seeing," the shapes and ideas associated with the object "blur off" and we observe only (an interplay of) colours and light. In this process, we can also become aware of the seeing consciousness, that is, it is only consciousness that sees colour; not a being or a self.

The same can be said for hearing and sound, smelling and odour, tasting and food, touching an tangibles, knowing and the object known.

Why do we usually note "hearing, hearing" instead of "sound, sound?" This is because sound is usually intermittent and scattered, and it is hard to follow. Trying to "catch" it will only cause one to become distracted and this will not help in the development of deep concentration. By noting "hearing, hearing," that is, by just being aware of hearing (of the sound) at the ear rather than "outside," we tend to bring our mind inwards and thus, help to make it more composed. But in some cases, it is true that we can note "sound, sound." This is when the sound is loud, persistent and unavoidable. In such cases, we will have little choice but to note the sound continuously and observe how it changes.

In noting the sense-bases and their objects, one must exercise bare attention and guard against the rising of concepts. This is clearly emphasised in the Buddha's advice to Bahiya: "Thus, Bahiya should you train yourself—In what is seen there must be only the seen; in what is heard there must be only the heard; in what is sensed (as smell, taste or touch) there must be only what is sensed; in what is thought there must be only what is thought."

*Whose life causes no remorse
And who sorrows not at death,
The wise one who has seen
    that state*
Sorrows not in the midst of sorrow.*

*For a bhikkhu whose mind is
    calmed,
Who has destroyed the craving
    for being,
The wondering on in births is
    finished;
There is no further being for him.*

Udana 4.9

_____

*Nibbana

Mindfulness of these internal and external bases tears apart our view of self. We see that there is no being, self, or someone behind them but just processes. This particular contemplation is especially relevant to the practice of developing insight with regard to anatta (non-self) in daily life.

Usually, defilements and fetters arise through the sense doors. This occurs when our mindfulness in noting "seeing, hearing, etc" is lacking, as is often the case in daily life. Hence, we have also to note the defilements that arise depending on the sense doors.

Aggregates

There are five groups of aggregates:

1 *Rupa khandha* (matter)—This refers to conditioned non-conscious phenomena such as the elements of rigidity, cohesion, heat and motion. They constitute the physical or material aspect of the world including humans.

2 *Vedana khandha* (feelings)—such as pleasant, painful or neutral feelings and sensations. They constitute the emotional aspect.

3 *Sañña khandha* (perceptions)—which constitute recognition and registering of sense stimuli. It includes memory.

4 *Sankhara khandha* (mental formations or volitional activities)—includes different mental states and thinking.

5 *Viññana khandha* (consciousness)—the knowing or consciousness.

Just as when the parts are rightly set,
The word chariot is spoken,
So when there are the aggregates (khandhas),
It is the convention to say being.

BUDDHA

These five aggregates consist of those of the past, present and future, internal, external, gross, subtle, superior, inferior, near or far. When "man" or "I" are seen in the contemplation of these aggregates, it is understood as being in existence only in the conventional sense. When the hallucination of view is abandoned, the defilements, together with the mass of suffering, are eliminated.

Contemplation of seven factors of wisdom

These seven factors—mindfulness, (penetrative) investigation of truth, energy, rapture, repose, concentration and equanimity—are wholesome mental states that lead one to Nibbana. As these occur clearly only to one with the fourth insight knowledge, they are not objects meant for the new meditator. When these factors are initially developed, we can become attached to them because of their peaceful and inspiring effects. Mindfulness of their presence or absence will therefore guard us against such attachments (that will not only retard but also destroy our practice). Rapture, repose, concentration and equanimity for example, can make us complacent and neglect to continue the Satipatthana practice; non-mindfulness of the wisdom factor when it arises can cause us to become conceited.

Besides stabilising our practice, mindfulness of these factors also helps to balance the faculties particularly between energy and concentration. We are told in a sutta that when one is lethargic, it is time to develop energy, rapture, and investigation of truth. However, when one is agitated, we should develop repose, concentration, and equanimity. Mindfulness, on the other hand, is always needed.

Being mindful of these factors as they arise and pass away is also in itself the practice for the development of insight. With continuous practice, the factors of enlightenment can mature to perfection and enable us to attain insight.

Truths *(sacca)*

This refers to the Four Noble Truths of suffering; its cause, its cessation and the path (leading to its cessation). Suffering is that which we should understand (as to its nature); the cause (craving) is that what should be abandoned and the cessation is to be realised by developing the Path.

For a bhikkhu whose mind is calm and peaceful,
Who has cut the cord (of craving for being).
The wandering on in births is finished:
He is freed from Mara's bonds.

UDANA 4.10

"Suffering" is one translation of the Pali word "dukkha." Some prefer to translate dukkha as unsatisfactoriness or imperfection. According to the *Anattalakkhana Sutta*, that which is impermanent is suffering and that which is suffering is not-self. Therefore, to be mindful of impermanence is to be mindful of suffering. So, what is impermanent? Mind and matter which include all physical and mental phenomena except Nibbana are impermanent. We should thus note all mental and physical processes as they arise and pass away.

When craving or defilements which are the cause of suffering arise, we also note them mindfully. By doing so, we will see them disappearing. As we see the three characteristics of impermanence, suffering and non-self, we also develop the factors of the Noble Eightfold Path till we experience for ourselves the utter cessation of suffering. These factors of the Noble Path are:

1 **Right View**
   the understanding of the origination and dissolution of phenomena in the course of one's noting.
2 **Right Thought**
   the application of mind to the vipassana object.
3 **Right Speech**
   abstinence from wrong speech (in the course of one's practice).
4 **Right Action**
   abstinence from wrong action (in the course of one's practice).
5 **Right Livelihood**
   abstinence from wrong livelihood (during one's practice).
6 **Right Effort**
   the effort exerted in noting.
7 **Right Mindfulness**
   the mindfulness during noting.
8 **Right Concentration**
   the concentration maintained during noting.

No permanent pleasures of sense are there among human beings
Here are charming things enmeshed in which a man dallies
And thus from realms of death doth never come to that
Wherefrom there is no coming back again!
Desire—born misery, desire—born pain
Desire disciplined is misery quelled.
When misery is quelled, pain too is quelled.

They are not the sense-pleasures—those beautiful things in the world
Lustful intention is man's sense-pleasure
They endure as before those beautiful things in the world
But the will thereto, 'tis, that the wise discipline.

Let him put wrath away and conceit abandon
And get well beyond the fetters all
that one, by name-and-form untrammeled
And possessionless—no pain befall.

He cast off reckoning, no conceit assumed
Craving he cut off in this name-and-form
That bond-free one—from blemish and longing free
Him no gods nor men, in their search could ken
Searching here and beyond—in heavens and in all abodes.

SAGATHA VAGGA 1.4.4

Mindfulness of the Body (Kayanupassana)

I n sitting meditation, we watch "rising" and "falling" of the abdomen. Beginners may find it very difficult to fix their minds on the "rising" and "falling" of the abdomen because it is not something they are used to observing. So, it would help if you put your hand on the abdomen, feel it as it goes up and down, or rising and falling. When the hindrances are less, you can follow it better.

One has to bear in mind, not to expect this "rising" and "falling" to be constant. It is not a constant object. It is not that easy an object to observe. Often, it can be very elusive. It comes and it goes. Sometimes it is fast, sometimes it is slow; sometimes it is there and sometimes it is not.

Your aim is not to control the "rising" and "falling." Your aim is to observe and follow the phenomena, the processes concerned with the "rising" and "falling." Usually the "rising" and "falling" is what we call the wind element, *vayo dhatu*. Here, *vayo dhatu* is the more prominent of the four elements—earth, water, fire, and wind. It has the characteristics of tension, vibration, and motion.

Whatever beings are born or will be born,
They will journey on leaving the body.
Knowing that all must be abandoned,
A skilful one, ardent, should lead the holy life.

UDANA 5.2

Perceiving reality

The main thing is to have mindfulness to perceive these things. It may be of help if you grip your hands very tightly to produce some tension there. Putting aside the idea of the hand, you note how the tension is. You then relax the grip and feel how the sensation of relaxation is.

Similarly, putting aside the idea or concept of the hand, you move your hand up and down quickly and then just note how the feeling of the motion is. That is the wind element—the element of motion. It has neither colour nor shape, it is but a sensation.

One should get a clear hold and perception of that. In the process of following that, the other elements also manifest. Heat sometimes manifests, cold sometimes manifests too—this is the fire element. Then, too, you feel hardness and softness—this is the earth element and they are connected by means of cohesion and stickiness—this is the water element.

When you can perceive these, the next thing is to observe it (rise and fall) from the beginning of its arising until its end. You find that the elements are just processes—they flow and the mindfulness should flow with them. The more mindful you are, the more aware you are of them as processes.

They come, as we say, moment-to-moment. However, they are not experienced at once. At the beginning, we are aware of conceptual forms. That is because our mind is so used to holding on to concepts. In other words, we are so used to the shape of the body, the shape of the stomach, who we are, what we are, and so forth.

In order for the mindfulness to perceive reality, you have to put away all concepts, including the idea of me or mine, the body, the shape of the body and so forth. Just follow the flow of the processes of the sensations. This is, in essence, the *vipassana* practice—to train the mind until you can do just that.

In the beginning, we will still feel the form of the body as well as the form of the "rising" and "falling." It cannot be helped because it comes with the thought processes. However, if you are able to single out the characteristics of the motion, then one will proceed deeper into the awareness of realities or the natural phenomena and the three characteristics.

This same process is done with all other objects—in your walking and your other activities. Another thing you have to bear in mind is that this "rising" and "falling" of the abdomen is not always there. However, the elements are there all the time. They arise and pass away moment-to-moment. Therefore, when you watch the "rising" and "falling" of the abdomen, it sometimes stops.

Applying Sitting and Touching

If you watch the feeling at the abdomen, the sensations could be there. You can watch these sensations. However, they sometimes become very subtle and you do not seem to be watching anything. To maintain the continuity of the awareness, you have to watch "sitting" and "touching." "Sitting" and "touching," however, is often not clearly explained. Therefore, I will have to speak a little bit more about it.

Generally, when we say "sitting" and "touching," it refers to the series of mind and body processes that maintain the sitting posture. In my view, the "sitting" refers more to the inner forces involving the muscles and the bones. The "touching" refers more to those at the surface of the body.

For beginners, of course, you do not see everything at once. You watch the most obvious, first. Keeping it simple, you just watch one "sitting" and one "touching." That way, you are aware of the whole mass of "sitting," the most obvious being the rigidity around the spine and the waist. And in "touching," the most obvious is the contact of the posterior on the cushion.

Again, the main idea is not just to do "sitting" and "touching" but to be able to feel the sensations or the phenomena concerning the "sitting" and "touching" in a regular, not too fast, not too slow pace. After a while, the "rising" and "falling" may stop for a longer period. When this happens, you will have to increase the touch points—"touching" at the legs, the hands and so forth in a systematic order.

Whatever doubts as to here and beyond
In one's own or another's experience,
The meditators abandon all these,
The ardent ones leading the holy life.

UDANA 5.7

When you do that, the "rising" and "falling" usually returns. The idea is to maintain the continuity of awareness and observation. The "sitting" and "touching" is a meditation by itself.

However, it has certain disadvantages, in that it tends to be more scattered and diffused and therefore, the concentration seems to pick up slowly. However, it has an advantage in that it is more constant and stable which therefore serves as a good back up for the "rising" and "falling."

Of course, when concentration eventually builds up, you will just be watching "sitting" or "touching" which is none other than the four elements in the process of "rising" and passing away. So, if you can do this properly, you will not lack a proper object to contemplate on.

Walking meditation

Now, let's talk about walking meditation. A fair bit about walking meditation, concerning brisk walking and moderate walking to build up the mindfulness of the footsteps has been touched upon.

Yogis take walking meditation as a preparatory practice or building up practice for the sitting meditation.

Here "slow" walking meditation and its contemplation to a deeper level will be examined. I have noticed walking meditation is very often overlooked or not taken too seriously. Yogis take walking meditation as a preparatory practice or building up practice for the sitting meditation. This should not be the case. Equal emphasis should be given to both walking and sitting meditation techniques.

In the scriptures, there are stories that tell us how monks were enlightened in the process of doing walking meditation. Therefore, enough effort must be given to improve on our walking meditation to lead to a state of deeper concentration, which is usually not an easy thing to do.

How do we do this slow walking meditation? There are a few simple guidelines to start with. Firstly, the body should be relaxed. It should not be tensed. When the body is tensed, you cannot really be mindful and therefore, you cannot really follow properly all the objects.

Secondly, to be able to walk slowly and mindfully, the walking should be stable. When you are wobbly, you cannot concentrate properly because your mind is not at rest. Therefore, it would help to take low and short steps. When the steps are short and low, you do not have to worry about stumbling or toppling over.

Thirdly, the mind should be in a very relaxed but yet concentrated state. To do this, one has to learn to build up the concentration. One way is to bring the mind to a pace that you are able to follow. That means, you have to walk as slowly as you can to stir up deep concentration but not too slowly that you cannot feel any sensations of movement. The pace of walking should be enough for us to feel the sensations.

Also, make sure that the sensation is there, not as you think it to be—it may be there but I am not sure, or "Now it is there, now it is not there." If you are not sure of the sensation, the continuity of the object and the flow will be broken. Hence, the concentration does not build up. But, if you can grasp and lock on to it, then the mindfulness keeps flowing with the object and the sensations and you lock the mind to that level of concentration.

In such a state, it seems as if the foot moves by itself and you cannot walk any faster even if you had wanted to. Once you are in that state, there is no problem following the footsteps. The effort can then be slowly applied to picking up the flow of the sensations.

At a certain level of concentration, only a certain degree of the sensations can be picked up. Therefore, after a period of walking, you slow down even further. You also have to be even more relaxed and more peaceful to make the mind sensitive enough to pick up the finer flow of sensations.

If you are locked in to that concentration, walking meditation would not be a problem because you are in *samadhi*. You will be very peaceful and quiet and time seems to fly. When you have done walking meditation, you could then go on to your sitting meditation and just continue being aware. Normally, the sitting and walking meditations are about one hour each, one alternating after the other.

With body steady and mind steady
Whether standing, sitting,
*   or lying down,*
A bhikkhu making this
*   mindfulness firm*
Shall obtain successive distinctions
On obtaining distinctions in
*   succession*
He goes beyond sight of the King
*   of Death.*

UDANA 5.10

I have noticed that in more advanced students; it may be better to do longer walking and sitting meditations.

Provided, firstly, they are able to get the concentration and secondly, the body is healthy and strong enough. If the body is weak, then of course, they will not be able to do this. If it is possible for the yogi to have these, then all the faculties could be built up very strongly and the moment they sit down, these faculties will sink into and follow the series of objects.

Seriousness in walking meditation and other daily activities

The main thing that I would like to point out concerning walking meditation is that it should be taken seriously. If you really do walking meditation seriously, you could go into *samadhi* or concentration easily in each of your walking and sitting meditation session.

The same goes for all other activities. When I was in Burma, I trapped myself, in a way, to do eating meditation properly because I had complained to the Sayadaw that people at the monastery ate so fast. There were so many monks and we, being the youngest and smallest in build, were at the tail end of the whole procession. By the time we reached the hall for meals, the senior monks were already leaving.

Due to my complaint, I was given a special table in front of everybody to eat. I had no choice but to eat very mindfully. But, it was a good lesson as usually after a meal, I would feel very sleepy and slothful, and wanted to sleep. Because I had been really mindful while eating, the sitting meditation session after the meal was the best. Although the stomach felt much distended, I would watch this and it became a very good meditation object. I did not feel sleepy at all.

So, it is possible that when you are mindful in each walking and sitting meditation session, you would be able to get into *samadhi*, or good concentration. This goes too, for continuity of mindfulness and the practice.

Endeavour must herein be made
By that arahat [saint] who knows no fatigue
That by abandoning sense-desires
He may not hanker for existence.

There is naught left to do, O Damali,
For the arahat—so said the Exalted One.
The arahat is one whose task is done
So long as he no footing finds
A creature swept by river-currents
Toils with all his limbs
But finding a footing, when on dry ground he stands
He toils no more: passed over, soothe, is he.
A parable this, Damali.
Even so the arahat whose cankers are extinct,
Ripe in wisdom, given to absorption,
On reaching the end of birth and death
He toils no more: passed over soothe is he.

SAGATHA VAGGA II.1.5

Mindfulness of the Feelings (Vedananupassana)

UNPLEASANT FEELINGS

There is one more object, which I need to elaborate for the sake of beginners. This is the pain. What we have been speaking of, all this while, comes under *kayanupassana satipatthana* or the mindfulness concerning body or the body activities and processes—"rising" and "falling," "sitting" and "touching," walking, eating and so forth. This comes under *kaya* and this kaya comes under *rupa*, which comes under material qualities. It will eventually end up mainly on the four elements (earth, fire, water, and wind elements) and you will find that, largely, it is the wind element—which is more prominent—the element of motion, tension, vibration, and so forth.

When you can single out that characteristic and watch it as a process, you may be mindful enough to comprehend the three universal characteristics of impermanence, suffering, and non-self; the clear experience and comprehension of which is insight.

Now, we talk about this painful feeling. Painful feeling is something that we cannot avoid. It is one of the things that comes with our body. Rather than trying to avoid it as in normal circumstances, we can make use of it here to develop our mindfulness, concentration, and insight.

What formerly was, later was not;
What formerly was not, later was;
It was not and will not be
And does not now exist. *

UDANA 6.3

*According to Comy., the first line of the verse refers to the defilements, which formerly existed and then ceased at the moment of enlightenment. The second refers to those virtuous and faultless qualities present at that moment. And the final two lines refer to the noble path as an unrepeatable experience, i.e. the path-moment (arahatta-magga) which occurs but once and is then immediately followed by its fruition (arahatta-phala). The latter, however, is repeatable throughout the remainder of life.

In pure insight meditation, pain is a frequent encounter. This is because you are very aware of the body processes. Therefore, when they arise, we have to note them mindfully.

What do you mean by noting them mindfully? Here, in order to note mindfully, the main factor for the mind to remember is, to be in a peaceful and undisturbed state. Usually, when pain arises, we get tensed up or frightened. We want to avoid it and escape from it. However, instead of doing that, you should welcome it like a friend or a stern teacher—a good, compassionate but stern teacher.

Many people need stern teachers. Therefore, when the teacher sits down and gives you a lecture or sermon, you should listen to every word because it is good for you. Your mind should also be soft and receptive.

Pain is something like that. When it comes, be peaceful and relaxed—like a cotton wool that absorbs everything yet remains undisturbed. It is easy to do this with lesser pain or smaller pain but when the pain becomes intense, then firm mindfulness—a firm but peaceful and undisturbed state of mind—is needed.

There will come a time when the mind does become agitated and this is usually accompanied by ill-will or anger. Then you should note "anger, anger, impatient, impatient." You take a deep breath, try to relax, stabilise the mindfulness, and keep watch.

Learning to be mindful of unpleasant feelings

When you are able to watch the pain mindfully, it does not just involve keeping the mind to the pain. If you just keep the mind to the pain, it is just concentrating on the pain and the pain becomes exaggerated and magnified. You will then see a small pain as a big pain, a giant of a pain or a mountain of a pain. If your mindfulness is not strong enough, you will give up.

The trick here is not to hold the mind to the pain, but to observe it. Observation starts by identifying the different types of pain that is present—sour pain, hot pain, and so forth. Ask yourself how many types of pain you can identify when watching this. How do you describe it?

When you can see these different types of pain clearly, you will also be able to see how they arise and disappear, how they seem to move from one place to another and so forth. When you can start perceiving the change, see it starting probably as a form of a throb, then you will be able to see the change more and more clearly.

This is also the same principle used in watching pain during sickness. When you are forced to watch pain during sickness, you do not just concentrate on it because it becomes more painful. The idea is to watch the *change* between the painful feelings.

People do not usually like to take pain as a main object of meditation because it is usually very stressful and not many people can do it. Nevertheless, when you do *vipassana*, you will have to face it eventually. You can watch it as long as you can be mindful. When it comes to the point where you really cannot be mindful anymore, or when you are just sitting there, biting your tongue and keeping on thinking "When is it going to go away?" then there is no more mindfulness. This has become pointless. It is then time to change the posture—either by stretching the legs and bending it into a different position or getting up to walk. There are, of course, some phases you have got to go through before you do that.

First, you watch the pain directly. When you cannot do that any more, watch it indirectly, and when you cannot do that any more, ignore the pain and watch something else. Only when you cannot do all of the above, can you then shift and change your posture.

The main thing is not to sit to want the pain to go away. The main thing is to sit and develop mindfulness concerning pain. Thus, you also develop concentration and insight.

Important points in watching pain

There are a number of things I have noticed concerning yogis when it comes to watching pain. Firstly, make sure that you are mindful. Secondly, be detached from the body. Sometimes, the pain is not actually that severe. It is the fear concerning the impairment of bodily parts or death that stops us from watching the pain.

Above, below, and everywhere released,
One not observing "I am this"*
Has crossed the flood not crossed before,
Freed thus with no renewal of being.

UDANA 7.1

**This implies the absence of conceit and wrong views, which have both been uprooted by the arahant; or it implies the contemplation with insight of all conditioned things as " This is not mine, this is not I, this is not myself, " by which one attains arahantship.*

In most cases, the pain does not go to such an extent that you actually become disabled. It is more of the fear concerning it. The instruction is not to sit ten hours. The instruction is to sit one hour. Usually, when you sit for one hour, nothing will go wrong with the body or legs.

When you can take pain as a vipassana object, then insight knowledge may arise.

There are also different types of observation that I have noticed concerning watching pain. The preferred one is the one-pointedness, which means, you pinpoint the most painful part and zero your awareness into it. This is called the direct encounter. Awareness is like a surgeon's knife that goes into it and observes it. Usually when your mindfulness is one-pointed and really focused, then it is very strong. You are usually able to see some degree of change there, and if you are able to bear with it long enough, then the pain will disappear.

Failing that, another approach is to adopt a wider perspective or view. This happens when your whole leg is in pain. Not one single part seems to be more painful than the other. The whole situation seems to be "here pain, there pain, everywhere pain." Then you have to focus your mindfulness as if it is covering the whole part of your legs. Otherwise, when you watch one part, another part of your body will be in pain. You watch another part, still some other part of your body will be in pain. The mind may then start running about and get distracted.

Of course, in the case when the pain comes because of a physical cause—you are sick—then those types of painful sensations can be more persistent and stubborn. It will not go away because it is not a pain made obvious via meditation. It is not a pain that comes through a posture. There is something physically wrong with the body. In such a case, it is advised that one does not pay much attention to it in the beginning because it will not go away, and it can be very distressing.

Therefore, it is advised that you try to ignore it, build up the mindfulness and concentration on other easier objects such as "rising" and "falling." If you really try to put your mind to the "rising" and "falling," you can actually ignore the pain and you will not feel the pain at all.

When the mindfulness and concentration is developed, you can have insight and experience the three universal characteristics concerning pain. When you are able to apply the same knowledge onto the sickness, you will also be able to handle it and may be able to even overcome and cure it.

Therefore, this meditation on painful feelings actually has many advantages. Firstly, we will be able to face pain in a more peaceful and dignified manner when we cannot run away from it. For example, when we come into a serious illness, we can still maintain a peaceful and happy mind until whatever happens next.

Secondly, pain is a very strong object. It is very peculiar to *vipassana*. It can bring about *vipassana* concentration quickly if you can bear it. The trouble is, it is quite oppressive, and it saps a lot of energy. However, if you can bear it, then *vipassana* concentration will come up very quickly because the object is very strong. When you can take it as a *vipassana* object, then insight knowledge may arise and you move closer to your cherished goal *Nibbana*.

Pleasant and neutral feelings

Of course, we do not only meet with painful feelings. We also meet with pleasant or happy feelings. Happy bodily feelings mean physical comfort. This is not so obvious to the beginner except, probably, for when you go to sleep. When you lie down, you feel very comfortable and that is why you sleep very quickly. By right, you should also note mindfully until you fall asleep.

What is more important is when pleasant feelings arise in the mind. This occurs when the concentration builds up and joy arises. When joy and the peaceful states of consciousness arise, and you feel happy, then you have to note it mindfully. You have to build up your energy and alertness; otherwise, you will fall asleep or get attached to the pleasant feelings, in which case you do not progress. Worse, you may go into wrong concentration and hallucinations because craving has set in.

Therefore, you have to note. Make sure you note very energetically when happy feelings arise. If you can note the happy feelings as they

He has cut the round, won the desireless,
The dried up river flows no more;
The severed round does not revolve—
Just this is the end of suffering.

UDANA 7.2

arise and pass away very mindfully, then you can proceed to noting the happy feelings, and you will also be able to attain the knowledge of the three universal characteristics. Alternatively, when we say *vipassana* insight or insight knowledge, it is with regards to the rising and passing away of pleasant feelings.

But, if you note the pleasant feeling and you do not see any changes, it is just happy, peaceful and nothing else, then it is better not to stay in that mental state, no matter how pleasant it is. It is "dangerous." Mindfulness will slip off and you may end up in a kind of wrong concentration. Therefore, it is better to pull the mind out of that happy state and make it watch the "rising" and "falling," "sitting" and "touching," or pain.

Finally, in more advanced meditation, you are able to note, not just pleasant feelings but also neutral feelings. You will find that the neutral feelings are the subtlest of all feelings. It is in the equanimity derived from neutral feelings that makes the mind become really peaceful and concentrated. In that state, the mind can also be very mindful. It is just like an undisturbed state of water, very still and very clear. There are no waves. The moment the waves arise, that means the feelings have become more pronounced.

Meditation on feelings is called *vedananupassana*, which is the second foundation of mindfulness. When you can be mindful of feelings, you become a master of feelings. You can make use of it for any noble purpose you wish to do. These are the two basic objects— the body foundation of mindfulness and feelings. You will notice that in both cases, it is bringing the mind finally to a natural mind or body process. In the case of body activities, it is the body process. In the case of the feelings, it is the mental process. If you watch the mental or body processes carefully, then you watch it as a series of phenomena. When you watch it as a series of phenomena, you see into the characteristics of impermanence. When the characteristics of impermanence become clear, the characteristics of suffering become clear. When both of these characteristics become clear, the characteristics of non-self become clear. In this way, you can proceed and improve on your meditation in order to go into insight knowledge.

Forms perceived* cause loss of mindfulness,
If we dwell on their endearing charms.
Passion grips the heart, and feeling flows,
Clinging has us firmly in its grip:
So emotions rise and grow in strength,
of divers kinds, all based on what was seen.
Some of greed and some of hatred born—
Grievously they all afflict the heart of man,
Heaping up his store of pain and woe:
Thus for him Nibbana's far away.

He who's not inflamed by things he sees, *
Seeing forms retains his mindfulness,
Not in passion's grip, just simply feels,
On him clinging cannot get a hold.
If he just observes the things he sees,
Not reacting to their shape or form,
He'll pull down the pile, not build it up.
Mindfully proceeding on his way,
Heaping up no store of pain and woe:
Then for him Nibbana's very near.

SAGATHAKA VAGGA XXXV, 95

---

*Similarly for sounds, scents, tastes, tangibles & thoughts.

Mindfulness of Consciousness & Mental Objects (Cittanupassana & Dhammanupassana)

The third foundation of mindfulness is mindfulness of consciousness or mind. At this point, we will not try to differentiate between what we call mind and mental states.

To digress a little on this matter; there is a fourth foundation of mindfulness regarding Dhamma, translated as *mental objects*. This fourth foundation of mindfulness is more general and there are different interpretations of what it means. Generally, there are two types of interpretations. One interpretation is that Dhamma means certain aspects of the teachings, whereby when we contemplate on it—insight ie vipassana may arise. The other meaning is mental objects. Concerning this, it may also be interpreted as Dhamma in the sense of phenomena because all phenomena can be made the object of the mind. Therefore, the field is very wide; it stretches beyond the fields of the other three forms of objects. For the beginner we will not deal so much with this. We will just deal with the mind. We will include the mental states, which have often been classified under *Dhamma* or *mental objects*.

What do we mean when we say "mind"—*citta*? *Citta* is often translated as consciousness, that which knows, or that which knows an object. When you know something, you generally say "we" know.

Nevertheless, here it is not that "we" know; it is the mind that knows because the mind is so defined as having the quality of knowing. All this is very abstract and metaphysical. For simplicity and ease of understanding, when we refer to it as "mind"—it means consciousness.

In the beginning of the practice, we may not be so aware of these mental states. We are more concerned with trying to hold the mind onto the "rising" and "falling," the "sitting" and "touching," on the walking and sitting and so forth. However, as we try to do this, we become very aware of the mind. That is so because we are trying to control it. In the past, we have been used to taking it for granted. We may know there is a mind but we do not really look into it. Now you have to control the mind, so finally you need to deal with it.

THE HINDRANCES

The first level of training concerning *Cittanupassana Satipatthana* is the mindfulness with regards to consciousness eg mental hindrances, sleepiness, and restlessness. When we talk about Cittanupassana—mindfulness of consciousness, the thing is that we have to be mindful of, is that we have to have a clear object of that consciousness or state of mind. This is not just to know that it is there but is the ability to watch closely, as if you are closely watching someone's face and you can describe it well. Similarly, when you are looking at the consciousness of the mind—such as sloth and torpor or restlessness—you need to be able to describe it clearly in your own words.

What will be more obvious for the beginner is the grosser phenomena—for example, anger, or hatred. Anger is indeed the grosser form of defilement. When you are angry—what is the state of mind like, what is the consciousness like? When you sit back and try to look at the mind when it is angry, you sense that the mind is in a very disturbed state. It is burning. The *Abhidhamma* describes it as a violent state of mind, a destructive state. It is just like a whirlwind or an explosion. It is very ferocious, very harmful, and very violent.

All these are different ways to describe the anger and the angry consciousness.

For example, when you are meditating and something disturbs you. You may become agitated, come out of concentration, and a little anger may arise. When anger arises, do not just say "anger, anger..." but watch the disturbed and agitated state of mind—the fierce state of mind. When you watch it, you will see how terrible it is.

Sometimes the evil root of craving is more difficult. When craving arises, we must also note the craving and watch the state of consciousness—the state of mind. For example, when you see very good food coming to you and you think, "Oh, this is so nice to eat," you find there is joy there. Now what happens is that the joy seems to mask everything. The craving for food is one thing, the joy is another. They are two different things. One is the consciousness and the other is the mind that comes with the craving. Normally when people eat their food, the taste brings joy. They are infatuated by the joy and so cannot see the actual state of mind. If one can look into the consciousness of mind, there is craving and then you are able to notice that this mind is not so wonderful after all.

A good picture of craving can be seen in one who is suffering from addiction. If you are a drug addict or are addicted to cigarettes but your drug or cigarette is not available, when you look at the state of mind you can see how terrible it is. When craving arises in the same way, you look at the nature of craving. It is a state of wanting, clinging, and so on. This craving and anger arises very often. If you can catch it every time and nip it in the bud, then it will not disturb you.

Sloth and torpor is a little more difficult because from the start it is subtler. As a point of interest, in the Abhidhamma one of these is interpreted as the unwieldiness of the consciousness citta and the other as the unwieldiness of the *cetasika*, the mental state. Both of them come together at one moment of time.

What is the difference? You see the consciousness. When you say the consciousness is unwieldy, it means the knowing itself is very blurred—there is difficulty in knowing something as if there is a

Ever grows the glory of him who is energetic, mindful and pure in conduct, discerning and self-controlled, righteous and heedful.

DHAMMAPADA 24

retracting from the object. It is like in the early morning when you may be very sleepy and you try to watch the "rising" and "falling" but you do not seem to see anything, it is just blurred and hazy. No matter how hard you try, it makes no difference. Finally darkness seems to fall and you go to sleep. In the case of the mental state, the noting itself is difficult. The mental state is activity and the activity has slowed down, is unwieldy, hard, and stiff. As you note, the noting becomes very slow and difficult until finally you see the mind and mental states as very dark clouds that are caving in. Sometimes people say the mind activity is like a blockage in front of them or somebody throwing a blanket over them until they fall asleep.

The important aspect is to have a clear perception of the hindrances and defilements when they arise.

Of course, in the actual practise we do not differentiate intellectually between mind and mental states. If we are sleepy, we note "sleepy, sleepy..." Sometimes you observe the mind consciousness and sometimes you observe the mental state. The important aspect is to have a clear perception of the hindrances and defilements when they arise. If you can do that, then you are able to nip them in the bud. If the slightest form of sloth arises, you can catch it. If the slightest form of craving comes, you can catch it. Likewise with anger.

This is something that has to be learnt; it is not something you see with your eyes. It is something you know by experiencing it with your mind. And you know it best if you are able to maintain a clear, calm and neutral state of awareness and compare it with that other state that is associated with defilements.

What is the difference between the clear and unclear mind?

When you are mindful, the mind is very calm, peaceful, and clear—it is very stable and aware, so the moment a little bit of agitation comes, you know it. How is the mind then, when it is disturbed? Possibly, it is vibrating. Certainly it is no longer the calm and steady mind. When anger arises you know it, the mind starts becoming violent. If sloth and torpor arises, the clear mind turns dark, hazy, and heavy. When craving arises, you know this craving—a type of clinging, asking for something or begging for something. When it is dull, it may be just pure ignorance and delusion; it becomes a dark and dull mind.

When you begin to train yourself in watching the consciousness, you are learning to look into the mind. It is another world by itself You can call it mindscapes instead of landscapes. There are deep valleys and high mountains. There are dark clouds and clear skies. Eventually, in meditation, you will have to go deeper and deeper into such states and become familiar with them. As a starting point, the states such as sloth and torpor come into play.

THE SENSES

Another important aspect of the consciousness that the beginner deals with—are the six senses ie seeing, hearing, smelling, tasting, touching and the knowing. Usually when people see something they say, "I see," but here, according to the Dhamma, it is not *you* who sees—the person is a concept—it is the seeing consciousness, a certain consciousness of mind which sees. It is a type of knowing which is the seeing of the eye object, the colour, and the light. Similarly with the hearing. The hearing knows the sound. The smell consciousness knows the smell. The taste consciousness knows the taste, and the knowing consciousness knows the mind object.

We do come across periods when we have to note "seeing," "hearing," "smelling," "tasting," or "touching." Take for example in walking meditation, the important aspect is to note the "seeing." If you do not note the "seeing" then what usually happens is that you start to think about what you see and when you start thinking about what you see, you are no longer with the meditation object. If you are not mindful, the defilements of greed, craving, or anger may arise. This skill has to be learnt. At the first level, it is just what we call

By effort and heedfulness, discipline and self-mastery, let the wise one make for himself an island which no flood can overwhelm.

DHAMMAPADA 25

"restraint"—you prevent the arising of the defilement. Because if you are not seeing "seeing" then you start thinking about what you see. At a further stage, we just note the process. There is only the seeing that notes the eye object. This can only come about when you do not cling to the idea that "I" am seeing. It becomes clearer when you are able to see the natural phenomena as they really are. (We will go further onto this later).

Similarly with hearing. A lot of talking and sounds may tend to distract you, so you have to note, "hearing, hearing... hearing" so that you know that hearing is a process and you do not think about the sound.

Of the five senses, the seeing, and the hearing play the major part. Smelling plays a lesser part and tasting only when we are eating. The touch, of course, is often our meditation object. Nevertheless, "seeing" plays a great part in the meditation in the sense that, if you are able to note it properly, a lot of thinking and restlessness will not arise, especially during the walking meditation. In further stages, one may actually gain insight by just noting these six senses.

THE IMPORTANCE OF NOTING INTENTION

The third thing you must not leave out—concerning mindfulness of consciousness and mental states—is the aspect of intentions. Before every action, an intention must arise. For example, after sitting for some time, you might like to get up and walk. The mind will have the intention to walk. It will tell you, "Get up and walk! You have sat long enough." After walking, you know it is time to sit, so the mind will say, "Go and sit." Because of the compulsion of the intention to sit, you go and sit. Similarly for all other actions—the intention to eat, the intention to drink, the intention to answer the calls of nature, the intention to sleep, the intention to talk and so forth—they will arise followed by the action.

Many of these intentions arise every day and they go about unnoticed. If you can mindfully note all of the intentions that arise, you will also be mindful of the action that follows. We start by taking note of the major intentions connected with the four major postures—walking, sitting, lying down and standing up. They usually occur between each of these four major postures. If you can take note of that then you can further extend your practice by taking note of the intentions prior to the minor postures such as bending, stretching, turning the head and so forth.

One way is to tell yourself, "I will not get up until I am able to observe the intention to get up," or "I will not sit until I am able to watch the intention to sit." If you can do that eventually the intention will become very strong and you will be able to observe it. It comes more like a strong urge, a strong desire, or a strong wish. One good example is when there is a lot of pain and you really want to move but you decide not to. Then the mind will tell you, "Move, move, move! What is the use of sitting any more? Who do you think you are? Are you trying to be a hero? You can be more mindful if you move to another posture." Then tell yourself, "Ah! That is the intention to move, the intention to get up." Take a good look at it. Then, if necessary, move. Likewise, possibly, with the intention to sleep when you first wake up in the morning and want just to stay in bed.

Once you have started getting hold of intentions, you find that the mind actually has a life of its own. You think you are controlling the mind but the mind is controlling you more than you are controlling it. If a person is not mindful, he acts largely on impulses. He is not aware of his actions. That is why things like addictions arise.

Sometime ago, a cigarette smoker told me that although he had tried to stop smoking cigarettes, the urge kept coming back. He said, "I do not know how the cigarette got into my hand." The cigarette just spoke to his head and said, "Come, let's have a smoke!" and he did not know when the hands moved. That is because there is a lot of desire in the mind that arose when left unnoticed.

Therefore, in a meditation retreat, the usual instruction is that when you go to one posture, stick to it. Strictly speaking, the

Do not give way to heedlessness.
Do not indulge in sensual pleasures.
Only the heedful and meditative attain great happiness.

DHAMMAPADA 27

instruction is that when you go to one posture like sitting, sit and do not move—not even a muscle. Some say you must not even move your eyeballs. We often move because we are not mindful, we are agitated or disturbed. If you want to move and must move then note the intention. For instance you may have an itch in the nose. At first, note it with, "itchy, itchy, itchy..." but if it gets too bad and you cannot stand it, and you really want to scratch it, then notice the intention to scratch. Notice the intention to move your hand and then slowly move your hand. Carefully notice the scratching, "scratch, scratch, scratch..." and then, while continuing to note, slowly put your hand down. Then you know that you have done a silly thing and that realisation is another feeling that replaces the itch.

Intention is very important in maintaining the continuity of awareness. If you are not aware of the intentions then you are usually unaware of many of your actions. It is like the link between one action and another. In the beginning, though, you do not try to watch every intention.

Two kinds of intention

One is stronger and more active; the other is more like an impulse. Start by watching the main intentions—the strong and active ones. When you can watch the main intentions, not only is the continuity there but other things follow such as the clear comprehension of the purpose and suitability of the intention. Take again the example of when you are walking and you notice the intention to sit. Why do you want to sit? Is it suitable for you to sit? Those things describe the nature of the intention and they will come with the intention. Possibly, you have walked too long and you are tired, or you are just lazy and do not feel like walking. You notice an intention to sit, so you ask yourself, "Why do I want to sit down?" and the answer comes, "Because I feel too lazy to walk. I do not get anything from walking. It is a waste of time." That is not the right purpose because

When you can watch the main intentions, not only is the continuity there but other things follow such as the clear comprehension of the purpose and suitability of the intention.

the intention is caused by laziness. Sometimes, of course, it is not a matter of being lazy but it is not suitable to stop because the time is not up. Therefore, every intention comes with its suitability and purpose.

Another important thing concerning the noting of intentions is that it helps to eradicate the sense of ego and helps to see into the nature of conditioning and non-self.

Normally people who are not aware of the Dhamma teachings tend to have a very strong ego—of self, "I," me, and mine. All their thinking revolves around it. In the Dhamma, it is different. Reality and right view replace the ego. So when one is able to note intentions, one realises that it is not "I" that intends to sit or walk. The sitting comes about because it is the intention that wants to sit.

Why does intention arise? This is because of other conditions. Why do you stand up, for example? Because the pain is too strong! Why is the pain so strong? Because you are very old or because you have stiff bones? In addition, you lack mindfulness, you cannot put up with it any more and so it is only wise that you stand up and walk, maybe for one hour. So you see all the conditionings that are present and when you clearly see the conditioning, you see that there is no person there. There is only the intention followed by the action and then the perception of non-self will be increased.

THE MINDFULNESS JOURNEY

So, there are these three basic things. There is mindfulness of the consciousness with regards to hindrances, mindfulness with regards to consciousness of the senses, and the mindfulness with regards to the consciousness of intention. There is also the mindfulness with regards to feelings and the mindfulness with regards to the body activities. These are the basic objects for the beginner to maintain continuity of mindfulness.

When one sits for longer periods such as one day, two days, three days or more, in order to be able to maintain the continuity of

The monk who delights in heedfulness and looks with fear at heedlessness advances like fire, burning all fetters small and large.

DHAMMAPADA 31

mindfulness, one eventually comes to noting one of these objects. Unless one is aware, that one has to note these objects—when they arise, how to note them and what these objects really are in terms of experience—the continuity of mindfulness cannot come about.

In this sense, it is like taking a journey. Sometimes we travel along a main road but when the main road is not available; we go by a side road. When the main road returns, we go back to it. Sometimes, as we travel on the main road, there is a flood—all the side roads and main road are flooded—so we travel by river. There comes a time when the water gets too rough, so we take a plane or helicopter. Why do we have to do that? Because time is getting short, the night is falling and dangers are approaching. Mindfulness is something like that. We meet with different objects. The objects are our path, our road. The further we go, the more advanced or nearer we are to the safe haven and to happiness. The main road is like the main object of the body—it is solid like the main road, more solid than the other foundations of feelings and mind. It is the main object that builds our concentration and mindfulness concerned with the "rising" and "falling." Then there are the other side objects like "sitting" and "touching" which are like the side roads.

The objects are our path, our road. The further we go, the more advanced or nearer we are to the safe haven and to happiness.

When there is no "rising" and "falling"—no matter how hard you try—then you watch the "sitting" and "touching." There will come a time when pain will become overwhelming or when the joy may become overwhelming, and the body objects recede. You have to take care to note the feelings. This is just like crossing the river. Feelings are like water—deep and turbulent. At other times, when you cannot watch the feelings or the pain is too strong then, you have to watch the mind. At other times, even the feelings and body objects are insignificant, then, too, you have to watch the mind. When you watch the mind it is like going into the air, it is more elusive.

NON-SELF AND THE DISCONTINUITY
OF CONSCIOUSNESS

With reference to non-self and the discontinuity of consciousness, we can say that the body is more solid but the key to penetrating it, is to penetrate beyond the seeming solidity. The body is more like fine particles of sand. When you do not look closely at it, the body seems like hard rock but when you watch closely, you see that it is made of many fine particles of sand. Then, when you closely watch the fine particles of sand, you notice that they are not stationary but are moving. So if you can put aside the seeming solidity of the body and the form, just watch it as a mere experience of sensations, you can transcend and see through the concepts of form and so forth. You can penetrate into the three characteristics such as impermanence, suffering, and non-self.

With the feelings, however, the main point is attachment to pleasurable feelings. If you are not attached to the pleasurable feelings—you will be able to watch the feeling as impermanent, suffering and non-self.

In the case of consciousness, the idea of the continuity of the mind and its mental states is involved—the idea that there is a self, an everlasting soul in the mind, an everlasting "I." That is because we cannot see the impermanence and the discontinuity. For example, people cannot experience the difference between the "seeing" and the "hearing," they think that the mind that sees and the mind that hears are the same thing, but with meditation you become very aware of the nature of the "seeing" and "hearing." "Seeing" is a type of phenomena, a type of knowing. "Hearing" is also a type of knowing. They are different types of knowing. More important is the ability to see the discontinuity of the consciousness. You cannot see the discontinuity of the consciousness at first. What you can experience is the discontinuity of the mental states. For example, we know that noting comes and goes. We know the mindfulness comes and goes. We know the thinking comes and goes, but you can still have the idea that though it comes and goes, the mind is still there and the

*Just as a fletcher straightens
an arrow shaft,
even so the discerning man
straightens his mind—
so fickle and unsteady,
so difficult to guard and control.*

DHAMMAPADA 33

mind is still permanent. If you keep noting and being very aware of the discontinuity and the changing of the mental states, noting "hearing," "smelling," "tasting," "touching," or "seeing," then you are able to see the discontinuity of the consciousness itself.

A good example is while you are noting the hindrances—like sloth and torpor, you note, "sleepy... sleepy... sleepy." The mind is very heavy and dark, but you persist with patience and energy. Then you may come to a point when the sleepiness goes away and the whole thing clears as if all the dark clouds have disappeared. Then there is a completely new type of mind. To use a mundane term, a layperson's term, you say, "I am a completely different person." When you see that the consciousness changes, it is so.

Take another example. You are very angry and cross with somebody. Somebody has done something terrible to you, for example, cheated or swindled you. You are very sad. Then you discover that they are innocent of the action. It was all wrong perception on your part. They did not cheat you, somebody else did. Then you are no longer angry with them. What happens to the anger then? It just went off. Isn't that strange? They are just two different minds. This, of course, is just an example but when you go into meditation, it becomes very clear. When it becomes clearer and clearer, you see not only the differences between the defilements and the pure mind, but also between the pure mind—one pure mind and another. The awareness itself changes moment-to-moment. It is as if every moment, every split second, is a different mind altogether, a different consciousness. The consciousness is more of the knowing mind. A mental state is like the noting mind. The knowing mind, the consciousness, is usually in the background, it is more difficult to perceive the change but if you can note it then your perception in impermanence is improved and the clinging to the self which is connected to that mind and the consciousness is slowly abandoned. Unless that happens, the deeper insights cannot arise. A lot of deeper insights are prevented because of this latent clinging to the self and the "I" which is connected with the consciousness; ie connected with the mind. Even among many Buddhists, there is such clinging to the idea that behind the mind somewhere there is something permanent.

When the concentration develops in meditation, the mind often slips into very tranquil states. Sometimes peace and joy may overwhelm it. Sometimes there may actually be absorption involved. These are very peaceful states, at times even blissful. When they arise and you notice the states, you should quickly note, "ah, peaceful... peaceful..." In the case of deeper concentration, you may go as if into a blank white state, there is nothing there and when you come out you think, "Ah! What a wonderful and peaceful state!" Some people may even believe it is Nibbana. When you are not mindful, you will cling to it and then craving arises. Whatever subtle states of consciousness arise, you must note them as they arise and as they pass away.

This consciousness is very subtle and very tricky. It is very deep but it is also that very thing from where you can get understanding into the nature of reality and into the path of freedom.

PRIORITY OF MINDFULNESS

When a person practises meditation to a deeper level, he becomes more involved with the realms of the mind and then he gets more familiar with these mental states. To a beginner who encounters them, some can be quite frightening and some can be very attractive. Many people ask me, "Am I doing the right thing? Am I experiencing what I should be experiencing?" I tell them that it is not important what they see. Rather, it is more important whether they are mindful or not. When you are mindful, you can do nothing wrong. When you are mindful and you keep noting these states as they occur, things will become clearer to you. For example, when people go into states as if there is a void—nothing there—note it. Go in again and be mindful and there will come a time when you will know the state you are in and very often, it is some kind of subtle state of awareness,

Few among men are those
who cross to the farther shore.
The rest, the bulk of men,
only run up and down the
hither shore.

But those who act according
to the perfectly taught Dhamma
will cross the realm of Death,
so difficult to cross.

DHAMMAPADA 85-86

there is some object there. Sometimes there may be a very fine and subtle thinking. Then you must be mindful of these things. When you have noted them then your mindfulness has improved and you have made more progress.

When one is able to take into account all these different states of mind, consciousness and feelings, then one is able to maintain the continuity of mindfulness. When one is able to maintain the continuity of mindfulness, concentration will become strong. The mind will become more workable, more flexible, and obedient. Because of the concentration, it becomes powerful. At this stage, it is able to sink into the concentration and observe deeply for a long and extended period, the nature of mind and body processes as they really are.

What is important is that if one develops insights they will arise very clearly and very sharply. There can be no doubt about it. Each level of insight has to be clear because the latter ones are based on the initial ones. For example, the first insight knowledge is insight into the discrimination of mind and body, seeing clearly the nature of mind and body according to their characteristics. There is no being, no soul. It is void of self. They are mere phenomenal experiences and occurrences. This has to be very clear so that they can be applied to all objects that one encounters. Only when that is so, the conditioning between one phenomenon and the other is very clear. Only when this is clear can the clinging of the self be further abandoned.

When one is able to maintain the continuity of mindfulness, concentration will become strong.

Of paths the Noble Eightfold Path is the best,
Of truths the Four Noble Truths,
The passionless of teachings is best,
Of humankind, the Seer.

This is the path, no other is there
for purity of insight.
Enter then upon this path
for this does muddle the Mara.

Entered then upon this path
You will make an end of suffering.
Freed in knowledge from suffering's stings
By me the Path is proclaimed.

Buddhas just proclaim the path
But you are the ones to strive.
Contemplatives who tread the path
Are freed from Mara's bonds.

DHAMMAPADA

Five Hindrances

The first one or two days in a meditation retreat is more of a time for spring cleaning. All the stress and fatigue accumulated will come for a showdown. So also, the habitual tendencies and thoughts. If they have not attended a meditation retreat before and have very little idea of what meditation is about, many people will easily get discouraged because it will be a very tough time indeed.

The moment they sit down, their mind will go haywire or it may just go blank when they try to concentrate or try to be mindful. This only shows our state of mind and the extent of control we exercise over it.

This is because of the power of the defilements, the power of the negative states of mind or the unwholesome states of the mind and the lack of the pure and wholesome states of the mind. These defilements have to be powerful to be able to keep us in *samsara*, the cycle of birth and death, since time immemorial.

Therefore, at no instance should their powers be underestimated! In terms of their general classification, we call them the three evil roots—greed, anger, and delusion. However, when it comes to meditation and its functions, we call them the five hindrances:

Clinging to sense pleasure, to sensual ties,
Seeing in fetters nothing to be blamed
Never will those tied down by fetters
Cross the flood so wide and great.

UDANA 7.3

1   sensual desires,

2   ill will,

3   sloth and torpor,

4   restlessness and worry, and

5   sceptical doubts.

They work in different ways to hinder or obstruct the progress of right concentration and the strengthening of the pure mind. In brief:

- Sensual desires are sensual indulgence of the five senses or pleasures of the five senses.
- Ill will is anger and hatred.
- Sloth and torpor is the laziness, indolence, and stickiness of the mind.
- Restlessness and worry is the agitation and flurry found within the mind.
- Sceptical doubts are the sceptical doubts concerning the practice and the Triple Gems.

To simplify things, hindrances can be classified under two main headings: Sloth and torpor, and restlessness and worry.

SLOTH AND TORPOR

In the first few days, when meditators come for retreat, they feel that these are very powerful indeed. Therefore, we will deal with it a little bit more to help you handle that. Of the two, sloth and torpor is the less dangerous hindrance, in the sense that it only brings you to sleep. When you sleep, it is not that bad. It is just a waste of time whereas the restless state of thinking is active and if it builds up, you can go mad. The mind "breaks" because of the excessive negative energy.

Nevertheless, when you come for meditation, you have to get rid of both of them. As long as they are present in some degree, mindfulness will not be able to work properly. The picture will not be clear. One has to get rid of them completely before the whole picture becomes clear and the work of insight can proceed.

How does one handle this sloth and torpor? Let us see some ways. In the first one or two days, sloth and torpor is usually of a very heavy kind of mental state. Very often, there is nothing you can do but just sit and ride through the storm. It is so heavy. The moment you sit, your mind is blank. If you had been rushing out a lot of work and you are very tired or you have had a long journey, it can be really heavy.

However, it is not altogether a permanent feature. If you sit long enough and if you try long enough, it will usually pass. Worse comes to worst, if you cannot sit any more, get up and walk. Nevertheless, after a few days of trying, it will become less and the sloth and torpor attacks will be more of the milder kind. It will be of the softer type. It is just like in the early morning when you are watching "rising, falling, rising, falling..." it is so clear and peaceful. But, somewhere along the line, everything has gone blank. Why? Because the sloth and torpor has crept in without you knowing. You said "I was very mindful but suddenly where did it go?" This is more of the softer kind of sloth and torpor and it can come on fast and attack suddenly.

So, when your mind is very peaceful, you have to especially stir up the energy or if you feel your mind is a bit slow, hazy, and fuzzy, then it is time to stir up the energy. The factor to counteract this sloth and torpor is energy or effort. The question is not whether we have energy or not. Mental energy is always there.

Here is an example. If you have overslept and you would be late for work but you did not know it, you would not be willing to get up. However, the moment you realised that you were late for work, or you were late for your examinations, all of a sudden within five minutes, you would be ready to go.

Where did the energy come from? The energy is always there. So, it is a matter of calling it up and a matter of will power to stir up and arouse the mindfulness. That is what we have to learn to do; to connect with the proper will power that can arouse the energy

From whom there is no root and soil
There are no leaves, how then
* creepers?*
Who can blame that heroic sage
Free from every form of bondage?
Even the devas praise such a one,
By Brahma too he is praised.

UDANA 7.6

whenever we want. Of course, there are other ways of bringing up this energy. Energy comes with what we call initial application, *vitakka*, that is, increased noting.

Therefore, when you cannot find the "rising" and "falling" because you are so sleepy, it may be wiser to use the "sitting" and "touching" method. Of course, because of the sleepiness, your "sitting" and "touching" objects are also not clear. Therefore, you hold on to a larger mass, the whole mass of the body as "sitting" and the contact point as "touching." So, you continue noting at a regular pace, "sitting, touching, sitting, touching, sitting, touching..."

Another alternative is to use more touch points ie "sitting, touching, touching, touching..." Examples of the touch points are the contact points at the posterior, legs and hands. You can also alternate the touch points in a rhythm or in an order. Usually, in the case of very heavy sloth and torpor, it may not work at all unless you are persistent.

With strong will power, it can go off. It may take some time. It may not be just five or ten minutes. It may take twenty or thirty minutes to break through. Nevertheless, once it is broken through, the mind usually becomes extremely clear. Failing that, of course, you use walking meditation.

In walking meditation, you are not usually sleepy unless you walk very slowly. It may be that the object is very subtle— when you are walking slowly and you cannot catch it, then the sloth will continue. Therefore, the idea is to take bigger steps, walk a bit faster and in a freer manner. If you are tense, the stiffness of the mind can influence you to be lethargic.

It is better to walk a freer, not too slow, nor extremely fast pace.

It is better to walk a freer, not too slow, nor extremely fast pace and take bigger steps. Over a period, when the mind has an object to catch, with one thing after another, it can become activated. When the mind is activated, sleepiness goes away and the energy comes about.

This is, of course, a simple method. Finally, it all boils down to will power and usually after a few days, say three to four days; the sloth and torpor will go away. In rare cases, it may persist for a week. Nevertheless, if you are diligent, it usually goes away after a few days.

RESTLESSNESS AND WORRY

The other hindrance involved is worry and restlessness. Here, you are advised to note 'thinking, thinking' with mindfulness and it should go away. Often, when we note 'thinking, thinking," it does not go away. We may just be saying 'thinking, thinking,' but we are not mindful. If you are mindful when you note, you would not be thinking. You should be clear and aware and the thinking would go away.

Sometimes, as we note, the thinking goes away but it comes back. It goes away again and it comes back again. A question may arise, why does it go away and then come back again? One possible reason is that the thinking goes away but a certain degree of defilement is still left. When you return to the "rising" and "falling," you are still not so mindful yet. There may still be a bit of craving, anger, or delusion. Therefore, in cases when the thinking is very stubborn and it keeps coming back, you should note its root (greed, anger or delusion).

This root is noted when you note the thinking—that is how the thinking arises. When you note the thinking and how it arises, you may be able to trace the root of it. That means whether it comes from greed, anger, worry, or any other negative defilements.

You will also be able to trace what it is that is troubling you. In terms of the object, it can be either specific or general. General is in the sense that there is no specific object that you are thinking about, and it can be just everything under the sun. Specific object means something is bugging your mind. Therefore, you should settle that problem.

Once you have found the cause, it is easier to solve the problem. If it is just a state of greed or anger, then you note it as greed, anger, delusion, and so forth. Noting of a more specific target is usually more effective than a general one.

This comes under *cittanupassana*, which means mindfulness of consciousness, which we will deal with later. It is more involved in actually being able to perceive the state of mind of greed, anger,

He for whom mindfulness of the body is always constantly established thus, "If there had not been, there would not be for me; There will not be, and there will not be for me,"** If he dwells upon that in graded steps In time he will pass beyond attachment.

UDANA 7.8

*This cryptic saying can be paraphrased with the help of the Comy. thus: "If there had not been" impure deeds (kilesa-kamma) that I had done in the past, then "there would not be for me" now, in this life, the experience of their ripening (vipaka). And since "there will not be" any impure deeds when he is an arahat, so " there will not be" anything to ripen in the future.

delusion, laziness or others with clear awareness as to the 'form' of the mind as well as the nature and state of the mind. When it is perceived clearly, it usually disappears there and then.

PRELIMINARY CONCENTRATION MEDITATIONS

There are, however, cases where these defilements are very stubborn. When defilements are very thick, you may have to tackle it with more seriousness. Take for example, people who are very troubled by certain problems. These problems are very nagging and if not taken care of, they may become psychological problems. Usually, it will not happen but if it does, you have to take special care. That is why it is recommended that in the beginning of the sitting meditation, one may do one or more of what we call the preliminary concentration meditations.

The four preliminary concentration meditations are firstly, *Buddhanusati*, the recollection on the virtues of the Buddha. This helps to overcome fear, sceptical doubts and instil confidence.

Secondly, meditation on loving-kindness. This helps to overcome anger and ill will and to establish a peaceful and harmonious atmosphere around one's sphere of meditation.

Thirdly, meditation on impurities for those who have strong lustful tendencies or desires.

Fourthly, meditation on death to overcome anxiety, laziness and complacency. Included in this category may be things like meditation on *Kamma* to overcome anxiety, fear, the loss of dear ones, sadness and so forth.

One must not underestimate the power of these preliminary meditations even though they are recommended to be done only in the initial five or ten minutes of a meditation sitting. When done properly, it can hold the mind. Truly speaking, the restless mind is actually only at a certain level of activity. If you can just hold the mind, make it still, and do its work long enough, then all those thinking, restlessness and hindrances will be put aside.

Restlessness occurs only in the initial stage, the first one or two days, or the first retreat. When one does not know how to deal with it, it seems as wild as ever—a hopeless case. Actually, it is not such a big deal.

However, we would always have to face these five hindrances as long as we are still not *Arahants*. When they arise, it is an opportunity for us to learn how to deal with them. If you are a beginner and you have not learnt how to deal with them before you leave, then you will always be faced with the problem. Learning how to deal with them does not come at once. It comes slowly. You will not be able to experience the pure state of mind until all these hindrances and defilements have been put aside.

Take for example, sleepiness. Sleepiness may be present in the mind and you note 'sleepy, sleepy, sleepy." It goes away but not completely. All the tendencies are there. You have not achieved up to what we call access concentration and therefore, it still lingers. On and off, it comes back. It is just like the sky where the sun is but there is still a thin layer of clouds there and you do not see the blue sky. Only when you note it off completely and when all the sleepiness has gone, you would then know how the blue sky is like. Then the sun comes through, shining with great clarity and you can see everything around you.

The five hindrances are the sloth and torpor, the thinking and so forth. To note them is like clearing the mind of rubbish. When you sweep the floor, at first, you throw away the large chunks of rubbish but still, the smaller chunks are there. Your work is not completed yet and when you remove the smaller chunks of rubbish, there are still dust particles. Even after the first sweeping, there will still be finer dust particles there. So, the effort must be kept up until all those hindrances and defilements are put aside.

Only then, will the mindfulness become clear, bright, and shining. One must be determined to fulfil this purpose of overcoming the hindrances. This is the first duty of a yogi when he practices mindfulness meditation. Having accomplished that, the basic objects become clearer.

What use is there for a well
If there is water everywhere?
When craving's root is severed
What should one go about
*   seeking?*

UDANA 7.9

There is, bhikkhus,
that base*
where there is no earth,
no water,
no fire,
no air,
no base consisting of the infinity of space,
no base consisting of the infinity of consciousness,
no base consisting of nothingness,
no base consisting of neither-perception-nor-non-perception;
neither this world nor another world nor both;
neither sun nor moon.

Here, bhikkhus, I say
there is no coming,
no going,
no staying,
no deceasing,
no uprising.

Not fixed,
not movable,
it has no support.

Just this is the end of suffering.

UDANA 8.1

———————

*Nibbana

Priority of Objects

SYSTEMATIC NOTING & CHOICELESS AWARENESS

Question: What objects do we watch?

Answer: We watch the object(s) that are easy for us to do so with mindfulness, watching their true nature.

This will differ with different people and conditions. In the Mahasi tradition one is taught to watch the "rising" and "falling." When one watches it mindfully one is actually observing not only the element of motion, but also many other conditioned phenomena connected with it. This is a good starting point because:

- Since "rising" and "falling" belongs to the material phenomena, it is gross and therefore, easy to observe. The mental phenomena like consciousness is more elusive and subtle.
- It is not painful so one can note longer without distress or getting tired.
- It moves and changes and so, it is not as monotonous as a stationary one. Moreover, it exhibits the characteristic of change clearly.

Having made some effort and time to watch it, one becomes accustomed to it. It will become dominant and serve as a primary

*The world is held in bondage by delusion
And only appears to be capable.*
To a fool, held in bondage by clinging
And wrapped up in darkness,
It appears to be eternal,
But for one who sees there is nothing.*

UDANA 7.10

---

*Of being able to act freely and independent of delusion.

object where one can use it as a base for developing mindfulness as well as concentration.

But as Nature will have its way, it will show inconsistency and irregularities. So at times it will either be absent or blurred. At those times other objects will dominate (eg sound, pain) and so they have to be mindfully noted. Another reason another object has to be noted is when that object is a defilement (eg attachment, sleepiness, anger, restlessness) and therefore it is necessary that it is dealt with and removed. These objects, which usually do not require long periods of noting (unlike the primary object), are called secondary objects. When the secondary objects need to or otherwise remain long, they are considered as primary objects to build up mindfulness and concentration.

For example, when the "rising" and "falling" objects are absent, one may use the "sitting" and "touching (sensation)" objects as the primary object. When pain later becomes very dominant and persistent, then it takes the central position of meditation objects.

In walking meditation, the walking process is the primary (1°) object(s). "Seeing" then is an important secondary (2°) object. (°) means degree—primary degree and secondary degree object.

The opposite diagram shows the shift of primary and secondary objects in systematic noting during a sitting meditation. In brief:

1 The first priority is the dominant object which is easy to watch mindfully for a long period of time.

2 The dominant object will be replaced, firstly, by an object which is necessary to be watched and got rid of—ie hindrance/defilement.

3 The first priority object may be replaced, secondly, by another very dominant object—eg strong pain.

4 In a choice between more than one secondary (2°) object that is of equal dominance, one gives internal objects eg "sitting/touching" the choice rather than external objects e.g. sound which is not conducive to the deepening of concentration.

FLOW CHART ON PRIORITY OF OBJECT IN SITTING MEDITATION
Shift of Primary and Secondary Objects in Systematic Noting

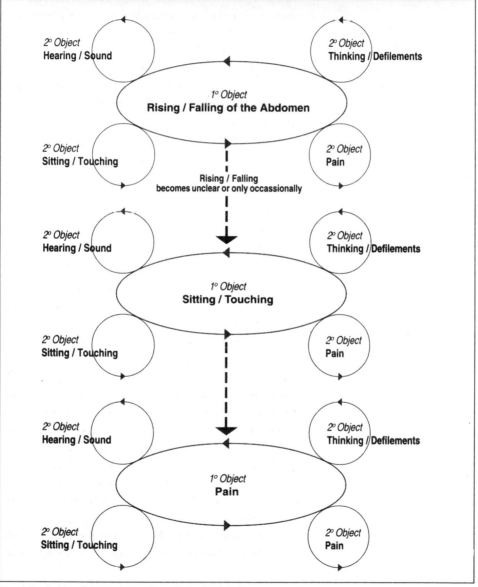

2° Object
Hearing / Sound

2° Object
Thinking / Defilements

1° Object
Rising / Falling of the Abdomen

2° Object
Sitting / Touching

2° Object
Pain

Rising / Falling
becomes unclear or only occassionally

2° Object
Hearing / Sound

2° Object
Thinking / Defilements

1° Object
Sitting / Touching

2° Object
Sitting / Touching

2° Object
Pain

2° Object
Hearing / Sound

2° Object
Thinking / Defilements

1° Object
Pain

2° Object
Sitting / Touching

2° Object
Pain

1° and 2° refers to primary and secondary objects respectively.

5 When mindfulness can become continuous, the mind becomes flexible and so, one may choose to watch an object that is conducive to build up insight better than another ie, they exhibit the three characteristics of impermanence, unsatisfactoriness and non-self.

Impermanence: The changing object is preferred to an unchanging one. *Unsatisfactoriness:* A painful rather than a blissful one which strongly encourages attachment. *Non-self:* One which exhibits non-ownership i.e. without active, personal control.

The above is done only so long as one can handle it. For example:

- Change may be so erratic and fast that one can become distracted or confused.
- Pain and unsatisfactoriness may be so strong and exhausting that anger arises.
- Things may happen in very uncontrollable and weird ways that they become terrifying or frightening.

6 If one's mindfulness and concentration do develop, then even subtle mental phenomena become clear, and subtle aspects of gross material phenomena are also observed. At those phases, mental phenomena are watched more frequently.

At such times the effort is made mainly to maintain or guard the mindfulness to ensure its continuity. The mind is left to choose its objects, and one has no time to think. With practice, mindfulness goes on by itself. This is also the time when labeling is dropped. This type of undirected mindfulness is called Choiceless Awareness which is often more stable but comes about only after much practice.

The beginner meditator must use the systematic way of noting (no. 1–5) to build up the necessary mindfulness and concentration.

Choiceless Awareness, however, can also be used at times when the mind is overactive or restless. It occurs with people

who run around a lot and become tensed up towards the day. Trying hard to direct the mind to its object often ends up *making it worse.* In such a case one may choose to be mindful of whatever that comes across the mind's eye. When mindfulness and tranquillity set in, then one may use systematic noting to direct the mind to its object.

THE FOUR FOUNDATIONS OF MINDFULNESS

In the discourse of the Four Foundations of Mindfulness, one can find the objects of Vipassana classified into four categories:

1   Body Foundation of Mindfulness—
              Material Phenomena (*Rupa*)
2   Feeling Foundation of Mindfulness—
              Feeling (*Vedana*)
3   Mind Foundation of Mindfulness—
              Consciousness (*Citta*)
4   Dhamma Foundation of Mindfulness—
              Mental States (*Sankhara*)

If one's mindfulness and concentration do develop, then even subtle mental phenomena become clear, and subtle aspects of gross material phenomena are also observed.

Generally, these are of progressive subtleties—and so, usually the meditator would tend to see more of the first foundation then increasingly more of the second, then the third and finally the fourth as one advances.

Yet within each foundation can also be found its own whole range of phenomena.

Feelings, for example, range from extreme pain to the very subtle neutral feelings not perceivable to the beginner. Consciousness ranges from angry consciousness to deep states of absorptions.

There are meditators who may choose to do more of one foundation than others which they claim to be more suited to their temperament. The Commentary also advises likewise, according to the suitability.

From experience, many have found that, even though it is interesting to explore into the foundations other than the often stressed Body Foundation of Mindfulness, it is still very important to find a firm foothold in this before proceeding elsewhere. This is because the Body Foundation is an easier base wherein to maintain one's mindfulness, especially when conditions are difficult, as in daily life, or when conditions are very strange, as in deeper states of intensive practice. Without it, one can end up at quite a loss as to what is best to do.

The uninclined * is hard to see,
The truth is not easy to see;
Craving is penetrated by one who
knows.
For one who sees there is nothing.

UDANA 8.2

---

*Some eds. read anattam, presumably understood as " non-self," but Comy. supports anatam: "It is craving that is called nata (inclining) because of its inclining to the various sense objects and to the various types of being, and also because, by its occurrence bent in that direction, it makes being inclined there. Where there is no such inclining is anata, 'the uninclined,' meaning Nibbana."

See the world with its devas,
Destitute of wisdom,
Established in name-and-form,
Conceiving this to be the truth.

Wisdom which leads to penetration
Is the best thing in the world;
By this one completely understands
The ending of both birth and being.

Devas and human beings hold dear
Those awakened ones ever mindful,
Possessing joyous wisdom,
Bearing their final bodies.

UDANA 4.1

The Five Controlling Faculties

The skill of balancing the faculties is very important in the practice of vipassana meditation. This is especially true when one goes for long retreats. As the mind becomes more powerful, the mental faculties are more worked up. It is just like when a car becomes more powerful and can go at a greater speed, you need to control the car better, otherwise you might just shoot off at a tangent due to complications.

THE FIVE CONTROLLING FACULTIES

First, let us look at some definitions. When we say "controlling faculties," we refer to the five controlling faculties of:

1 faith or confidence,
2 energy,
3 mindfulness,
4 concentration and
5 wisdom.

"Controlling faculty" means to exert control over the mind, or the mental powers. Like in the analogy of driving a car, there are different

Merit grows for one who gives;
No enmity builds up for one
    restrained;
One skilled abandons evil deeds;
With passion, hate, and delusion
    exhausted,
One attains release, final Nibbana.

UDANA 8.5

controls for different purposes—the steering wheel controls the direction you go, the accelerator controls how fast you go and so forth.

Of these five controlling faculties, the main controlling faculty is *mindfulness*. To give you an idea of how this operates, I will first give a linear or progressive relationship. When you start, you must first have confidence or faith in the practice. If you had no confidence in the practice, you would not have started anyway. The faith is based on the purity of mind and on the benefits of the way of practice. When you have enough confidence to practise, you make effort. Effort made in the practice can be considered as the energy-controlling faculty. Because of this, when you practise sufficiently, the mindfulness will arise. When mindfulness arises, it becomes continuous and concentrated. When the concentration occurs, we call it *concentrated awareness on the object*. This is what we call the concentration faculty. When the concentrated awareness focuses on the reality ie on the real object, when it experiences it, it is like a strong light that is focused on the object, you can really see what it is. When it grasps the meaning or the idea of what it really is—that is the insight or wisdom faculty.

Faith or confidence is based on the purity of mind and on the benefits of the way

of practice.

With the gaining of understanding and insight, more confidence is aroused and therefore, we can put even more energy into the practice. With more energy, more mindfulness arises and with more mindfulness, more concentration is focused on the object, and so forth until you get more insight. It is like a cycle that revolves, increasing in speed.

In the beginning, it is a matter of faith and energy. It is not so much of balancing; it is more of arousing. After a lot of practice, meditation becomes more a matter of balancing between the energy and concentration faculties. When we say "balancing the faculties," we usually mean the balance between faith and insight (wisdom), and the balance between concentration and energy. The balancing of faith and insight (wisdom) occurs more frequently at the very beginning because actual insight has not yet arisen. It is at a more basic and superficial level. The wisdom that is present is more theoretical and of mundane nature. The faith is also that which does not come with wisdom and experience, it only comes from thinking or devotion.

In Buddhist countries, the faith comes from cultural and parental influences. The person may follow the advice of monks with blind faith. This can be dangerous and it is not recommended. The methods taught may not all be correct and there is a tendency to gullibility. Therefore, one should exercise more thought before every action. On the other hand, in the case where the basic devotion and the faith is not there—like outside of Buddhist countries—where people are more intellectual, scepticism may arise because of the lack of faith.

A number of spiritual things cannot be fathomed by thinking. One has to try to experiment with a method for a long enough time to find out for oneself. Then, if the method is suitable to you there will be progress. If one only thinks and looks for one hundred percent surety and guarantee, one will never really sit down to practise properly and so, one will not get results.

CONCENTRATION AND ENERGY

As one embarks on the practice, the mental controlling faculties will become stronger. When this happens, the main concern for those in a meditation retreat will be the balancing of the energy and the concentration faculties.

What do we mean by "balance"? When I say, "the mind is balanced," it means that the mind is being as mindful as it can get and that it is at a point of optimal functioning of mindfulness.

When the mind is not well-balanced, one of the faculties is in excess while the other one is lacking. This is describing the faculties in terms of proportion. When one says that the concentration faculty is in excess, it also means that the energy faculty is lacking and vice versa.

In actual experience, however, it is not so much of a calculation. It is more of experiencing a certain state of consciousness.

Whatever recluses and brahmins have said
that freedom from being comes about through some kind of being,
none of them, I say, are freed from being.

And whatever recluses and brahmins have said that escape from being comes about through non-being, none of them, I say, have escaped from being.

This suffering arises dependent upon clinging. With the end of all grasping, no suffering is produced.

UDANA 3.10 (EXTRACT)

Let me give you a better idea. When we talk of the energy-controlling faculty, we are referring to the active aspect of mindfulness. Energy is active whereas the concentration faculty is the still and tranquil factor of mindfulness. When one's mind is at the optimal state of mindfulness, that means, one is following one's meditation object, such as the "rising" and "falling," easily. At the same time, the mind is also actively noting what is happening.

However, if energy is excessive and concentration is lacking, the mind may become too active. It is like when you are very excited and you try to follow the "rising" and "falling" of the abdomen but you cannot follow it very well because the mind has a tendency to jump about—a tendency to think and wander. It cannot stick to the object because the concentration is lacking.

However, if the concentration factor is in excess then one stays with the object for a long time. The mind is very calm and still but you cannot see many things. It just holds in there, not actively observing and following things around. Finally it becomes very still, calm, then the mind goes blank, and you fall asleep. Neither excessive energy nor excessive concentration is recommended. When either of these is in excess, the mind is not so stable.

If the process is further continued then, of course, excessive concentration would end up in sloth and torpor, whereas excessive energy would end up in restlessness. It would be very wise, when you notice that mindfulness is not functioning so well, to make effort to balance it.

In the beginning of the retreat, the balancing is not so much in question because there is not much concentration and not much wisdom at all—there is only energy. The thing to do is to make effort with mindfulness. Effort is like pushing, trying very hard to be mindful. The question is "How hard do you push?"

How much effort?

It is a matter of controlling the amount of energy. When you push too hard and you lose track of the mindfulness, you may become too tense. Whereas, if you do not make enough effort, you fall into sloth and torpor. So, there has to be a point whereby you try hard enough so that you reach the optimal state of mindfulness. This again has to be learned from experience. Some people push themselves very hard and become tense and sickly. Others are so lazy; they expect everything to work by itself. Then, of course, there is no progress.

By following the correct method of practice and pushing oneself long enough, the mental faculties—the mental powers—eventually become strong. Concentration will eventually arise and that is when the mindfulness and the balancing are essential. In other words, the mind becomes more powerful, and the concentration and other the mental faculties, become more intense.

What will happen then?

A number of things can happen. When the energy is too strong and your mind powers are strong, the mental energy is highly charged. Without mindfulness it becomes unbalanced and you will find that you cannot sleep. Your mind is very bright. You may be able to follow the object ie the "rising" and "falling" but it cannot sink in. This occurs, for example, when one is watching pain. When one is watching pain for an extended period, the mind becomes very highly charged, very energetic because you need a lot of energy to be able to face pain. After the period of pain, the body may be very exhausted but the mind is very bright. There is no trace of sloth and torpor there.

However, when you try to go back to the "rising" and "falling," you may be able to follow it but you cannot sink in. The mind is floating on top. It does not want to go in and is very bright. Moreover, when you try to go to sleep you cannot, you just toss and turn. Excessive concentration occurs more with people who have done samatha meditation, or with those who, while meditating, tend to place too much stress on concentration. What happens is that, the mind repeatedly goes into very still and calm states! At that point, there may be a certain degree of indulgence in that—it just stays there. You can sit for a long time but it does not penetrate. The mind is not able to follow all the details of the mind and body processes.

*Those who have made a bridge
Cross over the river flood,
Leaving the swampy pools behind.
While people are binding a raft
The wise are already across.**

UDANA 8.6

**According to Comy., the bridge is the noble path, the flood is samsara, and its flow is craving. The last two lines imply that without the knowledge of the noble path, there is no effective way of escaping from samsara. While still having attachments ("binding a raft") people experience sorrow (flounder in the "swampy pools") and are unable to extricate themselves from samsara ("cross over the river flood"). That the path-moment is immediately followed by its fruit is indicated by the instantaneous crossing by "the wise," i.e. the Buddha and his disciples.*

There will not be any pain at all. Sometimes, even visual images arise and they last for a long time. This is a state of stagnation. Therefore, when this happens, one has to balance the mind.

This balancing is not as easy as it seems. Sometimes it takes some time before the mind gets balanced because at this stage of mental awareness, of concentration, it works more under the influence of momentum. The many days of meditation build the momentum up until it flows in a certain way. The very moment when that happens, you may not be able to control the whole force that is working there. Therefore, you may need some time to redirect it or balance it.

Make your mind clear, alert and actively noting.

HOW DO YOU BALANCE THE FIVE CONTROLLING FACULTIES?

1 Employing the correct type of mindfulness

There are two ways to balance the faculties. One is to increase the faculty and the other is to decrease it. The safer way is in decreasing it, taking it easy, slowing down because you do not know where it is going. First, you have to identify which is more and which is less. Without experience, this is not easy. You only know that your mind is stuck somewhere and it is getting too intense. When this happens and you are not quite sure—just relax, relax the faculties, turn the controls down. Of course, if you can identify what it is, you increase that faculty which is lacking, and when you increase it, the faculties will keep building up.

Let us consider some of the methods of balancing the faculties. First, there is the type of mindfulness you apply and how you apply it. Increasing the energy is a more intense form of noting. Make your mind clear, alert and actively noting. For example, if you are feeling a little sleepy, then energy is lacking and you have to increase the energy. You may say "sleepy, sleepy, sleepy" but it may not work. If you say "sl-e-e-py, sl-e-e-py" then it is even worse. You have to say it very fast. It is like shooting a machine gun. Another example is if pain arises. When pain arises, you need a lot of energy. Without energy, you cannot face it. So what do you do? You say, "pain, pain, pain" but sometimes it does not work. You must say it very, very fast like the machine gun. Then active energy builds up, the mindfulness is balanced, and you can take off.

Of course, on the other hand when the energy is too much, you must go more to the concentration faculty. In such a case, you do not use such a strong intense noting; you use soft and gentle noting. For example, your mind is overactive. You have a lot of energy but you cannot sink in. There is a kind of excitement in the mind. When you say "rising, falling, rising..." it is as if your mind is floating on top. Therefore, what you should do is not to try so hard. Just relax, let everything happen and just watch softly, "rising" and "falling." You should not think of increasing the concentration or of getting results.

People who are very goal-oriented tend to push themselves too hard. They use too much energy. They should just sit back, relax, and see what happens. If there is nothing then you can tell yourself that at least you have some calmness and peace of mind. So, you just sit and relax. Then when you find that it fits nicely, you just follow it, and when everything is comfortable, peaceful, and nice and you do not have too much expectations, then the mind just sinks into it and follows the object.

One point to remember is that there will come a moment when you just need to maintain that level of balance that has been achieved. For example, if you have a lot of sloth and torpor you push in energy to gain progress. But you do not need to keep on pushing it. You only push it to a point where it settles into the optimum state. If you push it too much then you go overboard and it becomes too energetic.

Similarly, when you find you have too much energy, you relax up to the point where you settle on the object. Once balanced,

Whatever sorrows or lamentations there are,
The various kinds of suffering in the world,
It is because of something dear that these exist;
Without something dear these do not exist.

So they are happy and free from sorrow
Who have nothing dear anywhere in the world.
So aspiring to be sorrowless and stainless
Do not hold dear anything anywhere in the world.

UDANA 8.8

maintain that level. Do not try to relax anymore. If you relax any further, you will fall asleep.

So, it is not just a matter of relaxing or increasing the energy, it is to know how much to increase and how much to relax. There will come a point where it settles at a level and you maintain that level with equanimity.

2   Directed Awareness and Choiceless Awareness

There is another way of looking at the balancing of the faculties. We say there are two types of mindfulness. One is *directed awareness* and the other is *choiceless awareness*. Directed awareness is when we look for an object, go to it, chase it and note it actively. This is needed at the beginning of the practice where the concentration faculty and the mindfulness faculty are weak. When you push it after an object, it builds up faster.

When you sit, you must follow the "rising" and "falling" mindfully. If there is no "rising" and "falling," you must push to watch the "sitting" and "touching" sensations. This is called directed awareness—directed mindfulness.

The other type is choiceless awareness. That means that you do not choose any particular object to watch. You just sit still, remain calm, and watch whatever comes and goes. This method works well for those who tend to grasp, push too hard and try to get good results in a short period. Then you find that the mind becomes an obsessive grasping. When that happens, you just tell the mind to let go of everything because when there is too much energy, it becomes too intense and develops into craving. What you should do is to just relax and do not care about anything. Do not even care that you may lose your mindfulness because you really need to relax the energy. When you do this, the mindfulness will settle in but it may take some time.

The reason why mindfulness may take some time to settle in could be first, there is the fear that if you relax and have choiceless awareness, you will not progress and meditation will be lost and you will have no more mindfulness. Because of that you cling on to the noting, cling on to trying very hard to be mindful and consequently, tension is maintained. But, if you just let go, "do not care," and just relax— checking sometime after, to ensure that there is still awareness and mindfulness even though you had let go—mindfulness will settle in more easily and calmly. Over a period, the mind will be more open and relaxed. When the mindfulness has settled into a stable state, you can push if you want to and the tension will not arise. This is what we call "choiceless awareness."

This type of choiceless awareness occurs more frequently in more advanced practice. This is because when the practice becomes more advanced, the meditation objects may sometimes become random. The "rising" and "falling" becomes very subtle and as you try to watch it, many objects may arise—feelings, pains, sensations- and it is very difficult to pinpoint a specific object. Alternatively, it could happen that many objects arise and pass away very fast and you cannot watch any one of them specifically. You may try to, but your intentional noting is too slow.

Therefore, you just maintain a one-pointed awareness of whatever comes and goes. Usually, at this stage, it is just pure awareness of consciousness. If you can maintain that, the mindfulness becomes very stable. This, again, is another form of choiceless awareness. In choiceless awareness, the build-up of concentration is not so fast but it is more stable.

3 Other forms of balancing

Other forms can be used to balance the faculties. One is the use of the postures. Certain postures are associated with certain objects and certain faculties. Walking meditation, for example, is associated with the building up of energy because when one is walking, one is active. Moreover, to follow the footsteps, the mind has to be very energetic. Therefore, it is easier to overcome sloth and torpor by walking meditation.

The body disintegrated,
perception ceased,
All feelings become cool,
Mental activities were calmed,
And consciousness came to
*an end. *

UDANA 8.9

These are the five aggregates
(khandha), the groups of unstable and
impermanent components that
constitute what we call " a being." They
continue in process through the round of
rebirths but cease at the parinibbana or
passing away of an arahat.

Sitting meditation, on the other hand, is more conducive to concentration because the whole body is still and the "rising" and "falling" of the abdomen is a natural process. We do not have to intentionally breathe as we have to intentionally walk. It is therefore easier to keep the mind still and just watch the "rising" and "falling." Hence, by apportioning the walking and sitting meditation sessions, it is possible to balance the faculties. That is why it is often recommended that you do an equal amount of walking and sitting. If you sit for a long time, there is a tendency to just increase the concentration faculty. On the other hand, if you walk too much, there is a tendency to increase the energy faculty to an excessive point.

It is more important, though, to bear in mind the idea of mental proportion rather than of physical time. If you say that you want to increase the energy faculty and hence you walk for over an hour or possibly two hours, energy does increase but it is taxing on the body. You will get very tired. The main things here are actually the faculties within the mind itself. One need not, for example, increase the faculties by the change of postures.

As I have said, directed awareness and so forth can increase the energy faculty. Therefore, the change of postures or the proportioning of postures is a rather gross way of doing it.

Certain other objects would be more conducive to producing energy or concentration. Let us compare, for example, the "rising" and "falling" with the "sitting" and "touching." Between the two, the "sitting" and "touching" tends to arouse more energy than concentration. This is because sitting and touching are not moving activities—you really have to arouse energy and push the mind towards the "sitting" and "touching" by watching the points of contact and the sensations.

In contrast, the "rising" and "falling" tends to build up a momentum and a flow so that after a while, the mind will also be in the momentum and the flow. Moreover, you do not need much effort to follow it. That is why when you are very sleepy, it might be more

If you sit for a long time, there is a tendency to just increase the concentration faculty.

appropriate to do the "sitting" and "touching" with many touch points to arouse energy rather than concentration. Also, that is why we use the "rising" and "falling" as the main meditation object because it is more suitable for arousing concentration than the "sitting" and "touching." With the "sitting" and "touching," we tend to get many other sensations and therefore, it tends to be more discursive. However, when you do "rising" and "falling," it is like following one moving point. When you can focus long enough on one moving point, the concentration builds up.

Pain, on the other hand, arouses more energy. If you are able to watch it with a pure consciousness, it tends to arouse concentration because pure consciousness withdraws from all the other sense objects and goes only into the mind.

If one fails to make use of the vipassana objects to balance the faculties, then other things can be resorted to, such as, the samatha methods. For instance, if you are sunk in sloth and torpor, you can use the perception of light and recitations to motivate the mind. There are also other forms of samatha methods such as the kasinas or visualisations and even the breath. These latter ones are more conducive to calming the mind.

BALANCING OF FACULTIES IS DYNAMIC

The balancing of the faculties is not static. In fact, it is very dynamic. It is just like when we are going uphill on a bicycle. You need to balance and you must put in more effort. You will have to hold on to the bicycle handle absolutely still so that you will not fall over. This principle applies when we balance the faculties in meditation.

Why? Because as we progress, the mental powers have to be increased proportionately. Progress in meditation is actually an increase of all the mental faculties. Therefore, as you progress in meditation, you will have to make more effort. The higher you go, the more effort has to be aroused. It is not that frightening in the sense that by that time, there is also a considerable degree of

One who knows the "All "
in every way,
Who is not attached to anything,
Having fully understood the "All,"
Has overcome all suffering

ITIVUTTKA 7

mindfulness. In addition, energy can come quite automatically. Nevertheless, you will have to increase the energy faculty as you progress as the different types of meditation objects that arise can become subtler and more difficult to note. They can also be more horrible in the sense of more suffering.

The mind has to stay even more still and quieter in the advanced stages of practice.

So, you will have to keep increasing the energy faculty, otherwise you will not be able to deal with those objects. Sometimes, they can be so fine and pleasant that it is very easy to be attached to them. Therefore, you must really apply a lot of energy to face them until you come to a point where the energy is so strong that you can override all thoughts and objects. However, if the energy faculty or the active aspect of the mental powers just increases while the concentration is not there to keep it still, the mind becomes rather unbalanced, too active and too highly charged. Therefore, you will also need to increase the concentration faculty hand in hand. The mind has to stay even more still and quieter in the advanced stages of practice. This is what we mean by "the progress of vipassana consciousness."

AS WE PROGRESS IN MEDITATION

Vipassana consciousness is seeing things as they really are; being able to accept them and be detached from them. It also means being able to see them, understand them, transcend our attachments to them and therefore, go beyond them.

As we progress in meditation, the objects become finer and finer as well as deeper and deeper. Therefore, you must be able to hold them and note them. If the mind is not present in that moment, then you will not be able to gain the insight to reach final liberation.

However, once we are able to do that, the mind gains a certain momentum. We can then guide it further and further to the point where the mind is very calm and equanimous. At the same time, it is able to note all objects without any problem and see how they arise and pass away. The mind becomes very equanimous with deep concentration and deep understanding of the nature of impermanence and so forth. If we are to have any idea of what developed vipassana meditation is, then it would be this.

The state of the vipassana consciousness is where the five mental controlling faculties are highly developed in a balanced manner. When this happens, the energy faculty is such that when you sit, you can do so for hours without any difficulty. The energy and the mindfulness faculties are fully developed. The mind by itself is able to observe everything in minute detail. The concentration is present to hold the mindfulness in a concentrated state. At the same time, the concentration allows the mind to go deep into the meditation object for a long period. It is as if the observation keeps going on and on and keeps going deeper and deeper all by itself until it reaches the point where it can penetrate through all the mind and body processes to find realisation.

Sometimes, however, before that happens, the mind may go overboard ie it has either too much concentration or too much energy. This is because of the different conditions and also because the mindfulness is not yet strong and stable. In such a case, we have to take the appropriate action to balance the faculties.

This account will give you a brief understanding of the balancing of the faculties. Balancing of the faculties can be regarded as *cittanupassana* or the mindfulness of consciousness whereby you are able to detect all the subtle states of consciousness as they come and go.

But those who have abandoned conceit,
And who by destroying conceit are freed,
Have conquered the bondage of conceit
And overcome all suffering.

ITIVUTTKA 8

Or repeated birth, punabbhava. Bhava: being, becoming, or existence, is one of the factors in the formula of dependent arising (paticca-samuppada). Being arises from grasping and leads to birth, death and suffering.

There is, bhikkhus,
a not-born,
a not-brought-to-being,
a-not-made,
a-not-conditioned.

If, bhikkhus,
there were not-born,
not-brought-to-being,
not-made,
a-not-conditioned,
no escape would be discerned
from what is born,
brought-to-being,
made,
conditioned.

But since there is
a not-born,
a not-brought-to-being,
a not-made,
a not-conditioned,
therefore an escape is discerned
from what is born,
brought-to-being,
made,
conditioned.

UDANA 8.3

Balancing the
Five Controlling Faculties

THE BALANCING OF ENERGY AND CONCENTRATION

First let us look at the balancing of the Energy (E) and Concentration (C) faculties.

The E/C balance refers to how these two factors, when present together, give rise to a certain state of consciousness. When they are well-balanced (+C+E) or (−C−E) the mind is stable and so is conducive to mindfulness. If imbalanced, the mind tends towards one factor and so leads towards excessive energy (+E−C) or lethargy (−E+C).

This balance-relationship should not be confused with other mental factors that are also present at the same time. For example, in a normal person (not meditator) having a clear state of mind is balanced with E/C but it does not mean his mindfulness is very strong. Therefore it is necessary to include another variable (P) to clarify the situation. (P) represents the mental power or drive which increases with continuous and intensive mental exercise. I would clarify this as "*chanda*" or "wish to do" or as an Abhidhamma book defines it as "that phenomenon that wishes for the object."

*By fully understanding the
form element
Without getting stuck in the
formless,
They are released into cessation
And leave Death far behind them.*

*Having touched with his
own person
The deathless element free from
clinging,
Having realized the
relinquishment of clinging
His taints all gone,
The Fully Enlightened One
proclaims
The sorrowless state that is
void of stain.*

UDANA 5.1

Here we will label

P1 as presence of the drive

P2 as stronger drive

P3 as very strong drive

The vital play of these three variables can be best represented in the chart given together with the description of the types of consciousness that corresponds to the combination.

P1 Level

At the beginning of meditation when the momentum of the mental conditioning is yet to really pick up. This may occur in the first few days of a retreat.

−S **Without mindfulness, therefore mind is unwholesome**

−E−C Balanced state of E C, but as mindfulness is absent, it is unwholesome. This represents a weak state of consciousness represented mainly by dullness. Even though greed and anger may be present, it is nevertheless not pronounced.

+E−C Energy > Concentration, so the mind though not strong still tends towards restlessness and wanders to many irrelevant matters.

−E+C Concentration > Energy. This represents a sleepy, dreamy or lethargic mind, often appears when you try to meditate very early in the morning.

+E+C One becoming more tense and disturbed inside.

+S **Mindfulness present, therefore mind is wholesome.**

−E−C Mildly mindful but as the faculties are not strong, the mindfulness is also not strong. Such a balanced state is like that of an ordinary man's mind in a sane state as having just recovered from a shock.

+E−C Energy > Concentration: mindful but unable to remain long at one object, tends to note many objects yet not particularly intending to do so.

−E+C   Concentration > Energy: where one's mind calms down with meditation although can still be easily disturbed. One is also not particularly alert to the nature of the object.

+E+C   Mindfulness becoming better and concentration begins to deepen. Mindfulness is more or less continuous.

P2 Level

After the first week, the momentum picks up. The mind becomes more powerful which may be either good or bad! Of course, with the proper method, it should be good.

−S   **Without mindfulness, therefore mind is unwholesome**

−E−C   as above in P1 (+E+C).

+E−C   Mind becoming extremely restless, runs all over but you cannot stop it. Just like one who has been thinking a lot about many problems but cannot solve them, tension builds up.

−E+C   Mind becoming very stiff or heavy. Objects usually magnified and overly sensitive. Nimittas or visual mental objects may be plentiful and remain long. A lot of heaviness builds up in the head.

+E+C   Mind almost hysterical. Feels like screaming, or depressed. May last for hours (Danger point).

+S   **Mindfulness present, therefore mind is wholesome.**

−E−C   as above in P1 (+E+C).

+E−C   Mind very bright and alert and mindful but cannot go into deep concentration. Hovers above them or even runs to external objects. Occurs quite often after a very thorough walking meditation when the mind is charged up after a lot of active noting.

−E+C   Concentration deepens with some mindfulness still present and so no tension is built up even though heaviness may be present. One may not hear sounds and

No other single thing exists
Like the hindrance of delusion,
Which so obstructs humankind
And makes it wander on forever.

Those who have abandoned delusion,
Cleaving through this mass of darkness,
No longer roam and wander on;
In them the cause is found no more.

ITIVUTTAKA 14

wake up very refreshed. But one cannot note anything in detail or sharply.

+E+C Mindfulness is sharp and concentration deep. Good meditation is on the way. One is able to observe mental and material processes as they are with their specific and general characteristics.

P3 Level

After many weeks (or longer) of intensive practice, you may expect the mind to be in full gear. How far you have gone depends on the power (P) of your vehicle (mind).

−S **Without mindfulness, therefore mind is unwholesome.**

−E−C as in P2 (+E+C).

+E−C Mind is completely distracted and out of control.

+C−E Obsessive or compulsive mind over a subject matter. One is shut off, completely withdrawn. The mind may be completely hallucinated.

+C+E A mad person's mind; one has gone berserk.

+S **Mindfulness present, therefore mind is wholesome.**

−E−C as in P2 (+E+C).

+E−C Mind is extremely alert and bright. Cannot sleep. Keeps meditating through nights, but deep concentration does not last long.

+C−E Concentration is very deep and goes into very long and blissful absorptions, but mindfulness and insight does not develop fast or clearly.

+C+E Mind is like a saint's. Unshaken by worldly conditions because one understands the true nature of the world and as such, is detached.

From the above, it is obvious that when one undertakes meditation intensively it is very important to have mindfulness (S). This one factor serves to guard the mind from going astray into wrong concentration. It would do a world of good to have some degree of mindfulness even if one is undertaking pure tranquillity exercise which often overlooks this factor.

When (S) is present then one is at least safe. If one is not sure then one better make sure or else stop.

The next step would be to balance the energy (E) and concentration (C) faculties. This can be done by increasing one (+) or decreasing (−) the other. In the beginning of the meditation, it would be more appropriate to add (+) to the weak faculty. Not too much harm can be done as the power (P) is weak anyway.

Eg in case of Pl $(-E+C)++E = Pl (E+C)$

But should the faculties be in a more developed form, then one may weaken (−) the stronger faculty for a safer approach (ie to relax) especially when insufficient attention and time is available to keep one in check or one is lacking in expertise.

Eg in case of P2 $(-E+C) - - C = P2 (-E-C)$

However, if one is with ample attention and expertise, then one may go on to increase (+) the lacking faculty as this approach would promise quicker progress.

Eg in case of P1 $(-E+C) + + E = P1 (+E+C)$
Eg in case of P2 $(-E+C) - - C = P2 (-E-C)$
Eg in case of P2 $(-E+C) + + E = P2 (+E+C)$

An important point is not just increasing or decreasing any particular faculty. It is **how much** to increase or decrease **which** one. This comes with experience but as a general criterion, it is the point where the mindfulness is most stable and it proceeds to deepen with concentration. That is to say, with an increase in mindfulness, energy and concentration deepens hand in hand.

THE BALANCING OF FAITH AND WISDOM

Unlike the balance of energy and concentration faculties which often functions like a tug of war or a pair of weighing scales, the

A man companioned by craving
Wanders on this long journey;
He cannot go beyond samsara
In this state of being or another.

Having understood the danger
thus—
That craving is the origin of
suffering—
A bhikkhu should wander mindfully,
Free from craving, without
grasping.

ITIVUTTAKA 15

confidence and wisdom faculties are concerned with the beginnings and endings of the practice. This is so when the wisdom we speak of is that which arises out of meditation (*bhavana maya pañña*), and such wisdom does not come at the start, but is developed with practice. So, any tug of war or balancing that would actually happen would involve wisdom that arises with thinking (*cinta maya pañña*) and so does not come at the moment of actual noting or observation. In any case, we are not into the pure observation practice in all of our waking hours. Therefore a balance of faith and wisdom at those lower levels are a necessity to provide a stable base, otherwise sceptical doubts (because of perplexed and speculative thinking) may arise to paralyse the practice or excessive faith leads the gullible into wrong practice. Such a balance can be brought about by proper interviews with a good teacher who can provide inspiration and encouragement when your faith is at its low ebb and needs information and experience when wisdom is lacking. In the actual practice, it may therefore be more appropriate to ask:

Balance can be brought about by proper interviews with a good teacher who can provide inspiration and encouragement when faith is at its low ebb.

In what way does faith/confidence play in building up the faculties to lead towards emancipation?

Faith or confidence is like a starter or spark plug. It is the beginning of spiritual life. In Buddhism, faith is faith in the Triple Gem (Buddha, Dhamma and Sangha).

Through this we perform meritorious deeds (of *dana, sila, bhavana*) that bring us happiness. It is like a key to a treasure box. So, it has been said: *faith is the greatest wealth*.

But if our faith can only take us so far as to do charity and the observance of precepts, it can only offer us the happiness of humans and sensual heavens. If it takes us to practise pure tranquillity meditation that lead to mundane absorptions (*lokiya jhana*) then it will bring us to the happiness of Brahmas. All these are impermanent, though much better than suffering in the woeful states. It would be much better if it takes us out of the cycle of birth and death (*samsara*) and be completely free from suffering and attain everlasting peace— Nibbana. As such it must necessarily not only lead us to practise Vipassana but also practise it to the very end. This is like crossing the ocean, and so it has been said that, it is by faith that a man crosses the ocean.

Therefore the faith faculty must not only generate the energy to practise, but one must be confident enough to practise long enough to also generate all the other faculties of mindfulness, concentration and wisdom.

Those who think, "We cannot simply have enough time to practise", cannot be said to have enough faith, for if there is faith one can find the time.

Again, if one is to say, "Nowadays people cannot reach the holy path," one may say he does not only not allow himself the chance, he also writes off the chances of his fellow suffering beings. We cannot say he has enough faith either.

One should be more positive if one wants to achieve something worthwhile. Of course, one has also to be realistic. That is why blind faith is not recommended in Buddhism. So we need to have theory (but be selective of reading material) and teachers (of whom we often have to be selective too) and not to forget—that not so common "common sense." With experience, faith will strengthen as wisdom grows.

As aforementioned, wisdom that is derived from excessive thinking is more appropriately described as misdirected or speculative (ie wrong type of wisdom). In fact, the more the wisdom (derived from noting and observation) grows, the closer we are to our goal. It gives a better and better picture of the way, our mistakes, how to correct them, our good points and how to improve them. Finally it makes the truth known to us.

Wisdom is therefore the means to the end though not the end itself. This speaks just as well for wisdom born of cultivation—that often-talked about insights or insight knowledges. Therefore it will be a mistake to be attached to any of these.

For a bhikkhu who is a learner
There is no other thing so helpful
For reaching the highest goal
As the factor wise attention.
Wisely striving a bhikkhu may attain
The destruction of all suffering.

ITIVUTTAKA 16

With regard to the faculties, wisdom strengthens all of them like the cement that holds them all together in the required shape, for it gives light to the true meaning of all things. Therefore there is never an excess of this type of wisdom. They are too often badly lacking (except in the perfected ones).

WAYS OF BALANCING THE FACULTIES OF ENERGY AND CONCENTRATION

With special reference to the balancing of energy and concentration faculties, the ways which can be done are described below:

1 The type of mindfulness applied

Together with the consciousness (*citta*) in which mindfulness is associated, there are also other mental factors (*cetasika*) which will give rise to the type of mindfulness present here. Those that concern us here are none other than energy (*viriya*) and one-pointedness (*ekagatta*) which correspond to the two faculties in the balance. Hence if we can know more precisely what type of mindfulness is required, we can will it up.

- If we are sleepy and lethargic, what we need is the more energetic form of mindfulness. It is light yet effervescent, quickly coming out like one who is full of zeal. One has to remember that mental energy is not to be confused with physical energy. While bringing up mental energy it is best if it can be done with a relaxed body rather than one that is filled with tension. Then you can know this alertness, which is ever ready to act or the active aspect of mindfulness.

- However, when one's energy is excessive and inclined towards restlessness, then a more relaxed and easy-going form of mindfulness will bring about a balance. One should bring one's heart to a peaceful rest, bearing in mind the blessings of detachment. It is the still, peaceful and one-pointed aspect of mindfulness.

2 The system of mindfulness employed

"System" here refers to either one of the two:

a   **Systematic** or **Directed mindfulness** means the cultivation of mindfulness by directing the mindfulness to objects in a way or system. An approach has been given earlier with reference to the priority of objects. For example, first the meditator notes the basic object, then the secondary objects that had become dominant for the time being, etc.

b   **Choiceless awareness** is mindfulness of whatever objects that may arise and impinge on the mind's eye. No effort is made in the selection of objects to note.

Usually one begins with directed mindfulness because it is more energetic and encourages a more rapid build up of mindfulness, hence concentration. With regard to the four right efforts, it corresponds to the overcoming of evil states of mind and the arousing of pure states of mind that have not yet arisen.

Therefore it is used when faculties are weak or when strength is needed to overcome defilements or make headway to new insights.

Undirected mindfulness or choiceless awareness is used more often when mindfulness is more or less continuous. That is also when the subtler objects have become as noticeable as the grosser ones. There will also be many objects which you do not have a name for. By choiceless awareness, the mindfulness becomes very stable. In the four right efforts, it corresponds to the avoiding of evil states and maintaining of pure states. As the application of the mind to the object is reduced in this system, the energy factor too tends to be reduced. Concentration can also build up in this system but mindfulness has to be continuous. Hence, if the mind is restless, choiceless awareness can keep the mind tranquil and relaxed.

When a bhikkhu has good friends,
And is reverential and respectful,
Doing what his friends advise,
Clearly comprehending and
mindful,
He may progressively attain
*The destruction of all fetters.**

ITIVUTTAKA 17

The fetters (samyojana) are ten in number; personality view, doubt, clinging to external observances, sensual lust, ill will, craving for form, craving for the formless, conceit, restlessness, and ignorance. The stream-enterer has cut off the first three; the once-returner has also weakened the fourth and fifth; the non-returner has removed the first five; and the arahant has destroyed all ten.

3 Trial and Error Method

In practice it is not so easy to pinpoint how the faculties are not in balance. So in such situations we may employ the trial and error method.

For example, when a meditator encounters a "stuck mind", ie a mind that seems clogged up, and is unable to note much of anything. It may be due to excessive concentration or energy, or the meditator may be in doubt.

The meditator may try to start making the mind more balanced by noting a number of other touch points and increasing energetic mindfulness. If this fails, then one can relax, sit back and do choiceless awareness, and even if nothing happens, just remain so.

If this fails again, the meditator resorts to the first step again. Sooner or later one of them has got to work.

Sometimes we exert too much and we end up with one type of problem or "stuck mind" or, we may relax too much and also end up with another type of problem. Through practice we can reduce the excesses and insufficiencies and refine it to a point of exact balance. This balanced state of mindfulness deepens with an increase of equal proportions in the energy and concentration faculties. It is the development of ever deeper levels of awareness. That is, we become increasingly relaxed or calm as the alertness increases.

Sometimes we exert too much and we end up with one type of problem or "stuck mind"

If one can do this ie, continuously increasing in a balanced manner for a long time, one's meditation progress will go far.

Stuck mind may be referred to minds which are dull, lethargic, too much intense energy or inflexible concentration.

4 Choosing the suitable posture or objects that will arouse or reduce the faculties

a   The postures are physical in nature but they can affect the balancing of the faculties by:

i   Physical effort exerted (which influences the mind).

ii   The nature of the objects present.

Though physical effort and mental exertion are different, it does influence the latter to some extent. Generally we can understand that if we are involved in a lot of physical activities, the mind is also activated to some degree.

Roughly, we may put into a table according to the physical effort which may also correspond to the mental exertion involved.

+++E	Standing	(a lot of energy)
++E	Walking	(fair amount of energy)
+E	Sitting	(lesser amount of energy)
OE	Lying down	(no physical energy exerted)

Hence if we are lethargic or sleepy, standing and walking can help. And if we are restlessly tense or distracted, sitting or lying down can help. The last of the four (ie lying down) is usually not recommended as one will fall asleep too easily even though it can be done if one is sick or intends to sleep.

The general procedure is to do equal amounts (ie time) of sitting and walking (eg one hour each). Too much sitting or walking (ie more than one hour) is not favoured. This is especially so for beginners because too often, they are unable to maintain mindfulness well after that. However it must also be borne in mind that the balancing of faculties is mental and not physical, and so if one is progressing well in one's mindfulness and concentration even after an hour, there is no reason why one should change posture.

b   The objects involved with the postures can also influence the balancing of the faculties.

i   **"Sitting"** and **"Touching"**
      Whilst "touching" refers to the physical sensations at the point of contact, "sitting" refers to those physical sensations which are not at the points of contact. These consists of many physical forces—pulling, stretching, twisting, etc. that maintain the sitting posture in place. These comprise mainly

The eye, ear, nose, tongue,
Body and likewise the mind—
A bhikkhu who leaves these doors
Unguarded here,

Immoderate in eating,
Of uncontrolled senses,
Experiences suffering
Both bodily and mental.

Being tormented by body,
And tormented by mind,
Such a one lives in discomfort
Both by day and by night.

ITIVUTTAKA 28

of the wind element. Besides these, heat, hardness, etc can also be felt.

How long one stays at each noting (S or T) varies with conditions. When one is sleepy and objects are unclear, then one may not stay too long, eg 5 seconds at each point, but if one is not sleepy one may watch longer eg 50, 100 seconds or more, to see the various sensations. If one is very persistent in noting continuously S, S, S... T, T, T... a lot of energy is aroused and in many cases, can overcome sleepiness. Then one can detect more sensations. Such as S1, S2, S3, S4... etc or T1, T2, T3, etc (refer diagram on page 117)

Another approach is just to watch the different touch points, T1, T2, T3... etc, and with more energy if one is sleepy or the objects are unclear. It is singled out to watch for a longer time (eg up to 100 seconds or more) if one's mindfulness is up to the mark. This approach can be useful to beginners who are yet to understand fully what is meant by "sitting" sensations.

As concentration builds up one will be aware of sensations all over the body and may, if suitable, revert to choiceless awareness.

Generally "sitting" and "touching" arouses the energy faculty because a lot of effort is needed to keep the mindfulness or to apply it to the points or sensations concerned.

ii **"Rising" and "Falling"**

"Rising" and "falling" refers to the outwards and inwards motion of the abdominal region as we breathe. As we follow the movements which may be very irregular, we tend to forget the rest of the surroundings. It will then become progressively finer. As such it is more conducive to concentration than "sitting" and "touching" which soon become associated with pain.

However, because of its irregularity and grossness it loses to the breath at nose tip in terms of ability to tranquillise

SITTING & TOUCHING METHOD

LEGEND

S   "Sitting" refers to general feeling of firmness of overall posture

T   "Touching" eg. at the base contact with cushion/floor

R   "Rising" movement of abdomen

F   "Falling" movement of abdomen

There are many ways of watching "sitting" (S)/ "touching" (T).
For a start, we may just watch generally S, T, S, T, etc.

the mind rapidly. But then it is also the same reason that it is easier to see the Vipassana object of insight meditation.

iii **Painful feelings**

This object arouses a lot of energy if not anger as well! This is owing to its sharp and strong nature. As such, we need to hold the mind onto the pain with strong and firm mindfulness, ie to be really alert. However, it can also be very tiring.

iv **Pleasurable feelings**

"Happiness" being the proximate cause of concentration shows that the concentration is more easily brought about in this case. Therefore, we have to be very alert or else we will fall into slumber.

v **Sound/Hearing**

Sound is normally not used as a primary Vipassana object because it tends to bring about scatteredness and dispersion. It is also extraneous. So definitely it is not conducive to concentration. It also does not really help to stimulate the desired right effort either. However it can help to provide a condition for alertness of the present moment, when all other objects are unclear.

vi **Walking**

Walking meditation tends to arouse a lot of energy and mindfulness because of the active nature of the process. There are many movements and intentions to be noted. For the same reason it is also often not easy to go into deep concentration. So one has to learn to be very relaxed when walking extremely slowly and stopping for longer periods, while both feet are on the ground.

vii **Seeing/Light**

Like sound, seeing of light has to be abandoned when concentration sinks deep. In walking meditation, the eyes are usually open and so seeing is unavoidable. This can be very distracting for beginners and so they will have to note "seeing" regularly to develop the restraint of the eye. However, because of its bright and expanding nature, it can arouse a certain degree of energy and dispelling sloth.

There is a different kind of light seen at the mind's eye when sitting with closed eyes. These are classified as mental images. In Vipassana, they are noted and so will pass away. In Samatha meditations, they may be utilised to develop concentration.

From here, we may gather that if we can choose an object, we can also choose one to balance the faculties. For example, watch pain, "sitting" and "touching" rather than "rising" and "falling" to rouse energy if we are sleepy.

We may also apply the reverse in that when any of these objects do not appear when we choose to, then we can increase or decrease the faculty needed to balance the faculties. For example, pain is likely to increase energy and so it will be balanced by noting in a more relaxed manner. Likewise if there is a pleasurable feeling, then more alertness and energetic noting is required.

Another point to remember that can influence the balancing of the faculties is the temperament of the individual. The more energetic type needs tranquillity whilst the slothful type needs energy.

*One who is not ardent, reckless,
Lazy, and of little vigour,
Full of lethargy and torpor,
Shameless and without respect—
Such a bhikkhu cannot attain
Enlightenment which is supreme.*

*But a mindful and discerning
meditator,
Ardent, scrupulous, and diligent,
Having severed the fetters of birth
and decay,
Can attain for himself right here
and now
Enlightenment which is supreme.*

ITIVUTTAKA 34

Two thoughts occur to him,
The Tathagata, the Awakened One
Who endured what is beyond endurance:
Security (for beings) was the first thought spoken of,
Solitude was the second announced.

The dispeller of darkness, gone beyond,
The great sage who has reached attainment,
Become a master, freed from taints,
Who has crossed over entirely,
Released by the destruction of craving—
That sage bears his final body,
And having left behind Mara, I say,
He has gone beyond decay.

As one standing on a mountain peak
Might see all round the people down below,
So having ascended the Dhamma-palace,
The vastly wise one, all-seeing,
Views the people of the world.
The sorrowless one views below
Those still immersed in sorrow,
Overwhelmed by birth and decay.

ITIVUTTAKA 38

Sharpening the Faculties

NINE WAYS OF SHARPENING THE FACULTIES

In order that we may get a better picture of the sharpening of the faculties, it would be useful to look into the nine ways as mentioned in the "Path of Purification." In a nutshell, these nine ways mean:

> One full of faith, bearing in mind the suitable external conditions and internal factors, strives continuously and seriously despite any pains, sicknesses and discouragements (that may come across one's way) until one's goal is reached.

1 One bears in mind that one will be able to see that all formations are impermanent.

To be able to seek the way out of a dangerous place, it would be most helpful if you have a good map at hand. This proper theoretical base has its importance in arousing confidence besides being a guide to avoid pitfalls and advance in development. One has to put aside all wrong views before one is able to receive what is right. One, however, should also put aside philosophising and thinking, or else, there cannot be direct experience.

A wise person should be urgently moved
On occasions that make for urgency;
As an ardent discerning bhikkhu
He should investigate with wisdom.

One living ardent thus,
Of peaceful conduct, not proud,
Practising tranquility of mind,
May attain the destruction of suffering.

ITIVUTTAKA 37

This initial acceptance of the truth of the three universal characteristics as to the nature of existence is the first factor in that it propels one in the right direction of insight development.

2 One strives carefully

To be able to strive on continuously, one needs will-power and patience, skill, versatility and flexibility of mindfulness.

Striving carefully and seriously is in line with the "thorough" characteristic of mindfulness. Having a correct understanding of the importance of this practice gives us this proper attitude.

The only way that brings one out of all sufferings, and a practice that gives peace, safety and purpose, ought to be considered as the most important part of one's life. Yet despite this, many are unable to find much time for their practice because of other commitments.

So, whatever precious moments available to us to carry on in this noble practice, let us be most serious about it. Only when there is such seriousness, no part of the process is left unnoticed, an essential condition for the arising of precise and deep comprehension.

3 One strives continuously

Whilst careful and serious striving promises quality to each moment of noting, continuity is necessary. To be able to strive on continuously, one needs will-power and patience, skill, versatility and flexibility of mindfulness. This is even more so in vipassana meditation because of the momentariness of the concentration and objects observed.

Continuity allows for steady increase in mindfulness, and the momentum produced is considerable. That is why most people can experience more marked and visible progress over a short period of time (of a week or more) only in intensive meditation retreats.

4 Remembering the way one has attained concentration

We cannot expect to learn everything from our teacher. A lot depends on ourselves and our common sense.

For example, how concentration arises from an experiential point of view is highly individual although several lines of development may be drawn. It depends on each one's temperament and idiosyncrasies. When it happens, we are the best ones to make a record of it. The same may be said also of the experiences of insight.

In remembering the process, it is like one who remembers landmarks after one has completed one's journey. It will certainly be much easier and faster the next time. Making notes after each sitting will furnish one with a record that can help your teacher help you during your interviews as well as your own assessment after that.

Mindfulness has been compared to a king's good counsellor who advises the king after having made a thorough and correct assessment of the situation.

5 Taking into consideration the seven suitabilities

The external environment around can influence greatly the minds of those who are less than a veteran. And even if he is one, a proper choice of these conditions could bring better results.

Briefly, the seven suitabilities are:

1 Suitable food

A balanced diet suitable to the health of the individual would be the sensible choice. We also have to consider it from the point of defilements, ie food that does not arouse craving. Then there is the consideration of morality. The important point here is the motive and proper reflection on the food we eat, mindfulness while we are eating and another reflection after eating will help in meditation with regards to food.

A common recollection before eating is to consider the food as nourishment for the continuation of the body, keeping it unharmed and for helping in striving. One reminds oneself that one does not eat for intoxication, beautification, fun or for fattening.

*Regard the ordered words
he spoke,
The Tathagata, the Awakened
One,
Compassionate for all beings,
And the two things he proclaimed:*

*"See what is evil" is one,
The other "Be detached from it."
With a mind become detached
from evil
You will make an end of suffering.*

ITIVUTTAKA 39

2   Suitable dwelling

Some requirements that make up such a dwelling has been mentioned in the Nikayas.

- neither too far nor too near the village.
- easily accessible.
- not crowded by day, calm and silent at night.
- availability of basic requirements and safety from disease and other vermin or hostile creatures.
- presence of a good friend ie guide.

The *Visuddhimagga* further describes eighteen kinds of unsuitable dwellings under the heading of impediments. In addition, it also says that the type suitable will also depend on the temperament of the meditator.

In brief, the eighteen kinds of unsuitable monasteries are places:

- which are too noisy,
- where there is too much work and people to attend to,
- where requisites are difficult to obtain,
- which are dangerous,
- where no teacher is available.

Some suitable dwellings mentioned include:

- forest dwelling,
- dwelling at the foot of a tree,
- dwelling in an open field,
- dwelling in an empty house.

With regards to temperament:

- The lustful temperament is recommended an ugly and unpleasant lodging.
- The hateful temperament is recommended a clean, pure and pleasant lodging.
- The deluded temperament is recommended a lodging which has a view and is not shut in.
- The speculative temperament is recommended a screened or closed up lodging.

- The faithful temperament is recommended a lodging similar to the one for the hateful temperament.
- Whilst for the intelligent temperament there is no unsuitable lodging.

3 Suitable Weather

Obviously, it is best not to be too hot or cold. In the tropics, most prefer a cool environment for comfort and can thus get better concentration. This is understandable for heat can be quite exhausting. Often there are those who resort to air-conditioners. Their use can be debatable as to it being an excuse for weakness. Here we may bear in mind that the Bodhisatta attained supreme enlightenment at the peak of the hot season. It is also common knowledge among meditators that the heat is not as disturbing as we thought. In addition, there is a wet season. This may cause concern to those with smaller dwellings though the coolness may be welcome.

4 Suitable posture

Usually one maintains a balance of walking and sitting postures. This helps in balancing the spiritual faculties. It also aids in one's physical health. However in the Visuddhimagga we are informed that some postures may be more suitable than others for different temperaments:

- Lustful temperament—walking and standing
- Hateful temperament—sitting and lying down
- Deluded temperament—walking
- Faithful temperament—as in lustful temperament
- Intelligent temperament—any
- Speculative temperament—as in the deluded temperament

5 Suitable persons—as guide or companions in striving

These are people who are experienced in the practice, endowed with wide and deep learning and filled with

*One who has completed
      the training,
Incapable of falling away,
Attained to the higher wisdom,
A seer of the end of birth—
That sage bears his final body,
And having left behind conceit,
He has gone beyond decay, I say.*

*Therefore ever delighting in
      meditation,
Concentrated,
      with ardent energy,
Seeing the end of birth,
      O bhikkhus,
Conquer Mara and his host,
And go beyond all birth and
      death.*

ITIVUTTAKA 46

compassion to impart to others the Noble Way with tact and maturity of thought. They can serve as inspiration to the weak and depressed, as good examples to willing learners and as pace-setters to the lazy.

The Visuddhimagga quotes qualities of a good spiritual friend:

- revered and dearly loved,
- speaks and suffers speech (ie good counsellor and patient listener),
- the speech the person utters is profound (ie speaker in deep discourses),
- the person urges not without reason.

It further recommends one to find a noble Arahant, and if it is not possible, one with lesser attainments. Failing, one may seek one with *jhanas* (absorptions) and failing in that, one versed in the texts.

6 **Suitable talk**

Usually only talk profitable to one's practice is allowed during the period of intensive meditation. This may even be narrowed down to talks strictly concerning meditation. The less profitable, not to mention all worldly talk unless absolutely necessary, is cut off.

However, in daily life, one is taught to avoid as much unprofitable talk as possible, as some degree is unavoidable when you are earning a living. But by all means, we have to try our best not to transgress the fourth precept of telling lies and other forms of unwholesome speech.

7 **Suitable resort**

This refers to the places where a monk goes to beg his food. For lay people, it may mean the place of work. It is important to find a situation of work where it brings out less defilements, considering how much time we have to spend in it.

6 Cultivating the seven factors of enlightenment

These seven factors of enlightenment are mental conditions that come together at the moment of illumination. They are separately treated so that we may study each in more detail and apply it according to circumstances. Much has been written on these elsewhere and here, we shall mention the conditions given in the Satipatthana commentary.

1 **Mindfulness Factor of Enlightenment** *(Sati Sambojjhanga)*
This is right mindfulness of the Noble Eightfold Path, ie of the Four Foundations of Mindfulness. It is also the mindfulness of things as they really are in insight meditation. As it is the most important factor here, there is little wonder why it is mentioned first.

The four conditions that lead to the arising of this factor are:

- To engage in the practice of mindfulness with clear comprehension as indicated in the Satipatthana Sutta
- Avoiding persons with confused (unmindful) minds
- Associating with persons who are ever mindful
- Inclination (of one's mind, which may be through understanding and will-power) towards the development of mindfulness enlightenment factor.

2 **Investigation of Truth Factor of Enlightenment**
(Dhamma Vicaya Sambojjhanga)
This is the penetrative aspect of the wisdom that seeks to understand the nature of phenomena.

The conditions for its arising are:—
- inquiring about the aggregates and so on
- purification of the (physical) basis (ie cleanliness)
- imparting evenness to the spiritual faculties (for insight)
- avoiding the ignorant
- associating with the wise

*Whatever bad bourns there are
In this world and hereafter,
All are rooted in ignorance,
Constructed by desire and greed.*

*Since one of evil desires
Is shameless and disrespectful,
From that evil flows forth
And he goes to a state of misery.*

*Thus by discarding desire and greed,
Along with ignorance as well,
A bhikkhu arouses knowledge
And abandons all bad bourns.*

ITIVUTTAKA 40

- reflection on the profound differences of the hard to perceive processes (of mind and matter)
- inclination towards the development of the investigation of truth factor of enlightenment

3 **Energy Factor of Enlightenment** *(Viriya Sambojjanga)*
This is the Right Effort of the Noble Eightfold Path. It is also the energy used in the striving in insight meditation.

The eleven conditions that lead to its arising are:

1 Reflection on the fearfulness of woeful states (or rebirth)
2 Reflection on the benefits of energy
3 Reflection that the path trodden by enlightened ones is not for the indolent.
4 Honouring of alms (and other requisites)
5 Reflection that the great heritage (of seven treasures) is not for the slothful
6 Reflection on greatness of master (thinking, "is one befitting to be a disciple?")
7 Reflection on greatness of race (of the Buddha and oneself as one's son)
8 Reflection on greatness of fellows in holy life (eg Sariputta and Mogallana)
9 Avoiding lazy folks
10 Associating with diligent folks
11 Inclination towards the development of the energy factor of enlightenment.

4 **Joy Factor of Enlightenment** *(Piti Sambojjhanga)*
This is the joy that occurs in insight meditation. Its close association with faith serves to arouse the energy for practice whilst its connection as a factor of absorption *(jhana)* encourages the development of concentration. The factor can be aroused by:

- recollection of the Buddha (qualities)
- recollection of the Dhamma (qualities)
- recollection of the Sangha (qualities)
- recollection of one's (good) morals
- recollection of one's (unselfish) generosity
- recollection of the devas (good qualities also present in one)
- recollection of the peace (of Nibbana)
- avoid coarse folk (devoid of faith)
- associating with refined folk (full of faith)
- reflection on discourses inspiring confidence
- inclination towards the development of the joy factor of enlightenment

5 **Calm Factor of Enlightenment** *(Passadhi Sambojjhanga)*
This refers to the quietness or peacefulness of mind and mental factors. Seven things lead to its arousing:

1 resorting to fine (ie beneficial and suitable) food
2 resorting to comfortable weather (ie beneficial and suitable one)
3 resorting to comfortable posture (ie beneficial and suitable one)
4 judgement according to the middle-way ie reflection on kamma and its result
5 avoiding restless people
6 associating with calm people
7 inclination towards the development of the calm factor of enlightenment.

6 **Concentration Factor of Enlightenment**
(Samadhi Sambojjhanga)
Concentration is the profitable unification of the mind with the object. In this case, it would directly mean that insight meditation, where it is momentary (at mundane levels) and its object, exhibit the three universal characteristics of existence.

The born, come-to-be, produced,
The made, the conditioned,
*   the transient,*
Conjoined with decay and death,
A nest of disease, perishable,
Sprung from nutriment and
*   craving's cord—*
That is not fit to take delight in.

The escape from that, the
*   peaceful,*
Beyond reasoning, everlasting,
The not-born, the unproduced,
The sorrowless state that is void
*   of stain,*
The cessation of states linked to
*   suffering,*
The stilling of the conditioned—
*   bliss.*

ITIVUTTAKA 43

The eleven conditions that lead to its arising are:—

1 purification of basis
2 imparting evenness to the spiritual faculties
3 skill in taking up the sign (object) of meditation
4 inciting the mind on occasion (of laxity)
5 restraining the mind on occasion (of excessive energy)
6 gladdening the mind on occasion (of dissatisfaction)
7 regarding the mind without interference on occasion (of evenly balanced faculties).
8 avoiding people who are not collected
9 associating with people who are collected
10 reflection (on benefits) of the absorptions and emancipation
11 inclination towards the development of the enlightenment factor of concentration.

7 **Equanimity Factor of Enlightenment** (*Upekkha Sambojjhanga*)
The equanimity here is the balanced state of mind that comes about through abundant mindfulness of things as they really are.
Conditions that lead to its arising:
- detached attitude towards beings
- detached attitude towards things
- avoiding people who are egotistical with regards to beings and things
- associating with people who are detached towards beings and things
- inclination towards the development of the equanimity factor of enlightenment.

7 Not worrying about one's body and health during meditation

When meditators undergo intensive practice over a long period of time, it is likely that sickness may befall some time or other. Too often we use it as an excuse to stop. If we understand that sickness and death are inevitable, then we will see no reason to stop. We ought to be practising till our last breath. There were many who watched pain and at death reached lofty attainments. There are also those who recovered as a result.

Of course, it does not mean we do not need medical help. It just means that we do not give up practising.

8 Overcoming pain with energy

Pain and sickness usually come together. But then, there are other causes such as staying too long in one posture. Increased concentration can also make a slight pain seem great. Even hunger is considered as a form of illness. We cannot escape completely from these physical pains and so we will have to face it sooner or later. To do so we need a lot of energy to be mindful as we observe them. When our mind is strong enough we may overcome pain, as we say, "Mind over matter." But before that happens—a lot of energy is required.

9 Not stopping halfway to the final goal

The final goal is the complete eradication of defilements at Arahantship. As long as this is not reached, suffering can still be frightfully oppressive.

To reach this, it most probably will have to take quite a while for a lot of people. Having the attitude of "not stopping halfway" allows the meditator to strive on for as long as he can hold out.

OTHER WAYS THAT CAN HELP
TO SHARPEN OR MATURE THE FACULTIES

1 Having a wider exposure of objects

Every object has its peculiarities. It may be more suitable to certain temperaments and one also gets trained in certain other aspects of the mind and techniques. If we stick to just the same object which we have been doing all the time, our training may be narrow and

*These two Nibbana-elements were made known
By the Seeing One, stable*
and unattached:
One is the element seen
here and now
With residue, but with the cord of
being destroyed;**
The other, having no residue
for the future,
Is that wherein all modes of being
utterly cease.*

*Having understood the
unconditioned state,
Released in mind with the cord
of being destroyed,
They have attained to the
Dhamma-essence.
Delighting in the destruction
(of craving),
Those stable ones have
abandoned all being.*

ITIVUTTAKA 44

**Tadi: "stable," is a term for an
emancipated one, the arahant, and
refers to his equanimity towards
agreeable and disagreeable sense
objects.
** The "cord of being" (bhavanetti) is
craving for being (bhavatanha), so
called because it keeps living beings
attached to the round of existence.*

thus flexibility low. We may never know if another object may be so very helpful. Hence after having developed one strong basic foundation eg body foundation of mindfulness, it would be good to dwell into more, and for a longer period of time on other objects, eg feelings, mind and mental states. This will enable us to reach the deeper levels of practice no matter what object we may come across.

This increase of flexibility and the increased selection of suitable objects will definitely leave an impact on the maturity of insight.

The different types of objects in samatha meditation have their own peculiar effects on people.

2 Samatha meditations

Though pure tranquillity meditations are different from insight meditation it can definitely be of help. One who has strong (*samatha*) concentration can go on sitting for longer periods and at deeper levels of concentration to allow deep insights to arise. Although this is possible also with the pure insight vehicle, with strong concentration, it should make it easier.

Besides this point, the different types of objects in samatha meditation have their own peculiar effects on people. For example, some are specifically suited to deal with certain strong defilements. One who has strong anger would find it easier to progress after having undergone a course on cultivation of loving-kindness.

It can also strengthen a particular moral state if weak. In another example, one with less faith may become more enthusiastic and confident after practising recollections of the Triple Gem.

Another point to mention is that most of these Buddhist samatha meditations can relate closely with insight meditation. The objects of samatha can switch easily to that of Vipassana. It is just a switch of attention. An example may be quoted from the wind *kasina** whose initial mental object (*uggaha nimitta*) may be indistinguishable from the wind element of insight meditation at the initial stages if one is not well-versed with both. In

---

* Kasina is a purely external device to produce and develop concentration of mind and attain the 4 absorptions or *jhana*.

another case, extremely clear mind developed from light kasina meditations can definitely help with one's observations.

Besides these, the object of some meditation can produce certain states of mind which can catalyse the arising of insight knowledge. It is known from the texts that after coming across certain objects that may be purely conceptual in nature, insights arise. For example, seeing corpses may give rise to feelings of strong detachment very much alike to the knowledge of disenchantment and so forth.

The question on samatha meditations here is:

- The time needed to reach the satisfactory level of concentration and whether or not one is able to preserve it.
- The skill in switching to insight meditation.

One consideration, however, boils down to time factor, since everything is uncertain and time passes too swiftly, we have to act fast. The other factor may be the availability of skilled and experienced guides in the method suitable for one.

3 By use of resolutions or aspirations

The power of resolution is not unknown. By making resolutions, the mind and mental formations and energies are inclined to achieve that aim.

In a way, it is also an assertion of the will, the most important mental conditioner. It is like feeding a programme for a computer to go in a certain direction.

The making of resolutions allows us to exert control over things otherwise beyond our reach. The mind is very powerful and can work wonders beyond our normal conscious awareness. Concentration is the source of power and resolution is the power line.

Many commercial methods use such positive thinking and programming to achieve more worldly objectives. Even the supernormal powers are trained along similar lines. Here we shall be concerned with pure objectives of insight meditation.

Those of peaceful mind, discerning,
Mindful, given to meditation,
Clearly see things rightly
And long not for sensual pleasures.

Those peaceful ones,
delighting in diligence,
Who see fear in negligence,
Are incapable of falling away
And are close to Nibbana.

ITIVUTTAKA 45

When making such resolutions that are far-reaching, one must bear in mind:

- The purity of motive—
  It must not be influenced by greed, anger or delusion in any way, or else unpleasant results may lay ahead.
- Precisely and clearly worded—
  If this is not done, results will be just indecisive or may even be shocking. It is like feeding a computer with vague request. I have come across an unfortunate instance where a meditator lost control of the mind for quite a while because of this reason.

Once I asked my teacher as to what is the best attitude for a meditator. The answer was that meditation is for the purification of the mind. It would be good if resolutions were made with this in mind.

To begin, I could recall the aspirations frequently recited after performing some meritorious deeds such as the giving of alms.

> *Idam me danam*
>> By this giving
>
> *Asavakkhayavaham hotu*
>> may I destroy the intoxicants.
>
> *Idam me silam*
>> By observing these moral precepts
>
> *Nibbanassa paccayo hotu*
>> may it bring about the realisation of Nibbana.
>
> *Idam me bhavanam*
>> By this meditation
>
> *Magga phala nanassa paccayo hotu*
>> may it bring about the Path and Fruition knowledges.

These aspirations reflect the will to channel all our meritorious actions to give the result of emancipation from all sufferings.

Sometimes I have observed that if a meditator whose mind is quite unsure of a direction makes the resolution below, it results in his meditation becoming clearer and better.

May I be diligent in the practice of insight meditation. By my diligent practice, may insight leading to the complete cessation of suffering arise quickly and clearly.

Then, there is also the practice whereby one makes resolution to see and develop each insight knowledge clearly, such as

May the knowledge of arising and dissolution arise.

This can be done only when one has actually passed through these levels. When done it helps one to be more matured and established in each knowledge. Unless the lower ones are well established, the higher ones cannot do so. Such a practice is done with an experienced guide.

MEGHIYA SUTTA

In the *Meghiya Sutta*, the Buddha advises Meghiya on the conditions that are conducive to the ripening of the mind unripe for emancipation.

First, the Buddha give five conditions:

1   A monk has a good friend, a good companion, a good comrade.
2   A monk is virtuous and dwells restrained by his precepts. He is perfect in behaviour and habit, seeing the danger in the smallest fault.
3   Talk which is serious and a help to opening the heart: talk on wanting little, on contentment, on solitude, on going apart, on strenuous endeavour, on virtue, on concentration, on wisdom, on emancipation, on the knowledge and vision of emancipation, a monk obtains at will, easily and without difficulty.
4   A monk dwells strenuous in purpose, putting away unrighteous conditions, taking to righteousness, persevering and energetic, he shirks not the burden of righteousness.

*Having seen what has come to be
As having come to be,
Passing beyond what has come
to be,
They released in accordance
with truth
By exhausting the craving for
being.*

*When a bhikkhu has fully
understood
That which has come to be
as such,
Free from craving to be this
or that,
By the extinction of what has
come to be
He comes no more to renewal
of being.*

ITIVUTTAKA 49

5 A monk has wisdom and is endowed therewith as to the way of growth and decay, with Ariyan penetration concerning the way to the utter destruction of suffering.

Having been established in those five, four more conditions must be developed:

1 Reflection on foulness to put away passion.
2 Reflection on amity to put away ill-will.
3 Mindfulness of in and out breath to cut off distraction.
4 Perception of impermanence to uproot the "I am" conceit.

THE SEVEN POINTS

In the above sutta, the Buddha said that a monk skilled in seven points and investigator in three ways is called one accomplished. We may perhaps keep these points in mind if we are to develop insight. "The Seven Points" are the full knowledge of:

1 The nature of five aggregates (ie body, feelings, perceptions, formations and consciousness)
2 Their arising (due to causes)
3 Their ceasing (due to cessation of causes)
4 The way to their ceasing ie the Noble Eightfold Path
5 The satisfaction (ie the pleasure derived from them)
6 The misery (ie the suffering derived from them)
7 The escape from them (ie the putting away of the desire for them).

The "Investigator in Three Ways" refers to investigation into the nature of:

1 Elements (*Dhatu*)
2 Basis (*Ayatana*)
3 Dependent origination (*paticcasamuppada*).

You vigilant ones hear this:
Wake up, you who are asleep!
Vigilance is better than sleep:
There is no fear for the vigilant.

One who is vigilant and mindful,
Comprehending and concentrated,
Joyful and calm in his thoughts,
By rightly investigating the Dhamma
With unified mind, will in time
Destroy the darkness of ignorance.

Therefore be devoted to vigilance,
An ardent, discerning, meditative bhikkhu.
Having severed the fetter of birth and decay,
One may here and now attain
Enlightenment which is supreme.

ITIVUTTAKA 46

Types of Concentration

When you have had enough experience in basic meditation exercises and know how to balance your five mental faculties, in time you will begin to develop concentration. "Concentration" actually covers a wide range of experiences. In Pali "concentration" is sometimes referred to as *ekaggata* or one-pointedness; as *samadhi* or concentration; and as *jhana* or absorption.

To be able to develop concentration, we must know what we mean. We start by looking at *mindfulness*.

At the beginning of a retreat we have to learn what we mean by "mindfulness" and "no mindfulness." No mindfulness means absence of clear awareness. Mindfulness means presence of clear awareness. Mindfulness is not just "knowing," it is "knowing something properly with a clear mind."

After some days of practising, you will be able to know the difference between the two. When your mind is not mindful, it is wandering and thinking, and in a horrible mental state. When your mind is mindful, it is clear and you will be able to follow your object properly.

Then comes the question as to how mindful you are. It is not difficult to differentiate between strong mindfulness and no

A disciple of the Buddha,
Concentrated,
    clearly comprehending
And mindful, knows feelings
And the origin of feelings,
Where they cease and the path
That leads to their full destruction.*
With the destruction of feelings
    a bhikkhu,
Without longing,
    has attained Nibbana.

ITIVUTTAKA 52

*By penetrative understanding of
feelings according to the method of the
Four Noble Truths and by attaining the
noble path of the arahant. Feelings are
seen as the truth of suffering. They
originate in contact (phassa) and lead
to craving, as stated in the formula of
dependent arising (paticca-
samuppada).

mindfulness. But one has to know how to differentiate between subtle mindfulness and no-mindfulness. This situation occurs in more subtle and deeper states of concentration. Once one has learnt how to differentiate between the presence and absence of mindfulness, the next step is to differentiate between concentration and mindfulness.

Concentration usually means one-pointedness. A more general sense of the word means the mind holding onto an object. Although both concentration and mindfulness can occur simultaneously, yet they may not.

Concentration is the mind holding onto the object.

Concentration is the mind holding onto the object. For example, when your mind is trying to follow the "rising" and "falling" of the abdomen, that is concentration or one-pointedness. Or when you are trying to watch and hold onto the pain, that is concentration on the pain. Mindfulness is how you hold onto it.

RIGHT AND WRONG CONCENTRATION

You can hold onto an object with a calm and stable mind or you can grasp and cling onto it in an obsessed manner. If you are holding it and clinging onto it in an obsessed manner, grasping it very tightly as if not willing to let go, this is concentration of the wrong type or wrong concentration. It is concentration that comes with clinging defilement. But when you hold onto it properly, with a clear and peaceful mind, with a hold that could be very firm, it is right concentration, concentration that comes with mindfulness. This is an important differentiation because you must be sure you are practising right concentration, not wrong concentration.

It is important that when we start to develop concentration, we are developing right concentration— concentration of clear awareness or pure mind. When a pure mind is concentrated, it becomes stable, strong, and powerful. Just like when clear light is concentrated, it becomes powerful and strong and will enable us to see many things.

IMPORTANT ASPECTS OF CONCENTRATION

1 Tranquillity

A better word to use for tranquillity is peacefulness. The mind is peaceful and tranquil because it is free of defilement.

We should take special care that during the process of concentrating, when we say "noting," we first have to be mindful. It is clear awareness first. Do not be too concerned with having strong concentration. Be concerned with having continuous mindfulness. A continuous mindfulness puts the mind into a more wholesome and pure state. It is malleable, flexible and obedient. Then you can push it further to deeper concentration.

2 Abandonment of the grosser mental factors.

This applies to people who practise higher concentrations. In the process of developing concentration, gross activities, like initial application (*vitakka*) or sustained application (*vicara*), will be abandoned. When this happens, then the mind becomes more subtle and peaceful.

3 One-pointedness

After tranquillity from defilement has been fulfilled, one-pointedness follows. That means fixing the mind to a single object and not letting it wander elsewhere. When you can do that, then there is less fluctuation and that is when the mind becomes stable and peaceful.

TWO DIFFERENT PATHS

The path you are going to take depends on whether you emphasise concentration or mindfulness. Concentration is holding the mind to the object. Mindfulness is observing the nature of the object carefully. Herein lies the difference.

Let's take the example of holding a mirror up to your face. When you hold the mirror to your face and you can look into it for a long

A disciple of the Buddha,
Concentrated,
*   clearly comprehending*
And mindful, knows searches
And the origin of searches,
Where they cease and the path
That leads to their full destruction.
With the destruction of searches
*   a bhikkhu,*
Without longing, has attained
*   Nibbana.*

ITIVUTTAKA 54

time, that is concentration—holding the mind to an object. If you keep on holding your mind to an object and emphasise more on **concentration,** your meditation will proceed or **develop onto the path of tranquillity meditation,** which goes into deep states of concentration

On the other hand, when you hold the mind to the object and you observe carefully the features that are found in the mirror, for example the long nose, moustache, buck teeth, bald head and so forth, you realise that this is the face of a demon. You ask, "This is the face of what? Of a human being?" This means you have observed carefully, you take note of the nature of all the features of the face in the mirror. That is mindfulness.

When you have taken in all the details and you can understand what it means—the essence of it, the **mindfulness becomes wisdom.** When you emphasise on mindfulness, and you observe with careful mindfulness the nature of the object, all the different things that occur there, the processes there, the mind will progress or proceed in the way of **insight or vipassana.**

The two different paths you can take become clear when we use the example of *anapanasati.*

Some people do *anapanasati* by counting the in and out breaths at the nose tip and concentrate on that. The mind becomes very peaceful. As the concentration deepens, you may see or feel the point of contact there as if of very soft cotton wool. You continue to watch it more carefully with some mindfulness but with more emphasis on concentration. You will stay with it for a long time because the mind is so peaceful and calm. So the mind goes into deep concentration and tranquillity meditation. The object, as the mind becomes deeper, will become subtler and more still.

However, if one wishes to proceed to vipassana from there, it is not just a matter of keeping the mind still. You have to push the mind to note very clearly all the sensations that occur at the nose-tip. In which case, you will see many processes and changes, especially those relating to the heat element at the nose-tip, arising and disappearing.

Thus you will not go into the pure tranquillity states of the absorption, but will proceed by way of insight.

Even when practising "rising" and "falling," some people tend to go into the direction of tranquillity meditation. This may be because they did not emphasize the practice of mindful observation. Rather they emphasize fixing on the mind and following it in the "rising" and "falling."

Usually the "rising" and "falling" of the abdomen—as a meditation object—is more gross and the changes are more obvious. Therefore, it is selected as a more suitable object for the development of insight. But even then because the development of the observation of insight is quite unique and you need a lot of energy, people sometimes fail to notice the changes. Therefore they just concentrate and feel the peacefulness.

Even though they may be able to notice some changes, it is not sufficient. Mindfulness is not enough and concentration is being developed and emphasized instead, and they still go into a form of tranquillity meditation.

SPECIFIC TYPES AND NATURE OF CONCENTRATION IN SAMATHA AND VIPASSANA CONCENTRATION

Both tranquillity (*samatha*) meditation and insight meditation develop concentration. Both develop one-pointedness of mind or absorption into its objects because both need to hold the mind to its object for long periods to give it strength, to serve their purpose. But they are not exactly the same.

Concentration is like keeping onto the road. When you keep onto the road and go north, you will see a certain type of scene. You go south, and you see a different scene. But you are still keeping onto the road.

Different aims will see you progress in different ways and achieve different goals or objects. Let us again recap the difference between the two types of meditation. The main aim of concentration

Sensual search,
*   the search for being,*
The search for a holy life of one
Who takes his stand upon a view
And holds it tightly as the truth—
These are heapings of defilements.

For a bhikkhu wholly dispassionate
And freed by the destruction of
*   craving,*
Searches have been relinquished
And uprooted the standpoint of
*   views.*
With the destruction of searches
*   a bhikkhu*
Is free from desire and doubt.

ITIVUTTAKA 55

meditation is to develop right concentration—concentration of the pure mind. As a result of this, we end up in deep states of concentration or absorption (*jhanas*).

When these are further developed, they can give rise to supernormal powers—like levitation, mind reading, recollection of past lives, and so forth. In the final stage, because of the powers of concentration, you will find rebirth in the Brahma realms. These realms are above the sensual heavens—very high and lofty forms of existence.

In insight meditation or *vipassana*, the concentration is used to develop understanding into the nature of the world, the nature of mind-body processes. Everything in the world is a mind-body process. And they are realised in their true nature as impermanent, suffering and non-self. When one finally transcends all these—the mind finds union with the absolute, the unchanging and the unconditioned, or as we say, the everlasting peace. In which case, we will transcend and abandon all sufferings forever.

Firstly, you see the aim is different. Secondly, the object is different. The object in samatha meditation is a concept conceived by mind. It is not real. It is something that is created by the mind.

Everything in the world is a mind-body process.

But in insight meditation, the object is real in the sense that it is a mind-body process. The mind does not think or conceive the reality. It is thereby the virtue of its existence.

Hence, there are two different objects. And when you concentrate, follow and dwell into the object, the faculties are different. For example, in tranquillity meditation, the main faculty concerned is one-pointedness of concentration, with the support of mindfulness. Whereas in insight meditation, the main factor involved is mindfulness and the degree of energy or exertion of activities is much more compared with tranquillity meditation. As illustration, let us look at some examples.

Tranquillity meditation itself is of many types, depending on what we concentrate on. Take the example of concentration on loving-kindness—when you concentrate on loving-kindness, you think of the person in mind. The person or being is a concept. The person in your mind is a thought. So you concentrate on the person, which is a concept and you bring loving-kindness to the person.

Another pure tranquillity meditation object is *visualisation*, for example the *kasinas*. *Kasinas* are visualised circles, for example, the light kasina where you visualise a circle of light. You know very well that the mind created that circle and holds it there. So the visualised circle in the mind is a mind-conceived, mind-thought-up or mind-created object. It is just as if you imagined a picture in your mind.

When one is able to create that object in the mind, visualise it and hold it there with mindfulness, there is a very calm and peaceful awareness that just holds it there. If the mind holds it there long enough, you forget everything around you. Your mind will be very peaceful, quiet and increasingly subtle.

As your concentration becomes more powerful and subtler, the object also becomes brighter as well as finer. There will come a time when there is unification—the mind and the circle of light are one. That moment, when one does not seem to be able to differentiate between the two, is what we call *samadhi*. It is a kind of absorption. As long as one is still consciously knowing and differentiating at that very moment, is it still access concentration. Only when it seems to sink into it, as if the mind is completely absorbed into it, is it more like absorption. It is a very deep state that one seems to fall into, it is very still and tranquil—a different type of consciousness.

There is no subject-object differentiation at the moment of samadhi. It can be described as in a deep sleep, no, deeper than deep sleep. And yet when one arises or emerges, one knows the nature of that visualisation, at that period of time when one seems to be "unconscious."

A disciple of the Buddha,
Concentrated,
    clearly comprehending
And mindful, knows the taints
And the origin of taints,
Where they cease and the path
That leads to their full destruction.
With the destruction of taints
    a bhikkhu,
Without longing, has attained
    Nibbana.

ITIVUTTAKA 54

VIPASSANA

Vipassana object is a reality–like "rising" and falling," an actual sensation or pain. You do not have to think it up and create it. It is there already in itself although you may have to look for it. And as you become more aware of its nature, you will notice that it is not a still or static object. It is vibrant, dynamic, changing, arising and passing away.

The more you are aware of it, the clearer the changing nature. It is different from the samatha object or visualisation where the deeper you go, the more quiet, unmoving and still the object becomes. The vipassana object fluctuates because of the nature of impermanence. When it changes the suffering and non-self aspect also becomes very clear. You keep on applying vipassana concentration on the fluctuating object until insight arises. This insight is realisation with regard to three universal characteristics–impermanence, suffering and non-self.

The more you are aware of it, the clearer the changing nature.

If this vipassana concentration does not arise then insight cannot arise. The starting point is usually the perception of impermanence. Impermanence has to be noticed first because suffering is not just ordinary suffering but the suffering that is impermanence itself. The non-self is the non-self because it is impermanent and suffering.

The perception of impermanence is as if you want to understand the nature of a moving or changing object. What is the change? You must be able to hold your mind to the change. The change is not a static thing. It is a moving thing, so the mind must move with the change and become absorbed in the moment-to-moment change. And because mindfulness is so clear and sharp, it realises the nature of change because it is one with it.

If you cannot follow and be one with it, how can you know what it is? If you cannot follow the moving object, how can you see what it is?

EXPERIENCING THE DIFFERENT STAGES OF VIPASSANA

The nature of vipassana concentration is unique in the practice. Another way of describing this concentration is in terms of experience. The concentration can be classified into three stages.

1 Struggling

Struggling in the sense of you trying to build up awareness to follow the object.

Say you are watching the "rising" and "falling" in vipassana. You are aware of "rising, falling, rising, falling." Then the "rising" and "falling" stops. You stop. Then you continue. And you stop again. Sometimes in the "rising" and "falling," there is no mindfulness— there is only tension. So you have to relax and start again. So it is a struggle.

The struggling is the first stage, a difficult stage because the concentration is weak. Struggling comes at the preliminary practice. Any concentration that develops with the "rising" and "falling" is merely preliminary concentration. After one has done enough of this preliminary practice, struggling, then one proceeds to a different stage where enough momentum on the concentration has built up for it to move by itself.

2 Sailing stage

The second stage, the sailing stage is easier. It is easier because here it is as if you are on a boat and your boat flows with the current. The concentration at this point is developed to a stage where it seems to have a life of its own. It moves. Just like when you are doing loving-kindness with the object being your loved one. The loving-kindness just keeps flowing, flowing, flowing along, as if in waves.

In the case of "rising" and "falling," after your mindfulness has been built-up to a continuous mindfulness, it just flows along with the "rising" and "falling." If "rising" and "falling" is long, the mindfulness flows with it in long waves from beginning to end. If it is short, the mindfulness flows with it in short wavelets from

One for whom the taint of desire
For sensal pleasures has been
  destroyed,
Who has eliminated ignorance
And exhausted the taint of being—
Such a one is released
  without clinging.
Having conquered Mara and
  his mount,
He bears his final body.

ITIVUTTAKA 57

beginning to the end. If the "rising" and "falling" jumps, the mindfulness jumps along with it. You do not need to struggle and make a special effort, because it is sailing along.

3 Feeling of taking off

The third stage is a feeling of taking off, "flying and disappearing," or a "sinking and disappearing." Usually the experience is a taking off first followed by a sinking. This is because the momentum has become so smooth, so fast, so easy, that a lot of joy arises, a lot of peace arises. Everything has become very light.

As a result, the mind takes off to a subtler object. As the object becomes subtler, the mind goes into a deeper state. When you shift the concentration to a different level, it is like taking flight, the mind becomes so subtle it can sometimes seem like unconscious. Actually it is a state of concentration with a very subtle and developed object.

Sometimes one feels—especially if the object is a heavier one—as if one is sinking inside. This is because the unification of the mind and the object is like sinking. So when you sink into it, it is as if you are falling into deep sleep.

But actually one's consciousness and awareness are there, except that they are of a different type—a deeper type. So the "sailing" or flowing stage is more like access concentration. The "flying and disappearing" or "sinking and disappearing" (I am not saying it is), are more like what we call absorptions.

Thus concentration in meditation is momentum build-up, moving closer and closer towards the object. Where you finally go would depend on the basic practices, the basic noting. For example, when you are doing metta, it is the momentum and the current of loving-kindness that keeps flowing on and on, going to subtler and more elevated states, until it becomes one with the object, unified with the object.

If you have been thinking of other things or if you have different states of mind, then the momentum and the object will not be so specific. It is difficult to develop that degree of concentration. And when you go into deep states, it is expected that you can only reach those deep states with mindfulness.

When you do loving-kindness meditation, it would not go into insight because all the energy is metta energy, not reality-awareness energy. And the metta energy is continuously moving to the person you are sending to. Similarly, if you are doing visualisations, the energy will continuously move towards the visualised object.

NOTING MOMENT-TO-MOMENT TO EXPERIENCE REALITY

If you want to experience reality—realisation of the three characteristics (impermanence, suffering and non-self) and nibbana—then the noting at the very start must be of the nature of reality. This momentum is built up. That is why you always have to note each and every mind and body processes from when you wake up in the day until the time you fall asleep—not just during walking meditation, not just during sitting meditation—but in every activity like eating and drinking.

All these are mind and body processes. Note them, watch them, and concentrate on them in the sense of noting moment-to-moment how they arise and how they pass away. Even while sitting, although there may be many objects that arise (all these are mind and body processes), just simply watch them arise and disappear.

When you have seen enough—when you see repeatedly by observing—will the mind concentrate more and more on the nature of change. Finally you direct your mind to change, the arising and passing away of mind and body. If you are not directed at this change, the mind will not flow and be one and unified. It will not concentrate on the change. When it does not concentrate on the nature of change, you cannot bring about realisation.

THE UNIQUENESS OF VIPASSANA CONCENTRATION

Most kinds of concentration are little more than just tranquillity—they are peaceful, they are powerful. They are very useful but they do

Those fettered by the bond
*   of craving,*
Whose minds delight in being
*   this or that,*
Are people in the bondage
*   of Mara*
Who enjoy no security from
*   bondage.*
Such beings continue in samsara.
Going on from birth to death.

But those who have abandoned
*   craving,*
Free from craving for being
*   this or that,*
Having attained the taints'
*   destruction,*
Though in the world,
*   have gone beyond.*

ITIVUTTAKA 58

not lead to realisation because the concentration developed does not lead there.

Vipassana concentration is unique. It is not common. It is not easy to develop because the object is a changing object. It is easier to concentrate on a still object than a changing object.

When you look at mind and body processes as changes, it is unavoidable that you meet with a lot of discomfort and oppressiveness Change is usually associated with oppressiveness. If something is very quiet and still, it seems happy to stay that way and the change is not obvious.

But if change begins to be obvious, then it would seem to be very disturbing, which is therefore suffering. A good example of this is a vibration. If a vibration is very intense, you will find it disturbing. If the vibration is very subtle it seems more peaceful. So when you watch change, you cannot avoid noticing unsatisfactoriness and oppressiveness. Because of that, vipassana concentration is not very pleasant to start with. It is also not so stable to begin with because of the nature of change.

Nevertheless, it can be done and should be done. Or else no realisation will arise. You must understand this and try to be patient. Otherwise you will end up like most people, saying "Oh, I cannot get anything from this. All I get is suffering, suffering and more suffering. I might as well go to have my sleep."

Those who have persevered and experienced these sensations will know the meaning and purpose of vipassana meditation. Of course, there are many levels of experiences and they are different.

LEVELS OF JHANAS IN SAMATHA MEDITATION

In samatha meditation, the difference in terms of experience is in the levels of jhanas. Starting with access, the first, second, and up to the eighth jhanas are absorptions where they are like frozen states of mind. The mind is frozen and one with the object. It goes into deeper and deeper states. Usually people describe it as going into a void because the object is so subtle it seems like being in a deep sleep.

In the beginning, you will not seem to know the state of the mind in the absorptions, but with repeated experiencing, you will come to know what it is after you have emerged. You will also come to know the nature of the object, the absorption it is absorbed in. This is different from reflection. Here, one knows the states, the nature of the consciousness, the mind factors, and the concentration factors that are involved.

Here is the differentiation, described in the five jhana factors. The first factor is initial application—the force that brings the mind to the object. The second factor is sustained application—a force that sustains the attention of the mind on the object; the joy you get with the object, the deep peace and happpiness that is with the object, and the fixation of the mind that is with the object. Since we are not dealing much with this, we will not elaborate.

LEVELS OF INSIGHT IN VIPASSANA MEDITATION

However, in vipassana concentration, the concentration is usually associated with levels of insight. More vipassana concentration will bring about more concentrated awareness on reality. The more the concentration on clear awareness, the clearer the understanding of the three universal characteristics would be. This is how the different progressive levels of insight knowledge are experienced.

Finally this would lead to the experience of nibbana or the unconditioned state. Now that the nature of concentration and the different types of concentration involved have been explained, let us look at the skills in concentration.

ASPECTS OF SKILLS INVOLVED IN CONCENTRATION MEDITATION

1 Entering into concentration

The first skill is called "adverting." It brings the mind to the state of concentration entering into *samadhi*. It brings the mind into the state where it is absorbed in the object and keeps it there.

Virtue, concentration and wisdom—
One in whom these are fully
developed,
On passing beyond Mara's
domain,
Shines forth like the sun.

ITIVUTTAKA 59

We begin by holding the mind on the object and forget everything else. Hold on to the object by just keeping your mind to it. It sounds very simple but it may not be easy because people's minds are very complicated.

There are some simple things we can do to help ourselves.

The first being physical comfort. If one is physically comfortable, concentration is easier. But you should not get too comfortable like lying down on a bed. You might fall asleep when you should be meditating. Be physically comfortable but remember to stay alert.

Pain, sickness or a lot of noise will distract and make meditation more difficult. If it is cold outside it may be difficult to do walking meditation. So ensure that you have body comfort and a quiet place.

Secondly, there should be peace of mind. You should not have a lot of anxiety. Tell yourself to be detached and let go. It is not too difficult. Think of all the sufferings of people in wars in Bosnia, of people starving to death in Ethiopia, Somalia and you will realise that you have no big problems. Stop worrying about small inconsequential things. Give yourself peace of mind.

If you have any anger, hatred, or grudges, throw them all away as you would throw away a hot potato. Do not hold onto the rubbish that would make yourself unhappy.

There should be peace of mind. You should not have a lot of anxiety.

After you have achieved peace of mind, counteract the undercurrent of defilement, tendencies, idiosyncrasies, etc in the mind with the current of mindfulness. Build up your mindfulness moment-to-moment, noting these things.

Thus the mind habitually notes and is mindful instead of continuously running over worldly things. When the mind habitually notes and is mindful, we say that a momentum of practice of mindfulness has been developed. When this momentum of mindfulness has been developed and your mind is at peace, the body is at peace.

So all you have to do is guide your mind to an object. When you guide it to an object long enough, just hold it there. Do not think of the past, do not think of the future, just do not think, forget everything. It is like you are going to sleep—except that you are not asleep. You merely observe the object moment-to-moment.

I can assure you that within one minute, you can get into concentration. Sometimes in less than a minute, you will sink into the object. This is what directing your mind at the object means. When we say, "rising" and "falling"—just hold it there (at the abdomen), the "rising" and "falling" need not be extremely clear. It can be just "rising" and "falling" because we are not talking about insight. We are only talking of concentration.

Instead of saying "rising" and "falling," you can say "rise" and "fall." But you must be able to throw away everything. If you are attached to the body, you may think "I am going mad if I forget my body." Then of course you cannot get into it (the rise and fall). You will think you are falling asleep and you are not aware of the "rising" and "falling."

Throw away everything. Do not care about time and place. Do not care about who you are. Just hold the mind there, hold the mind as if your mind is like a still and unflickering candle light on a windless night. Hold your mindfulness on the "rising" and "falling." Do not care whether it is subtle or gross, just know it.

If you hold it long enough, you will go into concentration. It is very simple. The important thing is to build up stable concentration as a continuous flow and momentum of mindful noting. Once you have gone through it, you can recollect how you got into concentration. Then you can very easily go into that level any time you want.

After having gained this first skill of entering into concentration, the next skill is to stay in the concentration.

2 Stay in the concentration

To stay in the concentration requires practice. Then comes preparation, and following that, attitude. Preparation is needed—for

Bodily pure, pure of speech,
Mentally pure and taintless—
A pure one possessing such purity
Is called one who has
*   abandoned all.*

ITIVUTTAKA 66

concentration to last a certain period, momentum has to be built up through sufficient preliminary exercises and experience.

For a longer period of concentration, you need a lot more energy, so you must build up the momentum more carefully so that the energy accumulated is strong enough.

After you have gone into concentration, there is the question of attitude.

Attitude here means patience. It has to be lasting patience. It is like holding the breath. Going into concentration is like taking a deep breath and holding it. It is like holding the mind in a certain way because if you hold it in a very tense manner then the concentration cannot last long. When you hold it in a peaceful manner then it can last long. You must have the attitude of not caring how long you sit, nor worrying about the time.

Preparation is important. If you want to go into long deep concentration for, say, three to four hours, you have to plan to do it after lunch so that you do not have to worry about lunch. Otherwise you will say, "I will miss my lunch. I cannot go for long."

You have to forget about the time. You must put away all the worries and things that are deep in the mind. And you must be willing to stay there and stay long.

For a longer period of concentration, you need a lot more energy, so you must build up the momentum more carefully so that the energy accumulated is strong enough.

If you are impatient and say "Oh, if I stay too long, I have no time to increase my insight," then of course you will not stay long and you will come out. That is why the mind has to be attuned with the correct attitude.

Once you know the nature of the concentration and the attitude of mind that maintains it for a long period of time, you would have gained the skill of knowing how it comes to be. How we can stay for a long time in concentration—what state of mind can stay for long and what state of mind cannot stay for long and so forth.

When you know the conditions, then you can last for a longer time in the concentration.

3 Skill of emerging

Then of course there is the other skill of emerging from the concentration at the right time. This is not as great a problem as sustaining the concentration. If one can sustain it, one should be able to control its emergence. You can do it mindfully. You get up at an arranged time. For example, when you go into deep concentration, say "I will go in for an hour or one and half hours or one hour forty-five minutes or one hour and forty-five and a half minutes." When your skill is developed, you can get up exactly to the second you wish to arise.

You can also train yourself to emerge in response to different situations like just before lunch or when somebody calls you. It is like programming the mind to respond specifically to certain conditions. To have this skill is a great advantage.

In order to attain insight, one has to have enough time and room for insight to develop. It needs purity of mind and concentration. Therefore you have to build up the skill of entering into and staying in that state of concentration for a long period of time. And you must practise frequently.

One who has destroyed attachment
Along with hate and ignorance
Has crossed this ocean
With its sharks and demons,
Its fearful waves so hard to cross.

He has surmounted every tie,
Left Death behind,
Become free from clinging,
Forsaken suffering and renewal
of being.
Vanished, he cannot be defined,
I say–
He has bewildered the King of
Death.

ITIVUTTAKA 69

With an unguarded body*
And encumbered by wrong view,
Overcome by lethargy and torpor,
One goes along in the power of Mara.

So one should be guarded in mind,
One should make right thought one's domain.
When he has put right view to the forefront
And understood rise and fall,
A bhikkhu who overcomes lethargy and torpor
Will forsake all bad destinations.**

UDANA 4.2

---

* By penetrative understanding of feelings according to the method of the Four Noble Truths
and by attaining the noble path of the arahant. Feelings are seen as the truth of suffering.
They originate in contact (phassa) and lead to craving, as stated in the formula of
dependent arising (paticca-samuppada).

** Because it is unstable and liable to change.

The Salient Differences between Tranquillity and Insight Meditation

I t is important that a meditator has a clear understanding of tranquillity (*samatha*) meditation and insight (*vipassana*) meditation. In the Dasuttara suttanta (the last discourse of the Digha Nikaya), Sariputta says there are the two states which are true dhammas, real phenomena which have to be developed. In Pali it is *dve dhamma bhavetabba*, which is translated as "the two dhammas to be developed." They are *samatho ca vipassana ca*—calm and insight. This development is called cultivation, *bhavana*, for which we often use the term meditation.

When we try to teach meditation to beginners, the first thing we must make them understand is mindfulness. Only then can we proceed to differentiate between the tranquillity and insight aspect of the practice.

MINDFULNESS TO DISTINGUISH BETWEEN RIGHT AND WRONG CONCENTRATION

There are obvious reasons why meditation teachers are adamant in making meditators practise vipassana. Whether you develop *samatha*

Beset by craving,
people run about like an
entrapped hare.
Held fast by mental fetters,
they come to suffering again and
again for a long time.

DHAMMAPADA 342

(calm) or *vipassana* (insight) meditation, you need a very strong base of mindfulness. Without this strong base, one may fall into wrong concentration. This means one may concentrate without mindfulness. It happens more often to those who develop pure tranquillity methods where the mindfulness factor is not emphasized. For example when they try to do visualizations they might be obsessed with trying to concentrate on and visualize the object. As a result they may get very strong headaches, like migraines.

Headaches can also occur in vipassana practice. In longer retreats of some weeks or even months the concentration that is developed is considerable. If there is no mindfulness, then these migraine-like tensions in the head can build up also and become very persistent. This is actually a form of stress. It can be quite bad. That is why before we go into some serious tranquillity or insight meditation we must have a clear idea of what mindfulness is so that we will know whether our practice is moving correctly or not. Otherwise we may be just developing concentration and the mind becomes more intense and more stressed. Hallucinations may arise. And when this goes too far it might be difficult to correct.

Mindfulness is a clear state of awareness, no confusion, no muddle-headedness, having full control.

Mindfulness is a clear state of awareness, no confusion, no muddle-headedness, having full control. Therefore, even when pain comes the mind is not disturbed, the mind remains at peace. When you are asked about the nature of the object you are observing, you can relate your observation clearly to others. Mindfulness therefore is important to distinguish right and wrong concentration.

SAMATHA AND VIPASSANA

Now that you know that right concentration is concentration with mindfulness and wrong concentration is concentration without mindfulness, let us go on to understand the difference between samatha and vipassana.

The word *samatha* by itself means tranquillity, and *vipassana* means insight or knowledge. When we refer to just *samatha* or *vipassana*, what we generally mean is *right concentration*. This means the factor of one-pointedness of mind has to arise with mindfulness. Not with obsession, not with anger, not with greed but with clear awareness. One-pointed clear awareness. In a single moment of experience there is this one-pointed clear awareness, and that we call samatha, tranquillity.

In insight, the awareness is sharper, a more thorough awareness which can experience reality and gain understanding from it. You know very clearly what you are experiencing. You can explain, if you want to, the nature of the experience.

SAMATHA BHAVANA AND VIPASSANA BHAVANA

The phrases *samatha bhavana* (calm cultivation or meditation), or *vipassana bhavana* (insight cultivation or meditation) do not refer to one moment of time. They refer to a series of experiences over a period of time. This also means a series of results. Because of the continuity, developed states of mind arise. This means if you develop samatha bhavana, deep states of concentration arise. We call them absorptions or *jhanas*. In developing vipassana bhavana, deep states of knowledge or understanding arise. We call them insight knowledges or *ñanas*.

There are similarities between the experience of samatha and vipassana bhavana. Although certain experiences are similar, the important thing to consider is the direction in which you are going, or which of the two types of meditation you are progressing to. When either of these two meditations are further developed, experiences peculiar to that respective type of meditation will arise more frequently and more distinctly.

With the help of some knowledge about samatha and vipassana experiences we can understand the nature of these two types of meditation and we can also understand how far we have progressed in each. This is important, because when developing this concentration or insight, we should have a clear picture of where we are going.

Those who are lust-infatuated fall back into the swirling current (of samsara) like a spider on its self-spun web . This, too, the wise cut off. Without any longing, they abandon all suffering and renounce the world.

DHAMMAPADA 347

Otherwise wrong understanding, wrong views, blunders and unnecessary delays may occur and cause a lot of suffering. It is not so easy to tell in which track you are advancing, especially for beginners. But this is so too for more advanced meditators. The beginner has to grasp the basic techniques. Only when they are understood, then the principles behind the practice and instructions are understood, and one can be more confident in going further to get the deeper experiences.

THE PROGRESSION IN SAMATHA BHAVANA

Here is a more detailed description differentiating the nature of samatha and vipassana bhavana. The **object in samatha meditations is a concept**. An idea. And the concentration involved will be either access or fixed. There are certain types of samatha meditation of which the objects are very clear-cut. Take for example the visualization techniques, like the colour kasinas. You visualize light. You visualize colours. Sometimes people go so far as to visualize images like Buddhas, *bodhisattas*, deities and so on. These are very clear-cut samatha objects because they are concepts. You try to create in your mind, with your eyes closed, a circle of light. When the concentration is strong, you can actually see, with your eyes closed, your mental creation as if it was a real light. Even when you open your eyes, and create the light, you can see it in front of you. You know very well that it is a creation of your mind. This is a very clear and simple example of a conceptual object.

Other clear types of concentration are those that use words. Like mantras or recitations. It is very clear that these are called word concepts. You may think of what they mean, which is your idea, not your experience. These objects are thus created, thought out by yourself. Something like an imagination.

The creation of these samatha objects begins with the preliminary practice. Take for example a light *kasina*. At first you see the actual light of the material disc that you put in front of you, with your eyes. This is called the preliminary image. Then you close your eyes, and try to visualize the light. That is the visualized image called "grasped image."

When this is done persistently and with mindfulness, then the mind become more and more cut off from other objects. After some time you do not hear anymore. Later on you even forget the shape and form of your body. All there is is the circle of light.

When the concentration is not yet very strong, the circle of light might oscillate. It might have certain pictures inside. This shows that although you might think you are not thinking, the mind is still flickering and fluctuating. It will come to a point when the circle is completely pure and the light is very bright. Everything else is forgotten, the body, sounds, where you are, even who you are. You only know that the mind is concentrating on the light, one-pointed, not thinking about anything else. There may be a lot of joy, a lot of lightness, but nothing else. This stage is called *upacara samadhi*—**access concentration.**

There comes a stage very close to absorption when the mind is very pure and the light is very bright and translucent like a glass, as if the mind is light and the light is the mind. This actually is the case because the light is a creation of the mind. This is called the "mirror image"—*patibhaga nimitta*. This occurs also when people visualize deities. Sometimes they visualize bodhisattas and similar objects. The image becomes glass-like. When they visualize the Buddha he also becomes transparent. Because of the strong concentration, the mind is as if it is the "Buddha" and "Buddha" is as if the mind. That is a very pure state of mind. So much so that you feel your body is in the Buddha image. Then the mind gets absorbed into it, the mind sinks into the nimitta. Through the study of the Abhidhamma, you can understand that this is the **fixed concentration,** called *appana samadhi*. This means that the mind is unified with the object. During this time there are no other thought processes occurring. Which means that at this time you are like completely asleep. You sink into a state like "not knowing anything." But when you emerge from the concentration you know that during the absorption the mind was very clear and it was all the time one with the object of concentration, the circle of light.

In this samatha meditation the mind should becomes more and more calm, more and more serene, more and more peaceful, and the defilements go farther and farther away. These highly developed states

Let go of the past,
let go of the future,
let go of the present,
and cross over
to the farther shore of existence.
With mind wholly liberated,
you shall come no more to birth
and death.

DHAMMAPADA 348

in samatha are something like half sleeping and states deeper than sleeping. Except that you know you are not sleeping.

In samatha meditation the mind should become more and more calm, more and more serene, more and more peaceful...

For example in the early morning sittings the mind is very calm, and peaceful. Sometimes you may watch without any problem the "rising and falling" of the abdomen for one or two hours. But you cannot describe the rising and falling clearly moment by moment. All you can say is "I had a very calm, and peaceful meditation, the belly just went up and down, up and down, very soft, and very slow, a very wonderful sitting." Then you become attached to it. You want to get the same thing again. If you cannot get nice concentration you complain, "The meditation is difficult now, terrible, a lot of pain." To that I say, "Very good, very good." You ask, "How come?" After some time, when you think the meditation is not good I say, "Very good," to encourage you! If a person begins doing vipassana and feels so calm and peaceful, then it may not be a very good sign—attachment may arise.

Some believe they have attained to *sankharupekkha ñana*, the knowledge of equanimity about formations, the knowledge just before *magga-phala*—enlightenment. But they cannot describe as well as the earlier insight knowledges. This is getting stuck in concentration. We therefore have to be very careful how we proceed in our practice.

ANAPANASATI

Certain objects can be used for samatha or vipassana meditation. One is the *anapana* object, watching the in-breath at the nose tip. People frequently ask, "Is the concentration at the nose tip (*anapana*) a samatha or vipassana object?" It can be both. This depends on the nature of your attention. In the beginning when using the preliminary object it can be a samatha or vipassana object as it is mixed. When you start counting the breath it tends more towards the samatha object. But there is still the sensation of the breath to be felt.

Vipassana objects, unlike samatha objects, are realities. They are not mind-created, that is you do not imagine them. They happen as a natural occurrence—as mental processes and material processes. When you see these processes clearer and clearer, of course the three characteristics of existence—*anicca, dukkha* and *anatta*—also become clearer. These are deeper aspects of the mental and material processes.

So when you are doing *anapanasati*—concentration on the breath at the nose tip—and these mental and material processes, which are often experienced as sensations, are not clear, then the vipassana object is not building up. I have observed that in a large number of yogis, the mind is inclined towards samatha. Why? Because most people do not understand what vipassana is. Secondly, because vipassana is more difficult, more painful and the object is more turbulent. So naturally the mind would incline towards what is calm, what is peaceful and to what people usually understand as meditation, namely concentration. They think that when they can concentrate the mind on the object for a long time they have done a very good job. The breath object, when you can keep to it, is soft, pleasant, and therefore the mind inclines towards samatha.

I am not saying samatha is bad. Samatha is good if you can do it. It is just that if you want to get insight knowledge you have to be able to differentiate.

THE PROGRESSION OF THE ANAPANA OBJECT

When the meditation on anapana progresses, one of the two practices becomes clearer and more predominant. Sometimes both practices may occur on and off. This depends on the individual tendencies of the mind. But, as has been said, people usually incline towards samatha.

Here is how anapana progresses as a samatha object. Start by counting the in- and the out-breaths as one-one, two-two, three-three, and so on. Or you can count in other ways. When the mind gets one-pointed, you will forget about the form of your body, you will forget where you are, and only the sensation, the point of the breath, becomes clearer and clearer.

Due to the inclinations towards peacefulness and one-pointedness,

He who has reached the goal is fearless, free from craving, passionless, and has plucked out the thorns of existence —for him this is the last body.

DHAMMAPADA 351

the mind will develop the samatha object. This means the conceptualized object. It is a developed mental object, a *nimitta*, a mental experience. Some may experience it as a cotton wool, others as a very soft feather, or as wind blowing in this or that direction. Still others may experience it as a very soft white light that is twinkling and so on. These are conceptualized images of the breath.

Initially the object may be moving or pulsating and this is then often mistaken as a vipassana object because of the movement. But in this case it is not a vipassana object. The samatha object in its initial stage *is* moving, changing. But not in the sense of a vipassana object which changes moment to moment. If one progresses further in one's concentration, the object becomes more and more still, more and more fine until it does not move any longer. At that point the mental image is extremely purified and absorption can occur, the mind sinks into the object, becomes one with the object.

Because the concentration factor is more dominant, more pronounced, it seems that in the initial absorptions it is not so clear to the meditator what has happened, especially to people who progress fast. But as soon as one has certain mastery over the concentration, the progression of the samatha object is very obvious. A person who has entered the jhanas frequently should be very clear in describing the progression of the samatha object, how the breath forms the samatha nimitta, the sign of concentration, and how it gets finer and finer up to just before absorption.

From such descriptions we can judge whether a person has gone into deep concentration or not. If a person fails to describe it clearly he could have simply entered into a kind of peaceful state, some kind of peaceful *samadhi* or even sleep. For example, a person might meditate on the in-breath and out-breath, in-out, in-out, in-out, and suddenly he finds himself, he does not know where, waking up and thinking, "Oh, so wonderful and peaceful." But it probably was just deep sleep. Or he might have been enveloped in joy, which became overwhelming, swallowing him up. So the object and the progression of the concentration are not clear.

This can be observed among vipassana meditators, because certain vipassana meditators have a tendency towards jhanas, concentrations. But not that many. There was a case where a yogi was doing vipassana quite well and he seemed to have a lot of light coming out. Because he was doing vipassana we did not encourage him to stay on the light, he had to note "seeing, seeing, light, light" and when it got too strong, he had to open the eyes. Still, the light developed side by side with vipassana objects and kept coming up by itself. He described it once, "This light came out and got very fine like a round mesh, like a spider web, but it was all light and very clear. After that the mind seemed like a fly, flying at fantastic speed right into the centre of the fine web of light. And when I was in the web, it wrapped itself all around my mind and I entered a completely unconscious state." When he came out, he was very peaceful.

Such a description is a clear progression of the object with the development of the concentration. When you simply say the mind becomes very calm and clear in deep concentration, then it is only a very general description of what may have happened. Only when you experience this process by yourself can you describe how exactly this calm and clarity is. And from such descriptions we can know whether it is actual deep concentration or even just imagination. Whether the samatha object is loving-kindness (one of the practices of the *Brahma viharas*), or *anapana*, or visualization, there is a general similar progression which is unique to samatha bhavana.

THE PROGRESSION OF THE VIPASSANA OBJECT

The progression of the vipassana object is quite different. In the beginning it does not progress fast. Therefore one gets a lot of concentration experiences first. Because of this, the experiences in the beginning bhavana are quite similar with experiences in initial samatha bhavana. But the yogis have been told or taught from the very beginning to meditate in the vipassana way and not to concentrate on a single object, but rather on a process, not the visualized forms.

Even then some people can go into visualizations. For example,

Let him associate with friends who are noble, energetic and pure in life, let him be cordial and refined in conduct. Thus, full of joy, he will make an end of suffering.

DHAMMAPADA 376

when they note "sitting-touching, sitting-touching," people start visualizing the shape of the body. They can see themselves sitting there. That has nothing to do with vipassana, that is a visualization process. Some people watch their stomach going up and down and finally that the stomach has a shape. They see one long line that goes up and down, up and down. Sometimes it appears like a round ball. After a while the ball even has colours. It is here where people get attached to the concept and end up doing something like samatha meditation.

In walking meditation some people pay so much attention to the toes, the heels, the knees that they tend to visualize the form of their legs. This is not vipassana. Vipassana is the pure experience of the mind and body processes. For example, when noting "sitting-touching" you do not see the shape of the body, hands, legs or head, but rather the sensations that make up the sitting posture. You experience pure sensations.

"Touching" involves the sensations at the surface of the body. The most prominent ones are at the posteriors, or where the legs press on the floor. "Sitting" involves more of the internal forces, a very strong force at the spine, the waist, the shoulders that maintains the sitting posture upright. It is a kind of rigidity. Some people feel it like a force pushing from the back.

When one goes deeper into "sitting, touching" one cannot differentiate any longer between the external surface and the internal sensation or forces, because they are just sensations, and "internal" and "external" are concepts. Pure sensations without shape remain.

In this way we can understand the object as the pure *paramattha dhammas*, ultimate realities. These objects occur moment to moment and are different from the samatha objects. That is, one moment is like this and the next moment all has changed, and the next moment is again different. In other words, it is a process—a flux—something appearing and disappearing. Then the three characteristics become evident and the pain can also become quite dominant. Because of this

In walking meditation some people pay so much attention to the toes, the heels, the knees that they tend to visualize the form of their legs.

the concentration in vipassana bhavana, insight meditation, does not develop so fast. The object is always changing and pain is frequently present. But we have to develop this type of concentration because it is unique to insight meditation. This type of concentration cannot be obtained in samatha meditation.

You have to understand that the insight knowledges that arise are part and parcel of the type of consciousness and of the concentration that arise. That is one reason why some people who have done samatha meditations are asked by the meditation teacher to completely put aside the samatha practice for the time of the meditation retreat. This is in no way a prejudice against samatha bhavana. This is because one has to learn the uniqueness of the vipassana concentration.

If one who has done a lot of anapana is asked to watch the "rising and falling" of the abdomen, he or she usually does not like it. Because doing "rising, falling" is at times very gross and sometimes, you just watch the "stuck feeling" in the stomach. Sometimes there is just tension in the stomach. And after that there is a lot of pain here and there. And then because the mind cannot hold the concentration, it starts thinking. So these meditators do not like that, they say, "I am regressing. I am getting worse in my meditation. I am not suitable for vipassana." So finally they run back to samatha bhavana saying, "It is so nice, calm and peaceful." Therefore insight neither arises nor progresses.

The mind has to be forced to look into the mind and body processes. When pain arises you have to keep to the pain. There is no vipassana without pain. During the Buddha's time, a lot of people were doing samatha bhavana and after that quickly attained to *magga-phala*. You can find many examples in the Buddhist scriptures. This does not occur with everyone so easily. Usually one has first to develop this unique vipassana concentration. That is why you have to watch pain when it arises. Then you learn to observe the nature of these mind and body processes.

The mind must be clear and open, without any concepts. The mind must be very fast and clear, to catch each and every phenomena. This ability does not come out of the blue, just by wanting it. It has to

By oneself on must censure oneself and scrutinize oneself. The self-guarded and mindful monk will always live in happiness.

DHAMMAPADA 379

be developed. Just like playing squash. Squash is a very fast game. You hit the ball and before you know it, it bounces back on you. You might hurt yourself. When beginners hit the ball they do not know where the ball will go. You have to develop the necessary skills.

Similarly, the vipassana object is a very fast changing object. The mindfulness has to develop to a stage where it is very fast, flexible, and clear before one can keep up with all the arising and disappearing objects. You have to watch and note so many different objects, the arising and falling of the abdomen, then pain, then thinking, then this, then that, etc. Sometimes there is a lot of suffering. Some people call vipassana "suffering meditation" and find it very difficult to practise.

But when you have gone through all these experiences the mind becomes very calm and is able to follow the objects moment to moment. You can then experience the mind going into the object, onto the "rising and falling," the pain, etc, and watch all the many various sensations. The sensations can be very clear and very intense but the mind keeps calm. When you watch further and further, the three characteristics of existence become clearer and clearer. The various levels of insight knowledge are none other than clearer and clearer experiences with regards to the nature of reality, the nature of the mind and body processes, the nature of *anicca*, *dukkha* and *anatta*.

Whether we practise vipassana for insight, or samatha for tranquillity, make sure that we do it properly, step by step.

As one progresses in the insight knowledges, the vipassana concentration also progresses. When such a state is attained, the mind does not go so easily to samatha meditation any more. Except for people who have the tendencies. Even then, let us say if light arises and you note it, it quickly goes off. With the appearance of very clear insight knowledges, you know that the mind is progressing in the direction of vipassana. When no clear insight knowledges arise, the mind does not progress clearly in vipassana. The mind may still be hanging around, going after this or that.

In this world you find more samatha practices and experiences. The experiences of vipassana are not so common. One example is the first insight knowledge, the discrimination of mind and body. This knowledge can arise very clearly in walking meditation where it is often more obvious than in sitting meditation. Being the first insight knowledge the beginner's mindfulness is not this sharp yet. Because beginners like the calm they tend to go towards concentration meditation during the sitting. In walking meditation on the other hand, it is a clear moment to moment process of mind and object, noting the seeing and the sensations that are experienced in the walking process. When the intention arises it is also noted. In this way the processes of the mind and the body are clearly differentiated with sharp awareness. As a result of that, one knows with experience that there is such an insight knowledge, that there is such an experience. It is based on this first knowledge that all the other insight knowledges can arise.

Some say, "Oh, we passed very quickly through all the insight knowledges and ended up with the last few." I say, "You are dreaming!" Often when I hear this remark I ask them what mindfulness is. Sometimes they are not even clear about what mindfulness is. Their mindfulness and concentration are not sharp. So how can they go so far in vipassana? It is like when a person who is not able to speak with proper grammar says that he is a professor in English. He should not expect me to believe that. The mindfulness which comes with insight knowledges must be very sharp, very clear, very thorough. Only then can we know for sure that a person is developing in the vipassana direction.

So the one most important thing to know is: Do not be concerned with one or two experiences that you find unusual. What is more important is to get a very strong base of mindfulness or concentration, whichever you are developing first.

SUMMARY

Here is a short summary of what we have touched upon: Whether we practise vipassana for insight, or samatha for tranquillity, make sure that we do it properly, step by step. For that we would usually have to undergo intensive retreats.

The craving of one given to heedless living
grows like a creeper.
Like the monkey seeking fruits in the forest,
he leaps from life to life
(tasting the fruit of his kamma).

DHAMMAPADA 334

In the case of samatha, remember that we have to develop it strong enough to act as a base for insight. That means the concentration must be strong and sharp and obtained easily before we can switch into vipassana. Otherwise it does not serve the purpose. It may take some time before we develop it to such a degree.

Finally, we have to switch to vipassana, insight meditation. When we do that we have to put away completely the practice of samatha for the time being and devote ourselves fully to the practice of vipassana. Otherwise the mind will keep running back to the concentration exercises. In vipassana concentration we have to face a lot of pain and discomfort.

There are some people with certain types of strong defilements who may have to undertake first some samatha meditation for vipassana to be effective. From my experience there are not many Malaysian yogis who need this.

Still we should not underestimate the preliminary concentration meditations, the four guardian meditations: Two minutes recollection on the virtues of the Buddha, two minutes loving-kindness, two minutes contemplation on repulsiveness of the body and two minutes of contemplation on death. If we do these for the first ten or twenty minutes at the beginning of one's daily sitting meditation, they become habitual and can help in our practice to a great extent. Especially in daily life.

In the intensive practice it may not be so relevant, because the concentration attained in pure insight practice during an intensive retreat is already very strong. If you turn towards these preliminary practices you will actually have a weaker concentration. But in daily life, when the mind is extremely restless, these guardian meditations are important in maintaining the practice to some degree.

The teacher, the great sage,
Is the first in the world;
Following him is the disciple
Whose composure is perfected;
And then the learner training on the path,
one who has learnt much and is virtuous.

These three are chief amongst devas and humans:
Illuminators, preaching Dhamma,
Opening the door to the Deathless,
They free many people from bondage.

Those who follow the path
Well taught by the unsurpassed
Caravan-leader, who are diligent
In the Sublime One's dispensation,
Make an end of suffering
Within this very life itself.

ITIVUTTAKA 84

Understanding Insight

S ince we are all here to practise Insight Meditation it would
only be appropriate for us to have an understanding of what
insight is. In order to make the talk more complete, I will have
to deal with certain aspects of the experience which many of you may
not be ready for yet; but you can take this as a kind of general
knowledge. What I am going to say may venture into "sensitive areas."
"Sensitive areas" because insight knowledge is normally not spoken
of for fear that it may be misunderstood and misinterpreted.
Nevertheless, I feel that one has to know a number of things, at least
theoretically or just enough to help you to handle things as you go
on, especially when there are not many experienced teachers around
all the time.

INSIGHT AND UNDERSTANDING

First, we will talk about insight, or understanding. What do we mean
by wisdom of insight? One can define understanding or wisdom as
that which makes known, that which reveals. It is like turning on
the light—when the light is turned on, it reveals what is around you,

*Having known the escape from sensual
desires
And the overcoming of forms,
One whose energy is always
ardent
Reaches the stilling of all
formation.*

*Such a bhikkhu who sees rightly
Is hereby well released.
Accomplished in knowledge, at
peace,
That sage has overcome all bonds.*

ITIVUTTAKA 72

and what is reality. To emphasise the point again, the commentary in the *Visuddhi Magga* (The Path of Purification), gives three similes on the three levels of knowing. These are "perception," "consciousness," and "understanding." Perception is defined as that knowing which takes note or takes the marks. This is compared to a young child knowing something. The second kind of knowing is consciousness. Consciousness does not approach the degree of knowing as in understanding or wisdom. The third kind of knowing is wisdom knowledge. At this point, the dhamma differentiates two types of understanding—

Spiritual understanding involves the purification of mind, the overcoming of greed, anger and delusion and the reduction of the defilements.

worldly understanding or worldly wisdom, and spiritual wisdom. The difference here lies in the control of the mind and the defilements. Although we can think very well in worldly wisdom, get many answers, and do many things, there is not much in terms of controlling the defilements. That is why you can have very clever people who can end up doing many terrible things like building atomic bombs. This comes under the worldly wisdom of thinking. Nevertheless, the main power, which is controlling the thought processes, behind worldly wisdom of thinking can be the defilements—greed, anger, and delusion. Therefore, such type of understanding is dangerous if it is misused.

Spiritual understanding is different. Spiritual understanding involves the purification of mind, the overcoming of greed, anger and delusion and the reduction of the defilements. This type of understanding can be further classified into three levels of the dhamma. The first level is that which comes from hearing, this refers more to information or theoretical knowledge. For example, when you read the dhamma you know what is good and bad kamma, what is greed, and why it is bad, and so forth. All this is theory. One step further is understanding which comes with thinking. For example if one studies the *Abhidhamma* and knows how many mental factors there are, how many types of consciousness there are, you may turn this around and round in your mind and analyse it inside out, and from there you gain a different kind of understanding. Alternatively, you can apply this learning in your daily life, you can think about it, and come to a new understanding. This is called the second level, which you do not normally get from books. This is the knowledge gained from contemplation and thinking. What needs greater emphasis, is the third level, the knowledge that comes from meditation because in meditation the mind can develop at much deeper levels than is normally possible in ordinary thinking.

There are two types of meditation—tranquillity (*samatha*) meditation and insight meditation (which is what we are writing about here). In tranquillity meditation, although the main factor involved is concentration, there still needs to be understanding and wisdom to be able to develop deep concentration. When deep concentration is developed and the mind becomes very powerful, one can develop skills such as telepathy, clairvoyance and know many things not possible otherwise. This is also an understanding, which comes from mental development. This, then, is wisdom from tranquillity meditation.

Vipassana meditation

In vipassana, the understanding, which comes about, involves the true nature of the world ie, of the mind and body processes. The whole world which includes us can generally be classified into two types of things; mind processes and material processes. When one develops deep understanding from thorough observation of these processes, the mind sees them as impermanent, unsatisfactory, and non-self. When the mind sees them repeatedly, one gains much deeper understanding in this regard. This type of understanding of insight into the mind and body processes as well as into the three universal characteristics of impermanence, unsatisfactoriness and non-self, helps us to develop dispassion and detachment from all that is impermanent, suffering and non-self. Therefore we go beyond the mundane and find the peace of the supramundane. This is the unique nature of *vipassana* (insight) meditation. It is only through this type of

Having known the body
as perishable
And consciousness as bound
to dissolve,
Having seen fear in objects
of clinging,
He has gone beyond birth
and death;
Having attained supreme peace,
With composed mind he bides
his time.

ITIVUTTAKA 77

meditation that we are able to see clearly, how one develops the knowledge and why one abandons the world to experience the unconditioned.

DEVELOPMENT OF INSIGHT

As I have said, insight knowledge is not knowledge which comes from thinking and it is not what you get from reading a book. It comes from practice. It is knowledge that can be considered empirical, or experiential. It comes from a level of the mind that is clearer and more deeply concentrated than at other times. That is why when we do insight meditation, from the very start we emphasise mindfulness and clear awareness that comes without thinking. It is not concerning the past nor the future but the present experience. If you go to the past, you tend to think about the past. If you go to the future, it is a mere projection of your thoughts. Insight meditation concerns the present—when you do not think—when you experience the actual nature of what is happening to your mind and body.

Insight knowledge is not knowledge which comes from thinking and it is not what you get from reading a book.

This type of awareness is built up over a period so that it can be continuous both when you are doing walking and sitting meditation, as well as when you are eating and drinking. From moment-to-moment, we develop this clear awareness of the present occurrence. When we do that, this type of awareness and noting becomes more powerful and more concentrated. Finally it becomes a strong current that keeps building up and experiencing what is happening moment-to-moment. If you can maintain fairly continuous mindfulness, it is only a matter of time before you can be more concentrated on the object. However, what must be emphasised is the nature of the vipassana object—which has to be a real object. It should not be a concept. So at this point, it is necessary to give you a better understanding of what a concept is.

WHAT IS A CONCEPT?

As I have said, a concept is what is thought out, imagined or created by the mind. One form which is very obvious is when we think and plan things which has not yet happened, or when we imagine and "build castles in the air." All these are mere concepts, they are not real, and they are created with our minds. There are other types of concepts, which are subtler, and we have to recognise them. These come not actively but passively. They come with the processes of the mind. One type is what we call **sound** concepts, eg, words and melodies. These are not real because they are created by the mind. For instance, the word "selfish" does not really exist in the ultimate sense. It is made up of consonants and vowels, which are only sounds. The word has two syllables, "self" and "fish." At one moment of time, you cannot hear the whole word "selfish." What you hear are different sounds passing away. It is only the sequence of sounds, which gives the mind the idea. Actually, there is only vibration of sounds following each other. Another type of sound concept is the melody, *"do-re-me... do, a deer, a female deer..."* At no one moment does the melody exist. There are only musical notes arising one after another. The mind gets a mental imprint and so a melody arises. These are sound concepts.

Another form of concept is that which involves **form**. A form involves distance, direction, and size. All this is ultimately not real. For example, if I say that this is my right and this is my left, from your perspective, which is really my right and which is really my left? Right and left are concepts dependent on the relationship of one object and another, which way you are facing and so on. Similarly, things like distance and time. Even the idea of form and shape are concepts. We seem to see whole things at once but in the thought processes, we know it does not occur like that. Pictures on television are an example. They occur rapidly one after another but we see the forms and shapes created as simultaneous. Form and shapes are concepts. In the case of form, we experience only the colour and the light, which comes and goes very rapidly. **Time** is also a concept—dependent on the functions of many things—which come and go. That

Desire born of association
Is severed by non-association.
As one riding on a wooden plank
Would sink in the mighty ocean,
Even so one of virtuous life
Sinks by consorting with an idler.

Therefore shun an idle person,
One who makes little effort.
Live with those who dwell
secluded,
The noble ones resolved and
meditative,
Who are ever strenuous and wise.

ITIVUTTAKA 78

is all there really is; things that come and go. They arise and dissolve, and then they are already in the past. If it has not arisen, then we say that is the future. When it is happening, we say it is the present. All these are concepts and in them we cannot find the ultimate reality and truth.

There is another important concept which I must mention too, that is the concept of the **person—"I"**. This is a very central concept. While the mind holds on to the concept of the person and is clouded with clinging to this concept, you cannot go beyond this level of thinking logic or experience. When we say a person—"I," "you," "Mr Smith," or "Ms Smith"—who is this person? You try to look within. What is there when you have been noting "sitting" and "touching," do you find yourself in the body? What you find is the body walking and sitting, the movement, the tensions, the heat and so forth. This is not you—you cannot find yourself there. Then when you watch the feelings—the feelings will come and go and they are not you either. Look at your mind. Your mind does not listen to what you say. When you do not want it to think it thinks, when you want to think it does not think. When you do not want to sleep it sleeps and when you do want to sleep, it does not sleep. It is as if it has a life of its own. What we usually say "I"—is a function of all these processes but if you hold on to the person as absolutely real, you cannot go beyond this view. When we say, "Who is this person?" and you look within, there are just these complex mind and body processes.

There are also other concepts we meet with. Those, for instance, that come with visualisations—these are more involved with tranquillity (*samatha*) meditations. Sometimes people visualise many things; they visualise deities and Buddhas for instance. All these are mind created. If you know you created them, normally you do not take them seriously. However, there are people who have created a Buddha in their mind and they think that it is the real Buddha. When you are able to recognise visualisations as concepts and when they arise in your meditation, you do not focus nor concentrate on them. You concentrate on the realities—the mind and body processes, body contemplation like the four great elements (earth, fire, water and wind elements). For example, in your sitting meditation you watch the "rising" and "falling," you attend to those realities rather than the shape of the stomach which is a concept. Likewise, the words "rising" and "falling" are also concepts. Nevertheless, in the beginning we have to have some tools for convenience. These are to help you concentrate your mind on the realities. Even when you are walking you say, "right step, left step," and the words "right" and "left" are concepts. As you watch the footsteps "lifting" and "stepping," you will have an idea of the form of the leg— those are also concepts—but in the beginning, this cannot be helped. After some practice when you concentrate on the footsteps you do not think of the shape of the leg, position of the toes and heels and so on; you are just aware of the movements and sensations which are the processes of the walking. Similarly, when you watch the "rising" and "falling" you do not think of the shape of the stomach but you get the feeling of the extension, of the expansion and the contraction, of the movement. What is important is to get a clear feel of the perception of all these. This is where mindfulness comes in.

MINDFULNESS

Mindfulness is like a very clear light that shines in the sense of knowing in a very thorough manner these sensations, these processes. If you ask a person to put his hand on the abdomen and watch the "rising" and "falling," he will know that it rises and falls. However, if you ask the person to describe in detail how the processes were, the person will not be able to tell you; he will just say, "Well, it goes up and down." That is a very superficial level of mindfulness and not penetrative. At most, it is ordinary knowing with a little bit of mindfulness—not sufficient to give insight. If you can follow the rise and fall for a long time, it will become a little clearer because you have a better hold of it. That mindfulness is a bit better in the sense that it is enough to build up the concentration but it is not thorough enough to produce the insight. Insight goes beyond concentration. For insight to arise, you have

A bhikkhu who enjoys activity,
Restless, fond of gossip and sleep,
Will never be able to attain
Enlightenment which is supreme.

Thus let him restrict his duties,
Give up sloth and restlessness;
Such a bhikkhu can attain
Enlightenment which is supreme.

ITIVUTTAKA 79

to watch the "rising" and "falling" in terms of the three universal characteristics (impermanence, unsatisfactoriness and non-self).

Take for example a person who watches the "rising" and "falling" so that he can follow it mindfully. When he is more mindful he must watch the different types of "rising" and "falling" which are sometimes long, sometimes short, sometimes fast, sometimes slow, so that he can detect the sequence of events. Then it goes further and becomes like waves "rising" and "falling," or goes this way and that way. All this shows that the form and the manner are getting clearer. At first, it is mainly the form. The whole abdomen rises, it expands like a balloon; then it sinks, contracts or deflates like a balloon—these are forms. It goes fast this way and that way, all that is the manner. These, though, are still concepts but the aspect of movements, the characteristics of tension, vibrations, and so forth will become clearer. When it becomes very clear, there is just the tension, there is no this way or that way. There is just one moment of appearance and the disappearance of the characteristic.

Take again the example of the "rising" and "falling." It has a beginning, it proceeds slowly, or quickly until the end, then it stops. If it proceeds slowly—the

When rising and falling of the abdomen becomes very clear, there is just the tension, there is no this way or that way.

"rising" and "falling" seems long. When it proceeds quickly—it seems shorter. They are related. If we talk in terms of long and short or slow and fast then we are aware of the movement but concepts are also involved. So, there can be no beginning, middle, and end of "rising" and "falling." If it is at the end, then it is not at the beginning. If it is at the beginning, then it is not the end. End and beginning are two different moments. In the middle, however, there are many points, many movements. So at one moment of time how can you experience a long or a short "rising" and "falling?" How can you experience a slow or fast one? These terms, long, short, slow, fast, etc are all useful at the beginning, otherwise it is not possible to see anything at all, it is not possible to concentrate and concentration cannot develop. When you have learned to concentrate you will be told to feel the movement (eg, the nature, the feeling, or the sensation) moment-to-moment. That is to be able watch the movement as if it is a point rather than a length. When you can do so, you will arrive at the point where just pure sensation arises and nothing else. Then you arrive at what we call the *paramattha dhamma*—the ultimate reality, eg, the pure element of motion, or as we say, the pure wind element. When you are able to watch it very clearly, you can also watch the three universal characteristics.

At this point, it is also necessary to emphasise that the ability to watch and get hold of the ultimate reality does not mean that insight will arise. Another ultimate reality for which you do not need too much effort to find is pain. Pain is a feeling. No matter who is having the pain, it is pain, it is not subjective, neither the past nor the future. In addition, when you watch pain it too arises and disappears. However, seeing pain itself does not mean that you have insight knowledge. Instead, you may be grumpier or angrier. Nevertheless, if you are able to keep your mind calm and concentrated on the present moment, on the present occurrence, on the feeling we call pain, and you watch it very clearly, then you can realise its nature.

INSIGHT KNOWLEDGES

The first insight knowledge is the knowledge of the discrimination of mind and body. They say that when you watch the "rising" and "falling," you will be able to notice the nature of the mind, which is doing the watching. The noting mind is one thing, whereas the rising movement is another. Insight knowledge is the ability to recognise phenomena according to their natural occurrences. We may see them as the pure ultimate realities that we call *paramattha dhamma* in Pali. A natural occurrence is present when you free your knowing mind from concepts. When you experience it free from thinking and concepts, whether they are active or passive concepts, it will be there

*He is one who lives diligently
With concentration undisturbed,
Both when homage is paid to him
And when he receives no homage.*

*Meditating continuously, gifted
With subtle view and insight,
Enjoying the destruction of
    grasping—
They call such a one a "true man."*

ITIVUTTAKA 81

because it is a natural occurrence. In addition, when you watch that nature very clearly you will note clearly that it is not you. The mind that watches is also another natural occurrence and that is not you either. There is no person there. Both observer and observed are natural occurrences. This is a very clear experience which, once you have experienced it, you can arouse it and bring it up to any other object. It is the mind having pure ultimate reality as its object.

When one is able to watch pain, what normally happens is that one may think, "My leg is painful!" Then the concept of the leg comes in two ways—"my" and the "leg." If the idea of the leg is put aside, then it is "I am painful!" left. When you put away the thought of "I" there is just the pain and the mind but if the mind is not mindful then the mind just gets agitated and cannot know anything properly. However, if the mind is mindful you can bear the pain and only know that the pain is there. If the mindfulness is very thorough and you watch the pain, it will be very clear and the pain in all its nature will be very vivid, so vivid that the pain will have nothing to do with you, it is simply a natural occurrence by itself. The mind that knows it is also a natural occurrence by itself—there should not be any disturbance. In this way, what you know will correspond more to what I think is the level of insight. Then you know this as truth, not because it is in the books, not because somebody says so, not because you think it is, but you know it with clear mindfulness, it is not ima-gination. The awareness is very clear and sharp. It is sharper than ordinary kinds of awareness.

What often happens with lower forms of knowledge is that conceptualisation follows after the experience. Especially when insight is very clear, it can give rise to other types of theories, which complicate matters. The experience is one thing. The thoughts that follow are another. You may start creating a theory of how all this happens and you may start relating the experience to so many different things, all of which may not be accurate. So, there are two things. One thing is the actual experience and the other is the impact of the thought processes in ordinary life. The impact of the initial insight experience can be very sharp and some people may not be ready for it. In this case, many unfavourable thought processes might follow. Fear may arise because in ordinary life a person may have, for instance, a lot of attachment. At this point, if there is no proper guidance or no support group, they may be completely discouraged. Your insight may be strong but it may not be strong enough to cut off all the defilements, and if the related defilements are very strong, they may complicate matters. They may encourage one to see things in a different light to the extent that one may become frightened. The original experience is a true experience but if the mind is not ready for it, the thought processes that follow may have a negative impact. Of course, this varies with different people. Some people will easily take to it while others will not. If one is in a retreat when this happens and the retreat is extended, the actual insight into the nature of mind and body, without concepts, without thinking, keeps deepening to the point where it is well established. It can even reach the level of *magga phala*—the level of enlightenment, total realisation.

Of course, this process does not come in a spark or in a second. Usually it is a long process. The whole process for all the stages—for example, are given in the commentaries and to some extent in the suttas—as the seven stages of purification or the sixteen insight knowledges.

The first insight knowledge involves the purification of views, the abandoning of the concept of "I." In one of the suttas, the Buddha gave us an idea of wise attention to the normal procedure and system of thinking that arises. Normally when a person thinks the thought processes revolve around one—the "I," "me" and "mine," the ego—everything one does and one's whole world revolves around oneself. This, the Buddha describes as unwise attention especially when there is a clinging to an "I." This is not correct view because with such a view, craving, anger, etc arises. But in the dhamma, when one is able to see that there is actually no "I" but only mind and body phenomena, the whole world which seems to be centred around oneself is not seen as related to the person but is seen dependent on the pure and unprejudiced mindfulness, a pure clear awareness, ie, just this nature of phenomena and characteristics. Everything is not

*On seeing that he has won the battle,
Even the devas honour him,
The Fully Enlightened One's
    disciple,
A great one free from diffidence:*

*"We salute you,
    O thoroughbred man,
You who have won a difficult
    conquest.
Having routed the army of Death,
You are unhindered in liberation."*

*Thus do the devas extol him,
The one who has attained
    the goal,
For they do not perceive in him
Ground for subjection to Death's
    control.*

ITIVUTTAKA 82

"I," not mine. They are just occurrences that arise owing to dependency. At this stage we say there is the purification of views from all wrong views and wrong opinions which are based on the clinging to the self; clinging on the idea of the person, the "me," the mine.

The sixty-two wrong views mentioned in *Brahmajala Sutta*, are dependent on this wrong view of the clinging to the self. When one is able to observe this phenomena according to the unique or specific characteristic, when one sees them very clearly one after another, the relationship of dependent origination or dependent existence, the conditioned aspect of life becomes very clear. This dependent origination or conditioning is concerned with the second purification of view and the second insight knowledge. This is in relation to the overcoming of the deep concepts concerning time, the past, the future, etc. It breaks down the concept of time and so forth. Once this is possible, the three universal characteristics can become clearer.

All the sixteen insight knowledges—sometimes they talk about as eighteen insight knowledges—can be classified under three. These are insight into impermanence or concerning impermanence, insight into suffering or concerning suffering, and insight into non-self or concerning non-self.

Perceiving what can be expressed through concepts,
Beings take their stand on what is expressed.
Not fully understanding the expressed.
They come under the bondage of Death.

But by fully understanding what is expressed
One does not misconceive the speaker.
His mind has attained to freedom,
The unsurpassed state of peace.

Understanding what is expressed,
The peaceful one delights in the peaceful state.
Standing on Dhamma, perfect in knowledge,
He freely makes use of concepts
But no more enters into concept's range.

ITIVUTTAKA 63

Insight Knowledges in Brief

Insight comes from the direct experience of realities. Reality is when we put aside all concepts and keep the mind aware only of the present occurrence. The mind finds that what is actually happening are what we call mind and body processes.

When you are clearly aware of the present moment, what do you know? If you watch the sitting sensation around the buttock area then you do not actually know the buttocks—you do not see the shape, you will only know the pressure there and that is what we call ultimate reality. Ultimate reality is the occurrence that can be experienced in the present moment without thinking or preconceptions. This is usually the characteristic of mind and body processes.

Only when the deep and clear awareness is placed and focused to observe this reality—mind or body phenomena—can we have a deep experience or understanding of the reality of mind and bodily processes. Only when the deep awareness is penetrative, do we have this experience of reality. You see all this experience as a natural occurrence. There is no person there, no "me," no "you," just a natural phenomena. When you can watch this phenomena clearly, you will find that they are not absolute entities by themselves but are dependent on all other phenomena associated with them. We

For a learner who is training
In conformity with the direct path,
The knowledge of destruction arises first,
And final knowledge immediately follows.

Freed by that final knowledge,
By destroying the fetters of being
The serene one has the certainty:
"Unshakeable is my release."

Endowed with this faculty
The peaceful one delights in the peaceful state.
Having conquered Mara and his mount,
He bears his final body.

ITIVUTTAKA 62

say we are aware of the conditioned nature and what is obvious is the flow. The mind and body flows, the processes flow and dependent on the flow is this thing called time (past, present and future).

As one goes on, it will be seen that all things in the universe finally end up in what we describe as the three universal characteristics—impermanence, suffering and non-self. We also say that the sixteen insight knowledges can all be classified as insight into these three universal characteristics.

The dhamma defines what is meant by impermanence—impermanence with reference to the five aggregates.

INSIGHT INTO THE THREE UNIVERSAL CHARACTERISTICS

At this point, it is necessary to give a clearer understanding of insight into these three universal characteristics.

To give a better understanding, the dhamma gives a few definitions. They are *anicca* (impermanence), *aniccalakkhana* (signs of impermanence), and *aniccanupassana* (contemplation of impermanence). The dhamma defines what is meant by impermanence—impermanence with reference to the five aggregates. These mind and body processes are materiality, feelings, perception, mental formations, and consciousness—all these five aggregates are impermanent. That means that the actual and true nature of these five aggregates, these mind and body processes can all be summarised as impermanence.

What is this impermanence? We talk of the *characteristics* of impermanence. The characteristic means the sign. They are not impermanence itself, just the signs. Just as there is a sign pointing to Katoomba." The sign itself is not Katoomba. Katoomba is the place you reach when you follow the sign. Another example is, when the finger points to the moon, that finger is not the moon. In a similar way, the signs of impermanence only point to impermanence.

So, what are the signs of impermanence? The sign of impermanence is that lasting only for a moment—it's that arising and passing away. What we normally call change is the sign of impermanence. There is a beginning and an ending to it.

What then is this impermanence? Impermanence is that when the moment arises, it then disappears. One monk defined it as when you can experience the arising as the disappearance to the extent where there is no differentiation between the arising and the disappearing—it is at that moment that you experience impermanence. This is also what we call moment-to-moment change. If, for example, when you watch the "rising" and "falling," first you say "rising, falling, rising, falling." As I said before, the word is a concept but it is a concept to bring you to the experience of the movement, of the flow of sensations of the abdomen. You may get the idea of a round abdomen expanding like a big balloon and deflating. The idea of a balloon is a concept and it comes with the observation. However, as you continue, what becomes more obvious is the change that comes with it. Sometimes it is fast, sometimes it is slow, sometimes this way and then that way. The manner though is a concept and it is still there, this cannot be helped. What you do is to keep pulling the mind to the actual sensation. When you can feel the sensation then there is just one point of sensation. It is as if the "rising" is made up of many points and all those points cannot occur at once, only one point can arise and disappear at the one time. If you can fix more on just the pure sensation, very clearly, what normally would happen is that you begin to see the "rising" as comprised of a series of movements and a series of sensations. This can often be seen as if in a straight line though it is not necessarily a straight line, because a straight line is also a concept. As you watch, it gets closer and closer to a series of sensations, and you come to a point where it is just a flow.

As another example, at first you can watch the "rising" in two parts, which seems to stop briefly in the middle. If you watch further, it seems to stop three or four times as if it is broken into three or four parts. Then if you watch more closely, it is as if it is broken into ten parts, then into a hundred parts; though of course, a hundred parts you cannot count. So finally, at one moment of time, there is just an arising and the arising is also disappearing. When that happens

Contemplating foulness in the body,
Being mindful of in-and-out breathing,
Ever ardent and seeing clearly
The calming down of all
formations:

Such a bhikkhu who sees rightly
Is thereby well released.
Accomplished in knowledge,
at peace,
That sage has overcome all bonds

ITIVUTTAKA 85

you cannot think anymore. The sensation, the tension, and the movement itself are no longer obvious. What is obvious is the moment-to-moment change and flow. It is just like when you watch a cinema screen. One frame on the filmstrip comes and then goes, then another and another. When this occurs faster and faster, then what happens? The frames come and go or switch on and off, on and off until you cannot see the individual picture at all, you just know it flips on and off very fast. There is no time to see the picture because the picture only lasts for such a brief moment. In other words, the mind first concentrates on the sensation and when one is aware of the nature of the sensation with pure mindfulness, with pure attention or with bare attention at the present moment, you then see only the flow. When you see only the flow, you see impermanence. Therefore, whatever it is, whether it be the material qualities of the four elements or the feeling, or whether it is the consciousness itself, or whether it is the mental formations themselves, when everything is reduced to this flow there is no real differentiation. When you arrive at that flow or moment-to-moment change, you see impermanence. That is why you can say that it is not just matter that is impermanent but the five aggregates of mind and body processes are also impermanent.

THE TRUE NATURE OF REALITY

This impermanence can be described as the true nature of reality itself, the true nature of phenomena. Impermanence is a word to denote reality but we have first to be able to observe these phenomena. You do not stay with the signs. You penetrate them and go into the actual reality. You watch the moment-to-moment change in the mind and body, the vipassana objects, but you do not cling to them. You direct the mind to observe these things but you need a clear and unprejudiced mind. Then you will have no preconceptions of what things will be when you push the mind, guide it, and sink it into the flow, into the process itself. You should not have any preconceptions that is like many bubbles coming and going, many particles coming and going and so forth. You should have no idea of how it would or should be. You should keep the mind in a way that is free and appropriate to your own unique state of consciousness as insight knowledge arises in a form that is peculiar to the environment and to the individual's temperament. Although there is a common pattern in that it arises and passes very quickly, each individual's experience is unique. If you have a preconception, then you are limiting the freedom to which your mind can develop insight. Some people with previous experience try to get back their past experience but we do not recommend that. If you have the right method and you practise accordingly, those levels of insight and experiences will arise on their own. If you try to conform to a certain way, as to how the experience should be, then you are actually delaying or limiting your own progress. It can happen in a slightly different form, even easier and faster without these self-imposed limitations. That is what we mean when we say you guide the mind by watching it observe the signs of impermanence. You do not have any preconceptions how the experience of impermanence will be. You have to have a really clear and open mind for it to happen. It is important not to have any expectations. Contemplation of impermanence comes about through the constant observation into the signs of impermanence and finally the realisation of its nature.

SUFFERING

In Pali, the word suffering is *dukkha*. When you say suffering, it refers to the five aggregates, in the same way that impermanence refers to the five aggregates of the mind and body processes. The signs of suffering are concerned with oppressiveness. The most obvious comes under what we call *dukkhadukkha*, "suffering-suffering" or pain of suffering. This refers to the pain of the body and mind. Examples are when you feel sad, have a toothache or a headache, or a back or leg ache. All these are the signs of suffering. That is obvious oppressiveness. However, when we talk of the suffering of

A bhikkhu enjoying the Dhamma
And delighting in the Dhamma,
Reflection upon the Dhamma,
Does not fall from the true
*   Dhamma.*

Whether walking or standing,
Sitting or lying down,
With mind inwardly restrained,
He attains to lasting peace.

ITIVUTTAKA 86

the five aggregates, what is implied is the five aggregates is suffering as they are impermanent. It equates impermanence with suffering. So there are actually two words with the same meaning but for people who have not yet experienced it, they would only be able to see the signs and not the reality. If one wants to penetrate the real meaning of suffering, in terms of the three universal characteristics, then one has to see into the impermanence. One has to see the signs of change repeatedly. When one is able to see the signs of change repeatedly, then one is able to see the signs of suffering more clearly. Finally, when you see into the impermanence clearly, you will see the suffering clearly as well. In other words, one has finally to bring the mind to see the moment-to-moment change, the actual flow of the mind and body processes, as clearly as possible. Then you will realise that the moment-to-moment change of the mind itself, is suffering and the experience of it, is like intense pain. This pain is more of a mental pain than a physical pain. Then the mind can realise, as given in the suttas, that whatever is impermanent is suffering.

If one wants to penetrate the real meaning of suffering, in terms of the three universal characteristics, then one has to see into the impermanence.

It is not so much that you suffer because you are attached to your property or body or when you change, grow old and fall sick. That is a more conventional form of argument and rationalisation. In the practice, because you see the moment-to-moment change—the real impermanence—very clearly, suffering is evident. This suffering is a moment-to-moment change that comes in the form of an unstable or restless experience. It is a real experience, something like pain and mental anguish. It is the very basis of the arising of all suffering in existence.

The aim of all this, bear in mind, is detachment—detachment from all that is impermanent, detachment from all that arises and passes away. Unless this can be experienced, the mind will not develop detachment from its conditioned nature to anything that has the nature of arising and disappearing. When you cannot have total detachment in that manner, the mind will still cling on to something that is conditioned, something connected with birth and death. You may seek refuge in something that may be very peaceful and very subtle. However, when one sees that anything conditioned is unsatisfactory, painful, or suffering, then the mind will be detached from it. In addition, when the mind becomes detached from it, the mind will be detached from all conditioned things. When this happens, the mind actually turns towards the unconditioned, heads towards what we call nibbana because the unconditioned is something that does not change. Compared to the suffering state of conditioning, this is peace that is absolutely everlasting. Then you also realise why we say vipassana meditation is the only way to the unconditioned.

It seems that many people do not like to think that vipassana is the only way to the unconditioned. However, if you consider this point, of the nature of impermanence and suffering, only this insight meditation can bring your mind to see impermanence and the conditioned nature of suffering. Only when you see this, will you turn away from all these conditioned nature. Unless the mind develops this really strong and powerful understanding, all the long deep-seated clinging to the pleasures of the world and existence will keep you there. You cannot be free because the mind does not want to be free. The mind does not see the need to be free, because it does not see the suffering and the intensity of suffering that are present in the conditioned nature—present in anything that arises and passes away.

This means that our development of the perception of impermanence has to be very sharp. It is easier to see something with the nature of matter, eg, heat, vibration and tension, arise and disappear moment-to-moment. It is easy to see painful feelings arising and disappearing, but it is more difficult to see things like consciousness, things like joyful and neutral feelings, which ordinarily a person does not experience clearly at all. Only when you can see this as impermanent, do you see the real meaning of suffering behind impermanence and this will become increasingly subtle as your meditation and concentration deepens. The feelings become subtler. The objects and mental objects become subtler. If you are unable to observe the moment-to-moment change in these, you will not see

Three wholesome thoughts should be entertained,
Three unwholesome thoughts rejected.
One who stops such trains of thought
As a shower settles a cloud of dust,
With a mind that has quelled such thoughts
Attains in this life the state of peace.

ITIVUTTAKA 87

suffering in them; and because you do not see the change in them, you see them as being so wonderful. Therefore, unless you can see the moment-to-moment change (impermanence), and suffering that is a result of the change, detachment cannot occur.

In the very beginning, although you have not seen into the moment-to-moment change, you can see the obvious changes, see the presence of the change more clearly, and then detachment will occur. At first, you cannot have the perception of non-self, because the mind is still clinging to the idea of an ego or self. As one sees change in the mind and body, the clinging to the self is slowly put away, and the non-selfness of the natural occurrence of the mind and body process becomes clearer. You will see more and more that the body sensations are actually not you; that the mind that watches, is just the mind that watches; as well as that feeling and the whole mass of pain does not belong to "me." "I" am not the pain and the mind that watches the pain so clearly is not "me" either, it is just the mind that is watching. This kind of experience can arise only when you can see the changes and the suffering that arises from the changes. Then the signs of impermanence become clearer, the signs of non-self become more obvious. Only when the signs of non-self become obvious, will the non-self become obvious. This non-self is equivalent to the five aggregates, which is a different word describing reality, in the same manner as impermanence and suffering.

To make it simple and brief, the signs are just indications of the direction in which you must bring your mind to watch, without expecting how they will be when you actually experience the flow. The actual impermanence, suffering and non-self is reality itself but the signs are those things which you observe, like change and oppressiveness, which actually leads you to the actual experience of reality.

THE DIFFERENT LEVELS OF INSIGHT KNOWLEDGE

So all this impermanence, suffering and non-self, which is a reality as well as conditioned nature, can be experienced at different levels according to the power and strength of the different controlling faculties. The five controlling faculties are faith, energy, mindfulness, concentration, and insight. As the mindfulness, concentration, and insight become stronger, you will experience the three universal characteristics at a deeper level. The deeper the level, the deeper the insight knowledge.

The general trend of the observation starts with gross change and oppressiveness. Then, when the natural occurrences are seen clearly as non-self, impermanence becomes clearer and the signs of impermanence also become clearer. The signs of suffering follow and then the signs of non-self. When all these three signs become clear, the experience of impermanence, the experience of suffering, the experience of non-self (not just the signs) becomes clearer. In other words, the **experience of reality** becomes clearer.

Please bear in mind that when we say the experience of reality becomes clearer, we do mean the *experience*, the reality has always been the same. It is the experience, which makes it seem clear or not so clear. Therefore, these different levels of experience in terms of reality can be considered as the different levels of insight knowledge.

Take for example, the sixteen insight knowledges. The first insight knowledge of the discrimination of mind and body is the obvious insight knowledge concerning non-self. However, the second insight knowledge on conditioning and the third insight knowledge of clear comprehension can relate to any of the three universal characteristics because the third insight knowledge covers all the three universal characteristics. In this situation any of the three signs can become clear in your experiences. When you go to the fourth insight knowledge of arising and dissolution, characteristics of impermanence becomes clear. When you go into terror, danger, disgust, and desire for deliverance, these four insight knowledges, the characteristics of suffering become clear. When you talk of the insight knowledge on equanimity of formations, the non-self aspect becomes clear. So you can see that although all three universal characteristics are involved in all aspects of reality, at certain times one characteristic stands out clearer. When you see more

Though closely following behind,
Full of longing and resentment,
See how far away he is—
The desirous one from the
  desireless,
One unquenched from the
  quenched, *
A greedy one from the one without
  greed.

But a wise person who by direct
  knowledge
Has fully understood the Dhamma,
Becomes desireless and tranquil
Like a calm unruffled lake.

See how close he is to him—
A desireless one to the desireless,
One quenched to the quenched,
The greedless one to the one
  without greed.

ITIVUTTAKA 92

*Nibbuto: quenched or cooled. One who has extinguished the three fires of lust, hate, and delusion has attained Nibbana, the state of extinction of being " quenched".

impermanence, you experience more suffering. As you experience more suffering, detachment arises and you experience more non-self; so the cycle goes on.

THE MAIN AIM IS PURIFICATION

What is important here is that the main objective for all these experiences is purification. Purification comes about through seeing non-self in all things. That means you abandon the clinging to all these mind and body processes. Not just a gross clinging but all the very fine and deep-seated clinging. When all this clinging that is deep within us is abandoned, then what is left is Nature. In addition, because one sees the suffering in all these things, one is completely detached from all these impermanent things; then the mind can free itself, and find refuge in nibbana, the unconditioned state.

This is a brief summary of the mechanics of insight meditation.

THINGS TO WATCH OUT FOR

Whatever experiences we come across, no matter how pleasant, how wonderful, or how profound, they are just to be noted.

In the process, of course, there are a number of things to watch out for. The meditation manuals always warn the yogi against the pitfalls. Some of them is described in the part on *upakilesas*, which we call the imperfections of insight. These can arise very sharply and very clearly when one reaches a certain level of meditation. The pitfalls is often described at the lower *udayabhaya ñana*, the lower knowledge, of the arising and dissolution. Not that it does not arise anywhere else but it arises very vividly here. The point here is that whatever experiences we come across, no matter how pleasant, how wonderful, or how profound, they are just to be noted, just like all other things. They just arise and pass away. Unless you can see its impermanence, it can become a pitfall. It can arouse craving, conceit, or wrong view. Craving is when you find it so wonderful that you keep wanting it increasingly, and attachment arises. You feel that you have something wonderful, so you are great, and you are so proud of it. That is another form of attachment and defilement arises thus. Alternatively, you think you have found the highest state because you experience very calm and beautiful mental states, and you think that is *Nibbana*. You cling to the view that this experience is the highest state. That is wrong view. When that happens, you not only stop progressing, but you can run into further problems. In the extreme case, you can become psychologically defective, a bit psychotic, or neurotic. Therefore, you must be really warned about this because although people hear about it, they are overwhelmed when it happens to them and they fall into this trap.

THE TEN IMPERFECTIONS OF INSIGHT

The ten imperfections of insight or ten "defilements" of insight, are actually results of good experiences due to a pure mind, with the exception of the last, which is a true defilement. Nevertheless, because of the attachment, a downfall can happen. Therefore, the moral behind this is that whatever pleasant experiences that arise, just note them mindfully.

There are ten imperfections of insight or ten "defilements" of insight:

1 *Obhasa*—illumination, seeing light
2 *Ñana*—knowledge
3 *Piti*—pleasurable interest, joy
4 *Passaddhi*—tranquillity of the mind
5 *Sukha*—deep bliss
6 *Adhimokkha*—resolution, strong faith
7 *Paggaha*—exertion, energy that lasts for a long time
8 *Upatthana*—strong mindfulness
9 *Upekkha*—equanimity knowledge (not the actual supramundane knowledge yet)
10 *Nikanti*—contentment, gratification, attachment.

*Fettered by both these bonds—
The sensual bond and the bond of being—
Living beings continue in samsara,
Journeying on to birth and death.*

*Those who abandon sensual desires
But have not reached the taints' destruction,
Fettered by the bondage of being,
Are declared to be non-returners.*

*But those who have cut off doubts,
Destroyed conceit and renewal of being,
Who reach the taints' full destruction,
Though in the world, have gone beyond.*

ITIVUTTAKA 96

YOU MAY MEET WITH DIFFICULT SITUATIONS

The other thing to bear in mind is, in the course of the practice you may meet with many difficult situations. This may have a lot to do with the meditation as well as with your defilements. It is said that if a person's defilements are strong, the progress of meditation is more difficult because the meditation progress involves the purification of the mind; for example if there is a lot of rubbish to get through, it is more difficult to purge. Another example, if a person meets with a lot of pain and the person's anger is strong, then it is more difficult to keep calm while watching the pain. Watching this pain and suffering is inevitable in vipassana. For example, if certain aspects of anger are strong, they will come up repeatedly. In addition, anger is also connected with attachment. Anger comes because you cannot get what you want. Attachment is also connected with ignorance and delusion, you cannot accept or see the real nature of impermanence, therefore you are deluded, and because of that, you are attached. When you are attached and things do not happen the way you want, then you get angry. So you see, all these three roots of evil are interconnected, it is a whole syndicate. That is why, if the defilements are strong, certain phases of the meditation can be very difficult. If you are not able to handle it, you can be stuck there, and if you are not careful, instead of getting more purified, the mind can become more troubled. At such times, it is important to seek the proper advice. If the mind becomes more disturbed than ever and there is no mindfulness at all, then you had better go back to the basics and relax a bit.

You may have read that there are certain insight knowledges such as the knowledge of fear, terror, or disgust. Some people may fear such a moment. It is not really feeling frightened, it is more of seeing the terror in the nature of mind and body processes, which is insight. Therefore, if you see something terrible, it does not mean you will be terrified. You are terrified when it is not an insight knowledge, then it becomes a form of fear. If your mind is not strong enough and this appears to you, then the impact immediately following it may not be good. Instead of being a blessing, it becomes something less favourable. That is why strong and stable mindfulness is very important. If it is just a matter of concentration, then any small experience will become magnified. When it becomes greatly magnified and your mindfulness is not strong enough to accept and observe it, instead of experiencing insight knowledge, defilements may arise. Therefore, strong mindfulness is important.

THREE MODELS IN THE PROGRESS OF MEDITATION

I would like to postulate three models in the progress of insight meditation, ie, the progress of penetration into the three universal characteristics. The first model is the model of the microscope. The progress of insight would be like a microscope that is consistently increasing its power of magnification. The more the magnification of the microscope increases, the more details can be seen into the nature of the matter on the slide. It is the same thing when you watch the nature of the three universal characteristics. As insight knowledge grows, reality becomes clearer and clearer. Of course, this does not happen all at once, it increases slowly. This model gives the idea that it does not come from thinking, but from pure, clear and concentrated awareness. There must be intention to see and to experience more deeply. If one is just contented to experience what there is, then one may not go further. One has to push on.

The second model is that of a growing tree, something conical in nature, like a cypress or a spruce. What happens is that this tree, when it grows, must first gain firm and strong roots. If the root system is not strong, then it cannot support the growth of a tall tree. The roots represent the entire good kamma and morality, etc. Once the tree grows, it does so according to certain levels. The first branches grow, then as it puts out branches at the next higher level, the lower level must expand, and the roots must expand further. When these two levels are more established, then a third level grows. When the third levels grows, the lower two levels must grow further. This means that a proper base

For those who are knowledgeable
This is a state making for joy—
Living the life of Dhamma
Under the noble ones perfected
in mind.

They clarify the true Dhamma,
Shining forth and illuminating it,
Those light-bringers, heroic sages,
Endowed with vision,
dispelling faults.

Having heard their teaching,
The wise with perfect
understanding
By direct knowing the end of birth
Come no more to renewal of
being.

ITIVUTTAKA 104

When you watch a certain new experience, you have to watch it longer and clearer before you can watch the deeper ones.

of the lower experiences must be developed further before the higher levels can grow. For example, your concentration must last longer and deeper, before you are able to watch more phenomena. Therefore, when you watch a certain new experience, you have to watch it longer and clearer before you can watch the deeper ones. For the third level to become stronger, the first and second level must become stronger too. You do not forget the lower levels. This means that there will be a constant repetition of the earlier experiences for some time, before a new experience comes. The lesson to be learned is that you must have patience.

The third model is the model of the elixir of immortality. Maybe you cannot find it in the west, but the Chinese usually make use of ginseng. The legend of ginseng is that when it becomes the elixir of immortality, the root will grow into the form of a human being. This becomes a sentient being and runs about. The idea is to catch it. When you catch it, it becomes a ginseng root again, and when you eat it, it becomes a cure-all. You put the root in water and you boil it to extract the essence from it. You must boil it slowly for a long time to extract the essence from it. Similarly, to get insight knowledges, you must start sitting on the boil, ie, start "boiling" yourself. You watch the pain, you watch the "rising" and "falling," the "sitting" and "touching," the thinking, the same things again and again. Slowly, understanding emerges and this brings detachment from all that arises and disappears.

A WORD ON NIBBANA

Finally, speaking more from theory, a word on nibbana. As one goes deeper and finds complete detachment from this mind and body, the mindfulness and insight become more mature. When all these supporting conditions and paramis (ten perfections) are ripe, then the mind will turn into the unconditioned state—supramundane . In other words, it will reach a state where it is cut away from all mind and body processes, and goes to a state where there is no change. We call this the absolute truth. However, there's a lot of hearsay about this and many misconceptions can arise. Sometimes it can be really bad. For example, there was one case where somebody went somewhere to meditate. She was at the top of a building and she looked out across a river. She could see that the sun was shining, the river was flowing, and the clouds were floating here and there. When she saw all these, she became so inspired that she thought she had become enlightened. She thought she really understood imper-manence and considered herself a stream-winner (*sotapanna*—first stage of sainthood). This is very strange, you know, because the nature of *nibbana* has nothing to do with what you see or hear, with any of the sense doors. If you had at least some theory, then you would know that such an experience could not be enlightenment. It may be a very inspirational experience, but it is still not the experience of the unconditioned.

Another person went to the extent that when he started seeing bubbles all over his body, sensations arising and disappearing all over his body, somebody helped him to come to the conclusion that he had become a non-returner (*anagami*–third stage of sainthood). It was not so much the extinction of defilements, but this experience of sensations all over the body arising and disappearing that brought him to this conclusion. Another yogi asked, "Is that so?", because she was not convinced, "I experience that all the time so I must also be *anagami*." The first one turned around and said, "In a way, you are!" This goes to show that when one clings on to an idea, one cannot let go of it. It is a form of wrong view.

Experiences can go on to very subtle stages. You can meditate very hard to the state where the mind becomes seemingly unconscious for a short while; and then you come out, you think it is sensational. Sometimes, you can go in for a long time; and when you come out, there is nothing there. One thinks that that must be *nibbana*. That is another pitfall. It can be asked, what is the difference between that and sleeping? Some people might say it is different, but in what way

A person companioned by craving
Wanders on the long journey
In this state of being or another
And cannot go beyond samsara.

Having understood the danger
thus,
That craving is the origin of
suffering,
A bhikkhu should wander mindfully,
Free from craving, without
grasping.

ITIVUTTAKA 105

is it different? These people can become very attached to their experience. However, remember that the experience of nibbana is not just getting a blank mind or going into the unconscious.

If you study the Abhidhamma, the process becomes clearer. After the path and fruition knowledge, which is the fourteenth and fifteenth insight knowledge, the mind goes into the sixteenth insight knowledge—the knowledge of retrospection. In the Abhidhamma, the retrospection knowledge, the consciousness is sense-sphere moral consciousness associated with knowledge. In other words, it is like the mind meditating and watching the "rising" and "falling" except at a deeper concentrated state, but it knows what is happening at that moment. In that state of mind, the object of the mind is nibbana. That means all the characteristics of the absolute truth become "shiningly" clear in that state of mind. You will experience the absolute truth while meditating and you know what it is. This is what the Abhidhamma analysis of thought processes and consciousness says. So, it is a very clear experience, a hundred percent certainty. One of my brother monks asked a senior meditation teacher in Burma about this and he said, "Oh! You cannot miss it. It is like lightning has struck you in the head!" So it cannot be a case of going blank then coming out. The important thing is that it is an experience of the supra-mundane—unconditioned state, and the person will be able to describe it in his own words. The most important test will be what happens after that, the degree of defilements that follow.

The important thing to bear in mind is that we just keep working. Suffering is in all of us and we have to get as much mindfulness as we can. Then if our kamma and time permit, one day we may reach that cherished goal. The scriptures and the teachers tell us that it is a possible thing. However, a lot of effort must be made.

ONE LAST WORD

However, as a last word I have a Zen koan for you in case you think you have gained enlightenment. Usually I give this Zen koan to people who imply that they are enlightened. I ask them, "Why is it that if a person is fully enlightened, then all the defilements can be completely uprooted and never arise again? Before enlightenment, your anger and craving arises again though for a time you may not have them. Why is it then, when a person becomes fully enlightened and experiences the supramundane, all of this never arises again? Why?" I ask but they just scratch their heads. The important thing is that the teacher is not there to confirm but to make sure that you keep practising until the day you die.

If by renouncing a lesser happiness
one may realize a greater
happiness,
let the wise man renounce the
lesser,
having regard for the greater.

DHAMMAPADA 290

Fettered by both these bonds—
The sensual bond and the bond of being—
Living beings continue in samsara,
Journeying on to birth and death.

Those who abandon sensual desires
But have not reached the taints' destruction,
Fettered by the bondage of being,
Are declared to be non-returners.

But those who have cut off doubts,
Destroyed conceit and renewal of being,
Who reach the taints' full destruction,
Though in the world, have gone beyond.

ITIVUTTAKA 96

Wilderness of the Mind

16

$\mathcal{S}$*uttas* are discourses given by the Buddha to various people from different backgrounds. They were initially passed down through oral tradition and later written down.

There are many of these Suttas. The one dealt with here comes from the Middle Length collection. It is the *Cetokhila Sutta*. "Ceto" or "ceta" or sometimes "citta" means "mind." "Khila" means callousity, hardness or rigidity. The hardness is just like when the ground is fertile but has a hard crust which is very hard and dry for a long time where nothing grows there. In common language, alternative words that describe such a nature would be "numb-skull," "thick-skinned" or "dense."

One translation of Cetokhila is "the wilderness of the mind," a rather poetic translation. But generally it means the mental callousity or hardness of the mind. It is reflected in stubborness, non-acceptance and so forth.

When the Buddha gave the Sutta, he was addressing monks in a place called Savathi. He clearly defines the reasons why a person does not really grow and progress in his meditation; and his advice.and reasoning here is very clear. The Buddha told the monks, "Bhikkhus, any monk who has not abandoned the five callousities," (here

Desiring future security from bondage
One should abandon sensual desire
However painful this may be.
Rightly conprehending with wisdom,
Possessing a mind that is well released,
One may reach freedom step by step.

One who is a master of knowledge,
Who has lived the holy life,
Is called one gone to the world's end,
One who has reached the further shore.

ITIVUTTAKA 109

translated as the five wildernesses in the heart), "and has not severed the five shackles of the heart will find it impossible to come to growth, increase, and fulfilment in the Dhamma and Vinaya."

The Dhamma is the teachings, the Vinaya is the discipline. What it really means is that to find success and fulfilment in the practice is to reach realisation, which is purification and sanctification to the highest level. If the five callousities and five shackles are not abandoned, increase in fulfilment will definitely not be possible.

THE FIVE CALLOUSITIES

The first four concerns sceptical doubt, and the fifth concerns anger.

The first wilderness of the heart, as it says in the Sutta, is when one is doubtful, uncertain, undecided, and unconfident about the Teacher. Thus the mind is not inclined to devotion, perseverance and striving.

The second wilderness of the heart is doubt concerning the Dhamma. The third is doubt concerning the Sangha. The fourth is doubt concerning the training.

So the first four of the callousities or the hardness of the mind comes from lack of confidence.

When sceptical doubt arises, there is no confidence and therefore no faith. With no faith there is no full effort and full striving. This is understandable. Because if you do not believe in what you are doing, you will not really do it wholeheartedly, and for one to progress far in this striving, one has to make a lot of effort.

Whether a person will progress or not at the beginning of his meditation practice depends on whether he or she makes an effort. When people ask me, "Reverend, why don't I progress?" I ask, "How long do you meditate? How often do you meditate?" The usual reply is, "Uh... one hour a week."

"How long does it take to boil a kettle of water?" I ask. The reply, "Twenty minutes." "How long does it take for the boiled water to cool down?" I ask. "In a day," came the reply. "How many hours have your defilements been arising and how long do you think it would take to pare them down?"

This is just a simile. Those who understand will know that you have to make a lot of effort before you see a little bit of progress. If you see a little bit of progress every day you should be happy. Let us look into the factors one by one.

1 Doubt, uncertainty and lack of confidence in the Teacher

Here the Teacher refers to the Buddha—the Sammasambuddha—Gautama Buddha, the one who has attained supreme enlightenment under the Bodhi tree in Buddhagaya. Naturally, you would wonder how you know that He has attained supreme enlightenment? How can you have confidence in the Buddha? We do not know even if He is really the Buddha. Even during the Buddha's time, people who actually knew Him personally, still had no confidence in Him until He had preached and they had listened and gained realisation. Then their confidence grew and became strong. Take for example, His first five disciples or the five ascetics.

When He became a Buddha, He went to the Deer Park to teach them. At first they were reluctant to acknowledge Him as a Teacher because they believed He had abandoned the austerities and resorted to indulgences. So they had no confidence in Him. They said, "If you cannot withstand this human austerity and suffering, how can you attain the superhuman state?" So they did not believe him. Of course, as the story goes, He managed to convince them. And when they listened to Him—they attained enlightenment—they had complete confidence in Him.

So even people of such calibre who have personally met with the Buddha and heard from him found it not easy to be convinced. This is because it is not really easy to understand, fathom or have an idea of the nature of the Buddha's mind. The Buddha's mind is very different. It is wisdom. But we can have an idea or a glimpse of it if we have clear and mindful awareness, and if we study the Dhamma.

Controlled while walking,
Controlled while standing,
Controlled while sitting,
Controlled while reclining,
Controlled in bending and
Stretching his limbs—

Above, across, and below,
As far as the world extends,
A bhikkhu observes how things
    occur,
The arising and passing of the
    aggregates.

Living thus ardently,
Of calm and quiet conduct,
Ever mindful, he trains in the
    course
Of calm tranquillity of mind.
Such a bhikkhu is said to be
One who is ever resolute.

ITIVUTTAKA 111

2 Doubt concerning the Dhamma or the Teaching

Confidence or faith in the Dhamma, His Teachings, is most important. The Teachings here refers more to the theoretical part, the scriptural knowledge obtained by listening. The Teachings in terms of practice is referred to in the fourth statement on practice or training.

The Dhamma is not something we can easily understand because it is something very deep. To really have confidence we have to really make an in-depth study of the Dhamma and put it into

practice. When we find that it really works and really gives beneficial results then the confidence will grow. On a more general and superficial level, confidence means confidence in what is good and pure and the faith that there is a path that leads to that. If we have learnt the Dhamma and read about it, we will find that it is in accord with such a path. It is necessary to have that initial confidence and faith to spur us to practice. Then we will grow.

The Dhamma is not something we can easily understand because it is something very deep.

3 Doubt concerning the Sangha

The Sangha refers to the community; more specifically it refers to the Ariya Sangha, which is the community of noble ones. They are those who have practised the teachings of the Buddha and have attained the stages of enlightenment and realisation. Only when they have attained those stages are they able to lead others satisfactorily and confidently along the way. Then again, we will not really know who is enlightened. So this is a dilemma.

But we can to a certain extent or degree, judge from the behaviour, the way the person speaks and his teachings, whether that person is learned in the Dhamma or not. A more general understanding of confidence in the Sangha is that you have the confidence that people can be enlightened, that they can achieve the state of the unconditioned, the everlasting happiness. You too can achieve and reach that state through the practice. Have this initial confidence, practise and get the results, and it will grow.

4 Doubt with the practice itself

If you have not done the practice but only think about it, there will of course be an endless number of questions. A lot of these teachings and experiences described come about only when you undertake the practice. Only when you have experimented, tried it out, and through the guidance of the teacher gained experience and progress, will you gain confidence in the practice and training.

All these activities lead up to the Teachings itself. First you must have confidence in yourself. You must have confidence in what is good and true. You must be able to look up to the Teachings and try the practice long enough to get the results. Once the results come in, sceptical doubt will all be put aside, and you can go whole-heartedly into the striving.

This sceptical doubt is really a stumbling block in countries which are not culturally and historically Buddhist. In Buddhist countries the devotion may be "blind," but if the method is correct and is accepted with a pure heart, the practice will give practitioners the concentration and understanding that follows. But as I have said, it can be dangerous if you end up with the wrong teacher. Then you can get stuck for a long time.

You are not asked to have complete confidence in the Buddha, Dhamma, Sangha, and the Training. It is not expected that you should believe or swallow everything connected to them. But rather, you are advised to carefully accept things. Carefully, try things out. If one has a clear and open mind, and if one really has the heart to progress and to improve oneself spiritually without any preconceptions and without any prejudices, then it cannot be possible that when one really tries out the real Dhamma, one does not see the results.

We have to take into account individual temperaments. Some people are more inclined to the Dhamma, while others are more inclined to other faiths.

*Heedfulness is the path to the
    Deathless.
Heedlessness is the path to death.
The heedful die not.
The heedless are as if dead
    already.*

DHAMMAPADA 21

But the important point is this—that one must have enough confidence and faith to put in the effort to get some results. With time more results come in and only then when you see yourself really striving and putting all your heart and soul into the practice will the real results come. Why? Because number one, when you put in more effort, it also means you put in more time. Naturally with longer time, the results will come.

5 Anger

It is like when a bhikkhu is angry and displeased with his fellow companions in the holy life. He is resentful and callous towards them and thus his mind is not inclined to others.

In the first four callousities where the mind is like a hard rock that cannot absorb, there is not enough faith and too much scepticism. Whatever comes into the mind is questioned, "Is that really so? Is there such a thing as Nibbana? Why must I watch the pain for so long?" and so on. The instruction does not sink in because he does not want to accept it.

The fifth callousity has nothing to do with the fact that the person has no faith in the Dhamma. But rather, when anger is present, the mind cannot calm down. When his fellow companions in the holy life, his fellow strivers, or yogis try to give advice to the angry one, he cannot accept it.

Anger is of course, also very much connected with pride. Firstly, when one has a lot of anger, there is no acceptance of any advice or help. Secondly, anger itself creates a lot of unwholesome kamma that can block one's practice. For example, anger usually leads to a lot of physical ailments like stress, pain and tension.

One special consequence to note is when a person has anger towards his fellow yogis. If the fellow yogi is a very sincere and a diligent striver, the evil in a person's mind towards such a striver would create things that block him, especially if the yogi is an enlightened individual. According to the Commentaries, the path is in danger, it is blocked. And only when one removes the grudge and asks for forgiveness, will the path be cleared. This is an important point to bear in mind.

When the mind has a lot of anger, it creates a lot of repulsion. There are a lot of bad effects due to his kamma and the mind cannot accept advice in the Dhamma. Finally the mind cannot calm down. So he becomes a very difficult yogi—a very difficult person to handle.

THE FIVE SHACKLES

Even after we have enough confidence and faith, acceptance of the teachings and no anger, there are another five things that prevent progress. These are the five shackles of the heart. The five shackles can be described as like a clenched fist that holds the heart which cannot be free. You do not have confidence, you say "yes" this is good, but you cannot move. You are tied down. You are chained.

1 Sensual pleasures

When a person is very attached to sensual pleasures, it is difficult to progress in the practice because you keep going back to the sensual pleasures or bodily comforts.

I remember the first time I went to Mahasi centre, I noticed many bedbugs. Everybody was catching bedbugs. During meditation, the body felt itchy because of bug bites. So instead of meditating, people concentrated on catching bedbugs.

If you are not careful, you could start to feel that you are missing out on your sensual pleasures. The most obvious being food. The food provided in "small" meditation centres is not very good. It may even be terrible. So if you are not used to it, you will start thinking of all your good food back home. Westerners miss their food. They miss their cheese, ice cream, cakes, and all the milk products. It was Christmas at the Mahasi centre one day. The Westerners missed Christmas and decided to have a Christmas party in Mahasi centre. They chipped in their money and bought a lot of ice cream and had

Just as one upon the summit of a mountain beholds the groundings, even so when the wise man casts away heedlessness by heedfulness and ascends the high tower of wisdom, this sorrowless sage beholds the sorrowing and foolish multitude.

DHAMMAPADA 28

a party. The next day, the meditation teacher called them up and gave them a good scolding. Why? Because they should be meditating—sitting, walking, sitting, walking, noting "rising" and "falling"—instead of which they were having a party.

Sensual pleasure prevents you from meditating. Even if you are able to push and pull yourself into a meditation centre and watch "rising" and "falling," "sitting" and "touching," or whatever object you are watching, you will find that in most cases, the main hindrance is sensual pleasure.

Of the five hindrances—sensual pleasure, ill-will, sloth and torpor, restlessness and worries, sceptical doubt—sloth and torpor dominates the first few days of your meditation and then it clears, followed by restlessness.

When a person is really detached from the senses and is not worried about what he had seen, smelt, tasted, touched or heard and provided there is some mindfulness, the mind will be able to concentrate.

If the thought is a strong one, it is rooted either in anger or sensual pleasures. Not many people have very strong anger, at least not the practitioners I know of in Malaysia. Their main hindrance is usually sensual pleasures. In the morning, they think of food, they miss their hot coffee. They get bored and think of their video shows at home—all the odds and ends of things. Then the mind gets bored and they want to go into more interesting stories or things to do. All these come under sensual pleasures.

When a person is really detached from the senses and is not worried about what he had seen, smelt, tasted, touched or heard and provided there is some mindfulness, the mind will be able to concentrate.

Think about this. Why do you think so much during a retreat? What do you think about? Very often it is because you are bored. The mind does not like to be bored. It likes interesting things and so it wanders into stories and creates things. All these activities are usually centred on sensual pleasures. That is why if you prepare yourself and do a certain type of preliminary meditation to calm down the mind, then you would not think so much.

2 Attachment to the body

Firstly, when a person is attached to the body, he cannot go beyond it. Secondly, he will not be able to stand much pain. Many a time you will find that we are unable to see through pain because of the attachment to the body.

Take for example, a pain sensation in the leg. Very often when the pain becomes stronger and stronger, the person gives up noting the pain. It is not because the pain is very painful but because he is attached to the leg. Or he thinks that the leg is his and if he sits longer, something will go wrong with his leg and he will never be able to walk again. This fear or concern is rooted in the attachment to the body. If it is somebody else's leg and you just watch the pain, do you think you will be affected? At the very least you would not be so concerned.

There was a time when I was meditating, there were a lot of mosquitoes. When a mosquito bites you, a lot of ideas go on in your head. You start thinking about the itch. It is only a little itch. But when you have a lot of attachment to the body, the itch seems to be very strong. Then you start thinking that perhaps the mosquito has malaria. Or perhaps the mosquito has dengue or perhaps it is better I chase away the mosquito, then maybe I can concentrate better. A lot of attachment comes and you cannot meditate anymore. But after a while you decide that because the itch is there you seem not able to concentrate. Instead of noting, "itchy, itchy, itchy," you may try noting, "hand, hand, hand" or "leg, leg, leg" or "nose, nose, nose."

By noting itchiness, the tendency will lean towards detachment. In that way, you look at your hand or leg very impersonally. Then you feel as though your hand or leg is just outside you. When you look at that, the itch is on the hand and it does not disturb you. It can itch all it likes, but it does not matter because the hand is not yours. But the very moment you think and get attached to the hand, you cannot meditate properly. You cannot watch the hand properly. Then you should think "What's so big about the itch anyway?" You will not die because of the itch. It is like a tickle, like somebody taking a feather and tickling you." It is just a feeling.

Wonderful, indeed,
it is to subdue the mind,
so difficult to subdue, ever swift,
and seizing whatever it desires.
A tamed mind brings happiness.

DHAMMAPADA 35

The thing about attachment to the body is that one cannot go beyond the body. That means one is chained to the concept of the body. In deeper forms of meditation one has to forget everything about the body, the hands and legs and so forth. If one can forget that, then one can go directly into the mind-door and it is only at the mind-door, that the concentration be very deep.

For example, when you watch "rising" and "falling," "sitting" and "touching," and so forth, you finally experience the wind element, the characteristic of motion. Only when you can concentrate on the characteristic of motion, can you then experience the three universal characteristics and develop insight. But as long as you still hold on to the concept of body, the hands, legs and so forth, you cannot experience the three universal characteristics and develop insight because reality cannot co-exist with these conceptual objects. Therefore if a person is very attached to the body, if he is not willing to forego the body, then the moment he finds he is losing shape of the body—sense of the body—he gets frightened and he cannot go beyond.

Attachment to the body occurs more frequently when people look upon the physical body as a reality and take the physical body as themselves.

3 Attachment to external things

The Commentary defines it as attachment to outer things like property and people. When you are attached to outer things like property and people, the attachment is in the mind. Firstly, you cannot let go of them and really meditate.

Secondly, the attachment prevents you from wholeheartedly putting aside all conditioned things so that the mind can be free to experience the unconditioned. When we say, for example, that at present we do not have any anger (or attachment) against anybody, that may be true. But it is there, deep-seated in our hearts and minds. If it is especially strong, whenever we want to go into deeper concentration and understanding, this attachment will stand in the way.

This explains why sometimes when people meditate, a lot of deep-seated neuroses may surface. Normally they do not encounter these but during meditation, the neuroses may surface, disturb and create a mess of things.

That is why in order to strive for progress in the Dhamma and Vinaya, it is better to be a monk. Monks do not have anything, they do not have to worry about anything, they just meditate and live day to day. Becoming a monk actually means you are prepared to meditate to death. You do not care about your past or your future. You just keep noting and noting, moment-to-moment. That is what being a monk is actually about. You do not have to worry about property or other people, only about practising detachment. So there is nothing to tie your heart down.

4 Attachment to inactivity

With reference to the Cetokhila Sutta in Majjhima Nikaya, it is like a man who eats as much as he likes until his belly is full and he indulges in the pleasures of sleeping, lolling and dozing, so that his mind would not be inclined to effort. He eats too much, then lies down to rest and sleep. There is no energy.

Of course, it does not mean we should not take a rest. We can. But rest, as prescribed in the suttas, means four hours at night. Other than that period of rest, we should strive every hour of the day. Of course you would take time off for a wash — you have to take a wash before reporting. There is time for eating when you have got to eat. But in the midst of all these activities, you have to practise mindfulness, keeping up with your meditation object.

The effort or energy needed to pull the mind up high is very great. In the meditation centres in the East, you can see how people really strive. Even then, it happens only in prestigious centres and under certain experienced masters. There, people are really serious. They go all out. In these places, people do not loll and rest after eating. They do not at the slightest excuse go in and rest.

In these places, they are reluctant to sleep. They are eager to get up. They find sleeping is a waste of time. Time is so precious, time is so wonderful, it must be made full use of. That should be the way.

Let the discerning man
guard the mind,
so difficult to detect and
*   extremely subtle,*
seizing whatever it desires.
A guarded mind brings happiness.

DHAMMAPADA 36

In earlier times many people put in more energy than concentration. Ananda, for example, was striving very hard throughout the night until he had to lie down for a rest, but not to sleep—and he got enlightened.

And Sona was compelled to walk. He did walking meditation until his feet became very tender. Yet he walked until the whole walkway was spattered with his blood, as if somebody had killed a cow there. That was the extent of energy expended by people during the Buddha's time.

In another story, there was a monk who was doing walking meditation during the night until he could not walk anymore. So he crawled—crawling meditation. And while he did crawling meditation during the night, a hunter who thought he was a deer shot the monk. When the monk was shot, he noted "pain, pain, pain." These stories serve as an inspiration to us to be more diligent.

So the mind is very good at getting attached to things.

5   Attachment to "glory"

This is like when a person lives the holy life aspiring to some order of gods. By his virtue, by observance of asceticism and by leading a holy life he strives to become a great god or deity or some lesser deity. Thus his mind does not incline to the highest, ie, enlightenment. In this fifth shackle, the mind really aspires to something less and gets a result short of Nibbana, the path and fruition, the actual enlightened consciousness or the one with Nibbana. It means that one gets attached to everything else, the body, feelings, morality, concentration, insight knowledge, but not the highest goal, enlightenment.

So the mind is very good at getting attached to things. When it gets attached to something lower than the highest goal—the actual nibbana experience—then one does not progress. One stops there. Instead of freeing oneself, one gets attached. In other words, any attachment chains the mind down and gets it shackled.

NEXT STEPS TO PROGRESS IN THE DHAMMA AND VINAYA

To make progress in the Dhamma, you must first be able to free your mind completely of all attachments in your striving. There is a return to the real state of things when one strives. After returning to the real state of things, all clinging must be put aside at least for the moment of time. You do not think of time at all. That's why a retreat helps. It provides a conducive condition for practice.

The Cetokhila Sutta says that when the five callousities are abandoned and the five shackles severed, it is possible for one to reach fulfilment. In the Dhamma Vinaya, "it is possible" does not mean "it will." Just that the things that prevent fulfilment are not there.

FOUR BASES OF SUCCESS FOR SPIRITUAL ACCOMPLISHMENT

The next thing the striver must do is to develop the *iddhi-pada*, the basis of success for spiritual power or accomplishment. There are four bases.

1 Concentration due to zeal and determined striving

Let us look into the first basis, which is accomplishment of zeal or wish to do. This is more like faith. It is like a push or intention—*chanda-samadhi*. This wish-to-do, to desire accomplishment of spiritual attainment is very concentrated. This faith and motivation brings about vipassana concentration or concentrated awareness of things as they really are.

2 Concentration due to energy and determined striving

The second basis for success is *padhana-sankhara*, where there are a lot of mental forces and a lot of energy and striving towards the goal. "*Sankhara*" are all mental formations, all mental activities or mental factors. "*Padhana*" is striving accompanied by all mental strivings, formations, forces that are involved with striving. This is how we build up mindfulness, make it continuous, build up a strong current of mindful noting moment-to-moment into our mind-body processes, and into the realities and three universal characteristics. This form of mental noting is very powerful and one-pointed and leads into the direction of realisation.

Better it is to live one day seeing the Supreme Truth than to live a hundred years without ever seeing the Supreme Truth.

DHAMMAPADA 115

Strong concentration arises because we have the faith, wish, and intention to push, and develop in that direction. Without this intention, which is not a craving but a wish, the mind may stop at some other point or at a level lower than or inferior to it.

Sometimes the development of forces to its point of accomplishment can be brought forward by energy. Of course you must have the faith and the understanding. But the predominant force that brings you to accomplishment is that you are very energetic. The main thing is that you strive and strive and strive.

3 Concentration due to purity of mind and determined striving

The third basis for developing spiritual power to accomplishment is mind. It covers the whole mental involvement. But it has got to do more with what we call strong will-power or volition.

4 Concentration due to investigation and determined striving, or enthusiasm

The fourth is insight. Accomplishment can come to people with strong good understanding and maturity of the mind. He is one who knows and is able to see into things.

To reach the goal, you must get rid of the shackles and callousities. Build up the four bases for success. Through the force of practice, bring up all those mental powers. Push your one-pointedness on and on, day after day unrelentingly.

To give you an understanding of how a person really strives to gain that realisation, the sutta gives the simile of a mother hen hatching her eggs, brooding on them. When the mother hen sits on the eggs, turning them over and over for a long enough time, only then can the chickens come out of the eggs. When a hen carefully covers, incubates and nurtures her eight or twelve eggs properly, only then are the chicks capable of piecing their shells with the point of their claws and beak and hatch out safely without her worrying about them. So too, a bhikkhu who possesses the factors including enthusiasm and strong energy will be capable of breaking out, capable of enlightenment, capable of attaining supreme security from bondage.

Those who enjoy what exists,
Those devas exercising control,
Those who delight in creating,
And others who enjoy sense-objects—
Being in this state or another
They cannot pass beyond samsara.

Understanding this danger
In objects of sensual enjoyment,
Let the wise person abandon all sense pleasures,
Those both heavenly and human.

By severing the flow of craving,
The flow so difficult to overcome
Of greed for pleasing, enticing forms,
They attain to final Nibbana
And overcome all suffering.

The noble seers, masters of knowledge,
Wise ones with perfect understanding,
By directly knowing the end of birth
Come no more to renewal of being.

ITIVUTTAKA 95

Important Points to
Vipassana Progress

H ere are some important points or factors to help bring the meditation practice to a higher level.

MORALITY

One of the first important points for my progress was morality. Not that I was immoral before. I took up the robes, not so much out of faith but more out of curiosity. However, when I did take up the robes, many things happened. Somehow, the mind in that sort of environment brought about changes. Morality for a monk is not just a matter of following the rules. It is obvious that when we follow the moral rules we abstain from many unwholesome deeds. But beyond that, morality for a monk means his whole lifestyle and whole outlook is changed. For example, before I became a monk, I was studying and was very goal-oriented. There were exams after exams and results after results. Then, once you get out of the rat race and you live a life that is spiritual, the goal is more of a spiritual realisation rather than material benefits. The way of life, as implied by the rules themselves, throws away all other things and the mind has only the thought of purification and realisation of seeking absolute peace.

For there is suffering, but none who suffers;
Doing exists although there is no doer;
Extinction is but no extinguished person;
Although there is a path, there is no goer.

VISUDDHIMAGGA 89

Things that were in the mind began to be phased out and I would get many experiences which I later discovered to be vipassana experiences. Before that I was more into Zen practice, not the Japanese Zen but the Chinese Ch'an. So if you look at morality from the monks' point of view, we do not think of it as simply following the rules. Rather it is a lifestyle, meeting the aims and objectives implied by the rules and the conditions that are given to us. A more ordinary example would be: if a person comes to a meditation centre or a temple, stays there for a while, does whatever meditation he or she can and lives a more spiritual life, then the mind will calm down and turn to its spiritual goals. On the other hand, if his or her morality begins to become decadent, there will be less restraint and everything begins to go down the drain. A good criterion is to look for morality itself in the practice.

BUDDHIST METAPHYSICS

A second important point that I found very helpful was when I began to study the *Abhidhamma*. The *Abhidhamma* is Buddhist metaphysics. It involves the study of *Paramattha Dhamma*, of the ultimate realities, different mind and body processes and characteristics, different consciousness and different mental states.

When I first went to Penang, I was very interested in *Abhidhamma* teaching, as I had not heard of it before. Although I had come across such books they were very technical, containing bombastic words which did not make too much sense to me, especially as my English was not too good. For example, *Cetasika* was translated as mental concomitant—"What is mental concomitant?" They used the word "perception" and I wondered what they meant by perception. The dictionary says "to perceive" is perception. What then is to perceive? Perceive is to know but then what is the difference between consciousness and knowing? It is not very precise. However, when you have grasped the knack of studying, you realise it is not just a matter of memory but rather the study has to be related to one's experiences, one's practice and so forth. Fortunately at the time, there was a teacher who taught *Abhidhamma* and he related it to daily life. When one is practising, it is helpful to relate it to the practice. When I had a number of questions and I was not in intensive meditation, I would analyse them and read whatever I could and then I would ask him the questions. This helped me to be very aware of the different states and conditions of mind. It also helped to define more clearly the meditation object.

For example, when one talks about greed and craving and one looks at the *Abhidhamma*, it gives clearer definitions with which one can relate to the different consciousness that operate. Then when I went out and looked at other monks I thought, well, there is greed, this one is having greed, look at him eating that way, he is having greed. Then I began to appreciate the *Abhidhamma*. Not many monks study the *Abhidhamma* so I was fortunate in being able to detect these things that happen in the mind and the body. That helps a lot in the practice, it cuts out many defilements, it increases the mindfulness and so forth. Of course, within the teaching itself, many things are said concerning the practice.

WAYS TO IMPROVE OUR PRACTICE

The third important point that is very helpful is what we call common sense and the intention to understand one's practice, to look for more ways wherein we can improve our practice. When I was studying *Abhidhamma* I would think, in what way will this chapter help me in my practice? I would look here and there and then I would devise ways and means to use it. Actually if you look at the Dhamma itself, the *Tipitaka*, the suttas, not just the *Abhidhamma*, you will find a wealth of knowledge and wisdom. I am often amazed that even though I have gone through a certain discourse and sutta, many times I would overlook its specific point.

The Great Sage did thus proclaim
This Insight stilled and purified,
That to emergence leads beside,
With many a neatly chosen name.
The round of rebirth's slough of
*   pain*
Is vast and terrible; a man
Wisely should strive as best he can,
If he would this Emergence gain.

VISUDDHIMAGGA 136

Then one day, on looking at it again, I found a revelation. I had not understood it before but going through it a second time, I could see so much relevance to the practice. I used to think it was a repetition of what had been said in other suttas but somehow suddenly, there is something new. Therefore, if you really research and think about many of the suttas, you find there is a wealth of knowledge and wisdom concerning the practice.

Sometimes, as monks, we do recitations and we would come across a certain recitation that was very agreeable to us so we would memorise it. Traditionally, the first step of study was memory. As you commit to memory it goes into recitation, then recitation and memory come in, and over a period, the mind becomes concentrated. When the mind is concentrated, the recitation goes into the mind and turns there. When it turns in the mind over a period, it deepens and we come to realise that there are so many things within the sutta that can be applied to the practice. Therefore, I found that the suttas were externally superficial but by going deeper into them, a whole wealth of knowledge that is useful to us emerges.

In the first few years, I was going repeatedly into the *Tipitaka*. Even now, I am discovering more points on the practice from the text. Therefore, the practice is like research. After you have covered the preliminary areas, you go into deeper aspects. With any sutta, there is a practical aspect at a deeper level.

CONCENTRATION

The fourth important factor involved in progress is concentration. Only with a certain level of concentration will deeper insight knowledge arise. Only then will the mind be powerful enough to do the work of penetration.

My first meditation retreat was a three months' retreat at the Penang Meditation Centre. I had not done a meditation or any vipassana retreat before. I just went in and did a three months' retreat. I found in that retreat that once the mind has reached a certain level of concentration, all kinds of things can happen. In the first month or so, although there was concentration, the experiences were not very clear. After the first month, all the thinking and the restlessness were gone and the experiences became very sharp. I noticed that I did an incredible amount of thinking. There was so much thinking. I did not know I could think so much! When you start to meditate and you have to really control the restlessness totally, you can see that the mind easily runs away.

At that retreat I came to the point where I was very determined to find out why the thinking came about. I noticed in walking meditation, for example, in between the moment of starting to step and the foot going to the ground, the mind slipped away. Because there was a certain degree of mindfulness to try to trace back what had happened, I found that at the moment it slipped away I could trace the process of the thoughts. Within that one or two seconds there were at least twenty or thirty thoughts, so many but because of the mindfulness I knew what the thoughts were, or at least a lot of them, one coming after another. "This is fantastic!" I said, "No wonder the mind does not go into deeper concentration!" When finally the thoughts stopped for an extended period, all the clear experiences arose one after another. The lesson here is that one should have a very strong determination to really note continuously and if the mind wanders, note clearly, where it has wandered. Bring the mind to a deeper level of concentration.

In this sense, later, in trying to make more progress I went into *samatha* (tranquillity) meditation. This happened when I went back to Burma for the second time. I found it very useful but the emphasis is not *samatha* meditation. When I went to Burma the first time, I wanted to do *samatha* as well as vipassana. I wanted to learn as much as I could. However, they were not willing to teach me. They said, "now vipassana is important and it is the priority." Therefore, I had to practise vipassana until they were satisfied. I can understand this because people have very little time. Even if you renounce the world and become a monk, you really do not know how long you will remain a monk. So given the uncertain nature of the world and its

The bhikkhu in whom there are no latent tendencies, in whom evil roots are destroyed, leaves this shore and the far shore as a snake leaves its old worn-out skin.

SUTTA NIPATA 1.1.14

conditions you have to choose and I chose to carry on with vipassana, insight meditation. Although some people say you need *samatha* (tranquillity) meditation, *jhanas* and so forth, before you can make good progress in vipassana insight, from personal experience I find that it is not necessary for initial levels of insight. It is sufficient just to do vipassana and go through the insight knowledges.

If one has *samatha*, that is of course, an advantage. The problem is the limitation of time. To reach the basic and necessary levels of concentration as a strong basis for vipassana may take a long time and there is not much time. In addition, when you go from *samatha* to vipassana, it does not mean that you will be able to shift objects easily. You will only have the advantage of a calmer mind.

I do agree that there are certain people who really need this tranquillity meditation before they do vipassana. This is so for people with very strong defilements and really need to control them. However, for most people I think it is not an absolute necessity. Nevertheless, as one goes higher in practice it becomes very helpful. For example, if one is able to watch the "rising" and "falling" break-up and if the break up goes into very fine particles with each fine particle arising and disappearing rapidly moment-to-moment, then if one gets into deep *samatha*, the small particle can be expanded into a big balloon and each big balloon will be as if within it there are even much finer particles. The speed of change seems to become very much magnified. It is known in the suttas for example, that people can practice on the insight vehicle to arahantship, the highest state.

It is known in the suttas that people can practice on the insight vehicle to arahantship, the highest state.

OTHER IMPORTANT FACTORS

There are other important factors for having the presence of a teacher. One factor is the question of faith and confidence. For the initial yogi the confidence is variable and erratic, it comes and goes. When things are going well, faith is high but when pains and problems starts then the confidence lessens. When things go well again, faith increases but when problems arise again faith lessens. With a teacher present somehow the confidence stays and you carry on.

Another important factor is that many things come in the oral tradition of these teachings. Much has been written but many teachers do not write their knowledge down. They do not have time to write down all they know. Those who do may have done it in Burmese, so you cannot read it. In addition, many things cannot be described. Monks in robes cannot imply they have reached a state of sanctification and so there are many sensitive issues that do not permit writing about. It is for the protection of the practitioners and the teachers themselves. Therefore, to some extent a lot of these experiences and techniques remain in the oral tradition. In this case, you need to learn from a teacher. Often we do learn from more than one teacher, each helping to hone your technique.

Other than that, the most important point is the practice itself. Usually the practice needs to be spread over a period of years, and intensive meditation is a must if you intend to reach the highest stages such as realisation and enlightenment. As such, the retreats should not be too far apart, and in between the retreats, you must be careful for that is a time when you can accumulate defilements, especially when the stress builds up.

Before a person goes to retreat, I would recommend that the person does regular daily meditation for at least one week otherwise when the person comes; the person has to start picking up the pieces. A person who has done regular daily meditation may take two to three days to get to where the person has left off at the previous retreat. For one who has done nothing, it may take four to five days and if just prior to that the person has been very busy and had a very stressful time then it may take even longer. However, if in between the retreats you had traumas and very bad experiences, then you may have to spend the whole retreat trying to clear it up before you can return to where you left off. Still, that is better than

*Just as a firm post sunk
in the earth
Cannot be shaken by the
four winds;
I say that a virtuous person who
Thoroughly perceives the
Noble Truths
Is similar to that.*

RATANA SUTTA V.8

rotting inside. When you start rotting inside it starts to stink and your mind becomes ruined.

Rest assured, it is evident from the many yogis whom I have seen that if you are persistent, go for regular retreats and meditate fairly regularly at home, over a period of time you will get somewhere, even if it is not *magga phala* enlightenment or the realisation of nibbana. At least you will get somewhere near it. That itself is very good. The actual factors that bring about the crossing over are rarely spoken of so there hangs a very big question mark regarding those factors. Personally, I think it has a lot to do with past perfections and past karmic accumulations. If you are patient, then over a period, progress will come and you will definitely get somewhere and you will definitely be much happier. In fact, you will be among the happiest people in the world.

A conscientious bhikkhu
Who never does wrong in any way,
Neither by body, speech, or mind,
Is called "one of lovely behaviour."

An unassuming bhikkhu
Who has cultivated well the states
That lead to enlightenment
Is called "one of lovely nature."

A taintless bhikkhu
Who understands for himself
The end of suffering here
Is called "one of lovely wisdom."

He who excels in these three things,
Untroubled, with doubt destroyed,
Unattached in all the world.
Is called "one who has abandoned all."

ITIVUTTAKA 79

Leaving on the Edge: Mindfulness in Daily Life

READJUSTMENT

After going back to daily life, there will be a period when the mind has to readjust to function in a more worldly situation. Some may become quite wild or irritable instead. These are more of the release of desires and tendencies suppressed during the retreat. It should not be a cause to worry us as they will subside soon enough.

A number will try hard to continue what they have been doing during the retreat. Here, some complications may arise. They will seem to be weird, removed or proud, by their associates. They do not talk or joke as they used to. They even move so slowly!

It is obvious that it is not practical to move so slowly while trying to be mindful in the fast-moving world outside. It, however, does not mean we have to engage in nonsensical conversations if we do not want to. If it is going to affect your job efficiency, studies or family life, then you will have to forego the practice to some extent. Let us face it, you are not a monk or nun yet. You can still practise mindfulness and it will have to be in a less intensive manner. This is not a matter of choice but the situation is such that you have to.

From craving springs grief,
From craving springs fear.
For him who is wholly free from
*   craving*
There is no grief;
Whence then fear?

DHAMMAPADA 216

FLOODS OF DEFILEMENTS

How then does one carry on the practice when one returns to the world outside? Practice outside could be looked at on two levels. The first level is, keeping afloat. The second level is living on the edge. Keeping yourself afloat means preventing yourself from getting drowned.

In dhamma we talk about floods, different types of floods. These are the floods of defilements. The world outside is flooded with defilements. In Pali, flood is "*ogha*" sounds almost like "ogre." There are *kama ogha*, *bhava ogha*, *ditthi ogha*, and *avijja ogha*.

Kama ogha is the flood of sensual pleasures. They come one after another and you get completely drowned in them. So you have to keep afloat. *Bhava ogha* is the flood of becoming—you wanting to be something, to exist. You want to be a lot of different people, you want to be a hero of all sorts, you want to be everything. *Ditthi ogha* are all those opinions and ideas that are wrong. In *avijja ogha*, the flood of ignorance or delusions, you drown in delusions. In other words, when you are not mindful and all the defilements are strong, you will get caught up in them and you drown in them. They drag you down. You cannot move. There is no freedom.

When you are not mindful and all the defilements are strong, you will get caught up in them and you drown in them.

KEEPING AFLOAT

So the first part is keeping afloat—keeping alive—is to be mindful. If you can just be mindful, that is already very good. It is not easy to maintain mindfulness all the time. Often, it is the nature of human beings that it is difficult to be mindful. For example, if you are very sick, with a lot of pain day in and day out, how mindful can you be? To help us be mindful, we have to set up basic supportive conditions. First is the physical environment. The quieter it is, the more conducive it is to be mindful. Other things like temples and images also help. You can slowly develop through these bit by bit.

The choice of livelihood, what we call Right Livelihood, is also important. If a person is involved in a wrong livelihood, where the morality is questionable, it will be more difficult to keep a pure mind or clear conscience. So something has to be done. Either change your profession or do something about it. Refuse to do unwholesome deeds. Another aspect you should consider about the job is the time factor. Does the nature of your job allow you time to practise? Some jobs may be considered right livelihood and does not involve killing, stealing, telling lies, sexual misconduct or intoxicants, but it takes up a lot of your time. You work from morning till night and you get only two weeks off a year. In such a case, you will not have time to practise, to come for intensive meditation like attending a retreat. You may consciously set aside time to practise every day, but at the end of your work day, when you return home, you are so tired you can not practise well. Such a job is considered not suitable because it is not sympathetic or conducive towards the practice.

Lay people have to earn a livelihood as well as try to get time to practise. It may be more difficult in the west where retreats are often very expensive to attend. You have to pay towards the rent of a place and you have to pay for the teacher's honorarium, his fare, board and lodging. It is easier in Asia where retreats are sponsored. The cost to attend one or two long retreats in Australia is enough to pay for a ticket to Asia and a stay of a few months. Sometimes yogis prefer that. They can get to a new environment and after their practice, they can go sightseeing.

Relationship

The third factor is relationships. When young people ask me about relationships, I advise them not to get married. Marriage invariably leads to trouble. There is an old Thai saying, "If you give your heart to a girl, you cannot be a monk. If you give your heart to a boy, you are sure to cry." But if you really can't help it and fate has a strong hand, then you have to choose carefully. At the very least, choose a partner who is sympathetic to the practice. You may decide not to have children

Let a man guard himself against irritability in thought; Let him be controlled in mind. Abandoning mental misconduct, Let him practise good conduct in thought.

DHAMMAPADA 233

when you marry. But when the children come, you can not leave them alone, throw them out. Even if they are not problematic children, you have years of responsibility to bring them up properly. If the partner turns out to be not compatible, there is the problem of separation or divorce.

It is best to surround yourself with people who are sympathetic to meditation, not necessarily just husband or wife. This may be a bit difficult because not many people meditate, so you have to influence them. Show a good example, show that you have improved as a better person through your meditation, and it will have some effect eventually.

Of course, it is better to build up a core group. People who have meditated before should make an effort to get together, to meet, discuss or practise together once a week. In the case where you find that people are very unsympathetic, you have to practise equanimity and solitude. Then it is going to be a lonely road. But it is better to be lonely than to join in a mad cap race for which you will suffer later, pay for, dearly.

Wholesome Activities

The fourth condition is, in our daily life, when we are not in meditation, to perform a lot of wholesome activities to develop good kamma. When you do wholesome activities, good kamma, pure states of mind and other qualities are being cultivated. Patience, loving kindness, compassion, equanimity, integrity, truthfulness—all these are being cultivated during wholesome activities. Helping the poor, helping the environment are wholesome activities. However, be aware that they do not keep you so busy that sometimes you can not meditate and do not feel like meditating. Then, at the end of the day, when you are not doing anything, bored, you sit in front of the TV and let the idiot box feed unnecessary sense objects into your mind until you become groggy.

Wholesome activities play a very important part in a layperson's life. For one thing, they develop certain skills that are necessary, occupy the mind with wholesome things and actually serve as a kind of good emotional release. If people keep their emotions bottled up, one day there will be an explosion. Music may be a good emotional release. Do things that use the extra energy and emotion in a good way to develop the mind. Finally, reading to provide a sound theoretical background for your practice is necessary.

Having established the base, you should try to practise to be mindful in all your activities throughout the day. There are certain points you have to realize. Firstly, your meditation in daily life cannot be as good as your meditation during a retreat. After a retreat, you will not lose 100% of your concentration—probably 90%, 95% or 99%, but hopefully much less.

But because the mind already knows the basic method, when you are free, or the conditions are suitable, it will spring back to some extent. Just like a plant. When you water it, it grows beautiful and bushy. When there is no water, or when a few drops of water drips in once in a while, the leaves will fall off until only one leaf, the root and stem remain. But all is not lost. When you are free, you will water it more and you will get three or four leaves. It is better than nothing. The plant has not died. If it is completely gone, your mind will be in a horrible state. The demon will have taken over completely. So you must maintain some mindfulness. The trouble is that most people, before they start meditating or before they attend retreats, do not know what mindfulness is. When you have a better understanding of the nature of mindfulness, you can at least maintain it or develop it to some degree outside your daily life.

Slowing Down

There are a number of things to help make it easier to maintain mindfulness. The most important is, do not rush. Rushing may seem harmless, but actually that is where mindfulness is lost. You got to do this, do that, rush, and you've lost your mindfulness. With its loss, anger, impatience will come out with all the other things that follow. If you do not rush, you will have time to think, ponder and observe and watch and keep calm. When you rush here and there, there is not

Make an island for yourself!
Strive hard and become wise!
Rid of impurities and cleansed of stain,
You shall enter the celestial abode of the Noble Ones.

DHAMMAPADA 236

enough concentration. The awareness does not arise and the concentration is not there so you can not go deep.

If you have been meditating before and your mind has gone into deeper concentration, find a period of free time, like in the morning or evening when you put aside everything and do your meditation. Because of previous experience, concentration can come up again to some extent. But you have to take care the whole day. Do not rush about and do or say things without mindfulness. Otherwise, when you meditate, all the things will come back to nag you. If you maintain awareness to some degree, instead of getting restless, mindfulness is

If you maintain awareness to some degree, instead of getting restless, mindfulness is there.

there. When you forget, always return to the present moment. Relax, let go, do not do anything. Just be mindful. Always return to this state of being mindful. Relax, let go and be calm ten or twenty times a day, or even for one moment. You will see the difference it makes in your life.

One Minute a Day

Not many people can actually meditate without fail. It takes a lot of determination. So, how can it be done? Follow this simple rule. Every day, make it a point to meditate for one minute. If you watch "rising" and "falling" for sixty times, it is already more than one minute. If you can meditate for one minute a day, first thing in the morning and last thing before you sleep, you can surely meditate for a longer time than that. If you sit and watch "rising" and "falling" sixty times, you will feel calm. Then go on to meditate for two minutes. If you can meditate for two minutes, you can go on for three minutes. After five minutes, you may have had enough, but it has already made a difference to your day. You start the day happier, more mindful. The secret is in getting started, getting the engine going. When it is cold, you may not want to meditate. But just start the engine and it will go on for some time. This daily practice can affect our daily life and the meditation practice is maintained to some extent. Even if it is not in-depth, at least it is expanding our experiences and building a strong base so that when the conditions are more suitable, like in a retreat, our meditation picks up very fast.

Sometimes, just through daily practice, some people can progress quite far. These people meditate regularly every day without fail. Another thing that can help in this one-hour-a-day practice is concentration to help calm the mind quickly. It does not take much effort to go from a really restless mind to a peaceful mind. Do metta lovingkindness, chanting for ten or even five minutes to keep thoughts away, and the mind will come to a calm state so that you can go into vipassana without wasting much time. This ability has to be developed. Those who know chanting can follow the chanting on a tape with mindfulness and cut off all thoughts, so that the moment they sit, the mind is already calmed down and they can watch with mindfulness. Otherwise thinking and anger will intrude and by the time your one hour is up, you probably had only five minutes of watching "rising" and "falling" and already feel dead tired.

If you are a very busy person and meditate at the end of the day, then you do not need to do much walking. If you have been expending a lot of physical energy during the day, you may be tired. If you are really tired, get some sleep before you wake up to meditate. The best time for busy people is to meditate in the morning. You would have had enough rest and your mind is calm. You must get into the habit of waking up early and allow yourself time to meditate. Otherwise if you only have half an hour to meditate, you will be thinking of what you've got to do in your job before the half hour is up.

Another strategy to help you in daily mindfulness is to have proper planning. When you organize your work well, you do not have to think so much. If you do not have to think so much, the mind will not be so restless. Being organized will also give you time to do a lot of wholesome things.

Aspiration

Making an aspiration can make a person progress even in daily life. With an aspiration, you will be really committed to your spiritual

Let a man be watchful of speech,
well controlled in mind,
and not commit evil in bodily
action.
Let him purify
these three courses of action,
and win the path
made known by the Great Sage.

DHAMMAPADA 281

practice. It is not a hobby that you do only when you feel like doing it. There is continuity. On the other hand, be careful that you do not push too hard. If you push too hard, it may be more like a punishment or torture. You may begin to dread doing it—meditating only because you know you should. Eventually you may give up. There is continuity in making an aspiration. You try your best. You do not expect too much of yourself. There is regularity and the mind is conditioned to go to a higher level, for more experiences. After sometime when the mind has enough momentum due to the conditioning, it will push through because deep in the mind there is this wish, this program to make it happen. Without an aspiration, the wish to progress is not there and the mind does not accumulate sufficient conditioning "energy." You may not feel like progressing and the concentration will not come.

LIVING ON THE EDGE

There is a deeper practice which is more than just keeping afloat. This is called living on the edge. Here you are trying to live on the edge between this world and the other world. Between convention and reality. Between person and no person. Between the level which is influenced by hindrances and one that is not influenced by hindrances. As has been mentioned before, the difference between daily life and an actual retreat is that in the retreat, you have lots of time to go into deeper levels of concentration. When you walk, you do not look left or right, you just look down. When you watch "rising" and "falling" no one tells you "it's your call," and no child comes and pulls your legs and hands. In a retreat, you have the luxury of putting all your mental effort into the practice. That is why the concentration picks up much faster. Outside a retreat, it is not so easy. However, if you are a serious practitioner, you would like to have deep levels of concentration and a wide range of experiences as possible. That means trying to live on the edge.

The beauty of vipassana lies in momentary concentration. In samatha you cannot have that, you have to cut away from all worldly activities to maintain those levels of absorption and concentration. Once you are out of intensive samatha practice, the mind becomes very sensitive. It can be "hurting." When people in *samadhi* get out of it, they get bombarded by sense objects. They may run back to the caves and forests. During deep samadhi, the experience is very peaceful, better than singing in a karaoke and other worldly pursuits.

If you want peace and tranquillity, you have to live a more reclusive life. Tranquillity practice is not suitable for daily life because when you get involved in daily activities you lose all concentration. Unless you live as a recluse, but not necessarily as a monk.

Clear Comprehension

Vipassana concentration can always be gained in daily life to a certain extent. Here the important part of the practice is clear comprehension. Clear comprehension of purpose, clear comprehension of suitability. Purpose is what you want to do. Intention arises and you note the intention. You know that some intentions are wholesome and some are unwholesome. If it is unwholesome, do not do it. If it is wholesome, you can. Then we come to clear comprehension of suitability. Suitable for practice, suitable for many other things too. In the case of living on the edge, it is the suitability for going into the deeper levels of experiences, to the other world, to the non-self, to the realities. So you are always mindful when you want to be mindful. When it is suitable, you switch to mindfulness. You will just know the mind and body processes as they are. For example, when sitting in a bus and you have nothing to do, you can be aware of "rising," "falling," "sound, sound," an ache here, an ache there,... But you cannot go too deeply or else you will miss your stop.

Therefore you have to know how to control, when to go in and when to come out. Once you have mastered the art, you can go in quite easily. It is a thin line. Especially if you can maintain a certain degree of mindfulness, and clarity, you can "go in." For instance, while

The idler who does not exert himself
when he should,
who though young and strong
is full of sloth,
with a mind full of vain thoughts—
such an indolent man
does not find the path to wisdom.

DHAMMAPADA 280

walking, if it is just a straight path, and there are no cars, you can just walk. If you are used to it, you walk on the path, not noticing anything else, and at the right moment, you come out. But if you are walking on a road with cars, you cannot do that.

The question of suitability applies when we ask whether it is suitable to go into the practice. There is a special kind of mind that is able to drop everything and "go in" for a short while, and come out again. Most of the time, it cannot be done because it takes time to go in. You

have to struggle with the thinking, then look for the "rising" and "falling," look for the breath, find it and go on. But once you are used to going into concentration and watching "rising" and "falling," you tend to want to cut off from other things. You will be "inside." Walking is difficult because you tend to look around. If your mind really wants to go into concentration and you can watch the object and forget everything else, you can control the moment. You do not go in if the moment is not suitable. If the next moment is suitable you "go in." It can be done if you practise longer and get used to it. The line is actually very thin.

Experiencing Concentration

If you can go into states of deep concentration even for one second and come out, it is good enough. The one second can be a very deep experience. The enlightenment may be

If you can go into states of deep concentration even for one second and come out, it is good enough.

just one second, but it is deep. So train yourself, so that at a suitable time, you can for a short moment be completely involved in an object and come out. This is called living on the edge. This occurs more often in certain traditions that emphasize practice in daily life rather than intensive meditation. The people in these traditions try to be mindful in daily life and over a long period of time. In a split second, while they are involved in their work or some manual labour, because they have the mindfulness, they can get into concentration and just as quickly, they wake up. They experience complete absorption in the experience. These experiences happen frequently in people who emphasize daily mindfulness. Which is why I am also emphasizing that. Too many people come for retreats, work hard, but when they go back they become devils themselves. So if you can be absorbed in an object for one moment and come out, you will have a lot of opportunities to develop the deeper aspects of meditation in daily life as well.

Here are a few hints. Once you have continuous mindfulness, look at an object, cut off the concept of the "I." It is the concept that brings about thinking and restlessness. When you cut off the "I", you cut off the concept of space. When you cut off the concept of space, you cut off the concept of time. Take for example a simple thing like walking. If you always have a sense of "I am there," "This is the body," and so on, you cannot actually go deep into the experience. So do not care about the "I." It is the mind that is experiencing it. Do not think of space any more. Do not think you are moving. Movement has already become an object. Then there is just the movement as if you are at the same spot, never changing, so the movement becomes the object. When you think of time, do not think of what is happening to you—you are going to walk forever or something like that. You have all the time in the world to walk and you do not think of time any more. Then the mind will go in deep. It is just a question of attitude. So if you can do that, while waiting for a bus or while casually walking for five minutes, the mind can go into fairly deep concentration. Even when you are walking, you will not hear sounds, do not see anything at all. It is just the mind and the object for one or two seconds.

Of course, if you can combine intensive retreat and daily mindfulness, that would be best. For a better intensive meditation, before you come for retreat, prepare. Make sure you do regular sittings, "start the engine first" and try to finish your work way before the retreat. Lots of people, because they want to come to the retreat but have so much work, rush off to finish their work. By the time they arrive for the retreat, they are so sleepy. All the stress takes some time to overcome. But if you are prepared, when you come, there will be a big difference. Instead of taking three or four days to pick up, you will need only one or two days and you are already progressing.

Of all paths the Eightfold Path is the best;
Of all truths the Four Noble Truths are the best;
Of all things passionlessness is the best;
Of men the Seeing One (the Buddha) is the best.

DHAMMAPADA 273

SUMMARY

What is this meditation? This meditation is the developing of mindfulness in a systematic way so that it can be powerful and sharp enough to gain the insight that purifies us of the defilements and liberate us from all sufferings.

At first, we have enough mindfulness to prevent us from committing evil acts at the body and speech doors. This is considered as morality.

Later, when mindfulness has become continuous and powerful, the mind can be kept pure, free from the defilements for an extended period. This is concentration.

Lastly, it can become sharpened to penetrate into the true nature of mental and physical processes. This is insight.

This three-fold training of morality, concentration and wisdom of the Noble Eightfold Path are inter-dependent; for morality is a base for concentration to develop, while concentration is a base for insight to develop. Morality will become stronger as insight increases.

All these sound very simple but anyone who has undertaken the practice knows for certain that it is easier said than done. It takes time and effort and so, sacrifices have to be made. However, one can be assured that it is worth every ounce of it. We need a lot of these accumulations of vipassana practice to get us out of *samsara*. And if we know what *samsara* and all its sufferings are, we will practise diligently.

Appendices

Five Hindrances (Nivarana)

In the first few days of an intensive retreat or the initial phase which beginners undergo, they will encounter the hindrances in their full force. These hindrances are mental defilements. They are classified into five groups:

1 kamachanda—sensual desire
2 vyapada—ill-will/anger
3 thina-middha—sloth and torpor
4 uddhacca kukkucca—restlessness and remorse/worry
5 vicikiccha—sceptical doubts.

These hindrances have to be overcome for an extended period of time before one's concentration is powerful enough to act as a base for insight. The initial difficulty encountered is not unexpected as one does not have not much mindfulness in the beginning. In the case of a retreat, one also has to get accustomed to the more rigorous routine. The initial phase is a critical period because the hindrances must not be allowed to stay on for too long, especially at the time when one's concentration is being built up. We must be careful not to have wrong concentration. It is therefore imperative that meditators who still have not grasped the method correctly be patient and not push themselves. This will enable them to be freed from hindrances. The safest way is to allow mindfulness to be cultivated with the least stress.

When the hindrances arise, there are two methods that can be employed to overcome them:

1 Vipassana methods:

    a Mindfulness is applied onto the hindrance concerned.

    b Mindfulness is applied onto objects other than the hindrances.

2 Non-Vipassana methods:

    a Development of the opposing wholesome mental states.

    b Other methods, eg, involved in creating conditions conducive to pure states of mind.

SENSUAL DESIRE (KAMACHANDA)

Sensual desires are cravings for, attachment to, indulgence in the five sense objects and the thoughts connected with them with regard to their beauty, delightfulness and so forth.

We are born into a world delighting in and enjoying these senses and sense objects—colourful paintings, enchanting music, irresistible perfumes, tasty food, soft-warm touch and a fantasy of sensuous thoughts. It is true that these come with a certain degree of pleasure and joy. But they are very fleeting and we have to pay a heavy price for them. This hindrance is compared to a debt because when we want it, we go through much suffering before and after the brief moment of pleasure. Yet that brief moment of pleasure is not in itself peaceful. Exciting, perhaps, but not truly peaceful.

Sensual desires can be clearly seen when one takes note of them when they arise. During a retreat, one observes precepts and so, certain attractions and distractions are minimised. But sensual desire can still be detected for one still desires to look around, to listen and talk. We should be really mindful of it by noting "desire" or "craving" when it arises. When we do this, we should be quite sure that we are noting mindfully the mental state and not the object. We should also make the mindfulness as strong and continuous as possible because the presence of sensual desire itself indicates the mind is weak. We should also make sure that we note the sensual desire with detachment or else we slip back into attachment without our knowledge. If we can do this, we will find that craving or sensual desire is one thing, and the pleasure which may accompany it is another. The pleasure, which lasts only a very brief moment and then passes away, creates an uplifting and exciting cover over the suffering state of which attachment is the governing mental state. If you can be mindful of this sensual desire whose specific characteristic is attachment to the object, you will see it as not only unsatisfactory but also truly suffering. It is a hungry state, hence, it has been compared to a hungry ghost. It is a burning state, "There is no fire like lust", as the saying goes.

If we are mindful, the sensual desire that arises will cease soon enough. The reason is, there cannot be mindfulness and sensual desire at the same time. Another reason is, we see its real nature. The trouble is, we sometimes still crave for sensual pleasures. But if we have right understanding and are resolved to overcome the desire, and not to indulge in it a second longer, we shall be freed from it.

This method of watching the mental hindrance directly will therefore serve two purposes:

1 purifying the mind of the defilement,
2 understanding the true nature of the hindrance with regards to the three universal characteristics of impermanence, unsatisfactoriness and non-self.

Watching sensual desire directly will also reveal other things which can help us overcome it. For example, we can see the conditions that bring about the many varied forms of such desire, the conditions that maintain it, and the conditions that bring about its dissolution. One of the main conditions for arising is the presence of an attractive object. As such, mindfulness of the six senses contributes greatly to the prevention and overcoming of sensual desires. Only when we are not mindful of the attractive object at the sense door does craving arise. So it will help greatly if we note "seeing," "hearing" and so forth when sensual desire arises. Then we will also know that the desire or the pleasure it brings is impermanent, unsatisfactory and non-self.

There will be times when the attractive object is very dominating. At such times, it may be better that we wilfully ignore it and shift our attention to another object that does not generate craving but mindfulness. For a vipassana practitioner, one can first note the object as a vipassana object ie with the aim to purify the mind by understanding the true nature of the object. An example is when a meditator experiences pleasant states of mind. If he watches it, he may become attached to it after some time. So, if it does not go away or subside but instead remain as strong as ever, the meditator is advised to shift to a less attractive object—such as "rising" and "falling" of the abdomen or the "sitting" and "touching" sensations.

This method of ignoring can be seen in the rather humorous advice given by the Buddha to Ananda with regard to monks' behaviour towards women:

> "How are we to conduct ourselves, Lord, with regards to womankind?"
> "As not seeing them, Ananda."
> "But if we should see them, what are we to do?"
> "Not talking, Ananda."
> "But if they should speak to us, Lord, what are we to do?"
> "Keep awake, Ananda."
>
> —MAHAPARINIBBANA SUTTA

Methods of overcoming sensual desire which do not involve vipassana include meditation on conceptual objects. For example, in developing an opposing mental state (to sensual desire), one can do asubha bhavana, ie meditation on the loathsomeness of the body. When it is lust of the body to be overcome, one can do contemplation on the 32 parts of the body, the cemetery contemplations and so on. If it is greed for food, there is the development of the perception of loathsomeness of food. Similarly, we can also contemplate on the loathsomeness and danger of attachment to other objects. How these contemplations are done does not, however, come within the scope of this book.

Other non-vipassana ways of combating sensual desires include the thirteen austerities or ascetic practices of monks. For example, a monk may choose to observe having only three robes, a practice of contentment with regard to attire. Lay people can also observe a certain degree of austerity. We can also associate ourselves with the contented and dissociate ourselves from the greedy. Other minds or people can influence us.

These latter methods which involve concentration on conceptual objects are classified under samatha meditations. To what extent we occupy ourselves with them depends on individual temperament. Usually it is not necessary to dwell very long on such contemplations to overcome the hindrances and return to vipassana proper. However, if we do spend more time on them, concentration will increase, and this requires additional skill in handling the mind. This is also where one can draw the line between the practice of pure vipassana and one who uses tranquillity (samatha) as a base. If one wants to develop a strong base, then all the initial effort will first be directed towards a tranquillity exercise. But for a lay person who has not much time to spare, it is not difficult to understand why the person has to choose pure vipassana.

ILL-WILL (VYAPADA)

The second hindrance, ill-will, refers to the angry state of mind. It is a violent state of mind that seeks to destroy the welfare and happiness of oneself and others. It can come in many forms and is easier to detect than sensual desire because of its gross nature as well as the unpleasant feeling that comes with it. As in all defilements, it is easier to overcome when detected early. We note mindfully "anger, anger" or "fear," "jealousy" in whichever form it comes. While noting one should remain as calm and firm as possible. Being mindful of anger is like driving along a winding and bad road with many potholes and rocks. One has to be very alert, steady and firm. It is also like a meditator going amidst violent feuding groups to settle their differences. One must remain calm but not so lax which may lead one to be clobbered by both sides.

If we can be mindful of the characteristic of anger, which is savageness or harmfulness to its object, we will see that it is a very unsatisfactory state of mind. Yet people who bear grudges or remorsefulness cling to these adverse mental states, never willing to let go. Anger is never justified. Seeing its true nature will make one drop it like a hot potato.

One should also watch it detached from the concept of "I," "mine," etc, until the anger vanishes altogether. If the anger still stays, one will have to resort to other tactics such as shifting one's mind to another vipassana object.

One of the main conditions for the arising of anger is the repulsive object. A common repulsive object encountered by meditators is pain. Painful physical sensations are often objects of vipassana. After all, pain or dukkha is one of the three universal characteristics of existence to be realised. My Burmese teacher used to encourage meditators to make heroic efforts to watch pain. Another teacher calls pain a good friend of the meditator. No matter how we look at it, we have to be patient when watching pain.

Most of the unpleasant objects we encounter in the course of daily life can easily be handled with mindfulness ie if we make an effort to note them as soon as they arise. However, there are times when we may have to use other methods as our mindfulness and insight may still not be matured enough. Depending on the nature of the ill-will, the opposing mental state can be aroused. For simplicity, we can divide vyapada into three categories:

1   Ill-will towards living beings
2   Sadness, sorrow and lamentation
3   Fear

Ill-Will Towards Living Beings

There may be various reasons why a person bears ill-will towards another. But none of them can be considered justifiable. These emotions of ill-will can become so very deep that one may consider murdering one's enemy. The development of the sublime abodes (*Brahmaviharas*) would help one to overcome ill-will. That is the meditation of loving-kindness that overcomes anger and hatred towards any being. There is the development of compassion towards suffering beings that overcomes cruelty. There is the meditation of sympathetic joy towards happy beings. There is also the development of equanimity. Besides overcoming the hindrance and gaining concentration of mind, there are manifold benefits to be gained by practising these meditations.

Sadness, Sorrow and Lamentation

These are unhappy states of mind that are usually brought about in the event of separation from or loss of what is near and dear to us. These may be property or beloved ones. The deeper and stronger the attachment, the more painful it will be when the time for separation comes.

The meditation of equanimity will help one to appease these sorrows. Here, we reflect on kamma and its results with regard to ourselves and others. We can also reflect on the eventual coming of birth, old age, sickness and death. Mindfulness, when employed in such contemplations, should be very detached.

Fear

We fear the unknown, ghosts, mad men, heights, disease, and so on. There is a whole range of phobias and paranoia which people may suffer from. Fear is characterised by panic, shivering, and confusion. Mindfulness engaged to note it should be very firm to hold the shaking mind for a sufficiently long period of time. Confidence and courage are helpful—so when one is at a loss, one can quickly resort to the recollection on the virtues of the Triple Gem—the Buddha, Dhamma and Sangha. Frequent recollection also arouses a lot of joy.

What about other supportive conditions to overcome ill-will? The meditation manual, "Path Of Purification," suggests pleasant weather, pleasant dwellings, pleasant means in search of food, pleasant people, pleasant postures and so on for the hateful temperament.

SLOTH & TORPOR (THINA-MIDDHA)

Thina refers to the unwieldiness and indisposition of the mind, like one refusing to move, to do work or refusing to start to note mindfully in one's meditation. *Middha* refers to that same conditions in the mental factors. In such a state, the heavy and cloudy mind envelops, shrouding the meditator who finally dozes off to sleep.

These two arise together and make one rather "weak"—like a sick man who cannot sit up for long and walk straight. This "mental tiredness" is to be differentiated from physical fatigue. From experience, it is found that for a normal person during an intensive retreat, four hours' sleep is sufficient for the body to recover from physical fatigue (from the day's meditation). Of course, some may disagree, especially as we have been told a person needs at least seven to eight hours of sleep a day. I do not think this applies to normal meditators. But it can be readily agreed that the body must have its rest (much as some enthusiastic meditators would like to do without), especially when one's practice is not deep enough to go into deep absorptions for long periods of time.

We must learn to promptly note sleepiness when it arises. Often, we are not aware of it until we are badly affected. Sloth and torpor contribute to a weak, blurred, still and dull state of mind. So, some skills need to be acquired to overcome it. Some points to remember in noting sloth and torpor are:

1 Sharp Perception of Its Characteristic

Here one cannot be contented with just being mindful. One should note sharply and precisely the nature of sleepiness—an unwieldy, drowsy, heavy state of mind. Only by first noticing its specific characteristic can one later detect its general characteristic—ie its passing away.

2 Noting Energetically

Energy and effort are opposed to sloth and torpor. Energy can be developed through:

a   Contemplation on the virtues of the Triple Gem and the energetic endeavour of the Buddha and his disciples to arouse inspiration for oneself; reflections on the danger of sloth (such as being reborn in the woeful states) and benefits of energy.

b   Making a strong resolution to note energetically to overcome the hindrance. The energy aroused should be light, ie not heavy, and smoothly flowing.

c   Increased initial application of mind to the object. This can be brought about by the increased number of notings, continuously without a break and at a rapid pace. Such notings can be especially effective if applied to clearer and grosser objects such as pain or the touch points. For example, one may note the touch points—three or more—in a systematic and rhythmical manner to increase the momentum of the mindfulness. If sleepiness still persists, one can get up and do walking meditation with an increased but clear pace.

Standing meditation has been recommended for meditators frequently plagued by obstinate bouts of drowsiness. It has been found to be quite effective as a lot of energy is required to maintain one's meditation in the standing posture.

Methods other than vipassana in overcoming sloth include the development of perception of light. The nature of light is bright and expanding as opposed to sloth and torpor. The practice involves *kasina* meditations. Meditating in a bright, open room is also helpful.

Thinking and reciting the Dhamma also stimulate the mind to be active. Suitable conversation falls within this method. Then, there is washing the face, bathing or rubbing the hands and pulling ears. They are also effective to some degree. If everything fails, some meditators resort to sitting in a very uncomfortable posture to cause the arising of pain. This may sound repugnant but it is not as bad as those who are asked to meditate at edges of cliffs and wells. The chances of falling down cannot be ruled out!

RESTLESSNESS & REMORSE (UDDHACCA-KUKKUCCA)

Uddhacca means restlessness and kukucca, remorse. They refer to the turbulent and flurried state of mind that is running in all directions about many matters. The meditator becomes distracted and is unable to settle down to do his work of mindfulness.

This state of mind will occur in a beginner though he may not be consciously aware of his mind's wanderings. He is therefore reminded to make a point to note it as soon as his mind has wandered. Since his mindfulness is not yet sharp, he will have to note "thinking" or "wandering" until it ceases altogether. Again, the thinking, etc, should not be allowed to go on for too long, say, more than one or two minutes. If thinking or wandering persists, one should force one's mind back to watch one's primary object. If one is able to watch this hindrance well, one will also know the various types of restlessness, how it arises according to conditions, how it proceeds on and then ceases.

If one watches the restless, thinking mind, one may often find that at first there may seem to be no coherence but on close scrutiny, one finds that the restlessness often revolves around some unsettled or troubling points. It is like one or two stones thrown into the water, giving rise to many ripples and minor disturbances. Here, we shall attempt to discover some of the causes of this hindrance.

It frequently comes in the form of persistent remorse and worry over things done and left undone. Actually, a lot of these are really not very important and can be brushed aside. After all, there will always be problems to solve or things to be done in this world. Having taken the necessary steps, all we can do is to wait. Remorse and worry will certainly not help. But mindfulness certainly will.

If the restlessness is caused by one particular problem or matter, it is advisable to be on the alert for it. This is like setting a red-alert for a chief culprit running riot against the order of a place. If we can catch and subdue him, then the problem is solved. Such restlessness may arise many times in a minute, but every time it does, it is noted. In due time, its strength will weaken and disappear. This method can also be applied to a persistent habit or tune-ringing in the mind.

Persistent types of restlessness may arise because of a persistent disturbance present at one of the five sense doors—such as a continuous sound or pain. As a result, one is unable to note clearly one's primary meditation object such as "rising" and "falling." This problem falls on those with "square" mindfulness rather than the "rounded" ones; that is, people who are rigid and inflexible and also those who are obsessed with holding onto an object for a long time. Such restlessness can also occur when one's primary object becomes very fine and difficult to note, or when it takes an unexpected change or an unexpected interfering object slips in. As a result, the mind is confused and becomes dissatisfied. Restlessness is the result. One should therefore note mindfully and continuously; which is to say, one's mindfulness ought to be flexible enough to change its object to a more suitable or essential one when required. How this can be done will be dealt with in the following chapters. The vipassana object is a changing object: it also exhibits unsatisfactoriness. It behaves and comes about not as we wish it to. Be ready for it.

Another reason why restlessness may occur is when the mind faculties are unbalanced. For example, when there is too much forcing, the mind turns too active. The energy faculty is excessive. Even excessive faith can lead us to this state. In such cases, the relaxing of effort is important.

Last but not least, one may be able to spot the root which gives rise to the restlessness. There are these three evil roots—greed, anger and delusion which, when noted precisely, will disappear. It is more difficult for the practice if the three roots are not recognised when they arise. The greed, etc, which caused the restlessness may still be present even though the more active thinking has ceased. One should try to watch mindfully until it ceases altogether. Then the mind will be clearly rid of the hindrance. When abruptly freed of restlessness and worry, the mind experiences something like a sudden onset of silence. Similarly, being freed from sloth and torpor is like having the dark clouds dispersed and the bright sun revealed. However, if we are to leave traces of the hindrances behind, we will merely be inviting their swift return—the weeds quickly re-populate a freshly cleared ground—even more than before.

As can be seen, the whole affair of restlessness is quite complicated as all the defilements may be involved. Only through really continuous mindfulness can it be sufficiently put down. In summary, we tackle this hindrance by:

1. Noting "thinking, thinking" until it disappears.
2. If it stays on for more than one or two minutes, ignore it and pull the mind back to its primary object.
3. If the hindrance still persists, identify the nature of the restlessness—such as what is the evil root for its cause and deal with it appropriately, ie, by more noting.

Sometimes a meditator comes and asks: "I think the mind is really mad. Sometimes it thinks of really horrible things, even about my teachers and the Buddha. That is very bad mental kamma. Why does it arise and how do we handle it?" It arises because of defilements. To handle it, one has to recognise the nature of the defilement first and then take the appropriate measure.

There are also other means of dealing with distracting thoughts such as those set out in the Discourse on Thought Forms, the Satipatthana Commentary and so on. Some of these measures are: correct association and conversation with helpful and sympathetic companions, acquiring the right knowledge, considering the dangers of restlessness and benefits of concentration and so on. As a last resort, the Discourse on Thought Forms advised one to fight mind with mind. "With the teeth clenched, with the tongue pressed against the palate, if he subdues, restrains, dominates the mind by the mind, those evil unskilled thoughts associated with desire, aversion and confusion, these are got rid off and come to an end." By getting rid of these, the mind steadies, calms down and is one-pointed, concentrated.

SCEPTICAL DOUBTS (VICIKICCHA)

Vicikiccha, the fifth hindrance, refers to the confused and perplexed state of mind that makes one sceptical and disbelieve what is true (in this case, the Triple Gem). One should, however, differentiate this from the healthy doubts as referred to in the Kalama Sutta—doubting what should be doubted. This latter case is actually the wisdom faculty trying to understand the way.

Sceptical doubt arises in one who thinks beyond his ability to do so. The Dhamma is beyond logical reasoning that works on the conceptual level. As a result, such people end up confused and undecided. This paralyses the whole task of proceeding on the right way.

The method of noting doubts mindfully when they arise will solve the problem in most cases. The more persistent ones can be sorted out by an interview with the meditation instructor.

The real trouble occurs with people who come to meditate with little or no faith in the Triple Gem and without fully realising the purpose, practice and nature of the Dhamma.

Proper theoretical understanding removes, to a large extent, all these sceptical doubts as well as provide adequate faith for one to practise long enough to acquire more lasting faith gained through vipassana meditation.

SUMMARY

1 Sensual desires (kamachanda) can be cast out by:
   - Taking up an inauspicious subject of meditation.
   - Applying oneself to the development of Jhana on the sensuously inauspicious object of meditation.

- Guarded state of the controlling faculties.
- Moderation in food.
- Sympathy and support of good men in the endeavour.
- Stimulating talk that helps the accomplishment of the object in view.

2 Ill-will (*vyapada*) can be cast away by:
- Practice of loving kindness meditation.
- Applying oneself to the development of Jhana on the thought of loving-kindness.
- Reflection on ones' action as one's property.
- Abundance of wise consideration.
- Sympathetic and helpful companionship of the good.
- Stimulating talk that assists the development of loving kindness and the overthrow of anger.

3 Sloth and torpor (*thina middha*) can be cast away by:
- Seeing that sloth and torpor is caused by eating too much or gluttony ie practise moderation in food.
- The changing of postures completely.
- Reflection on the perception of light.
- Staying in the open.
- Sympathetic and helpful companionship of the good.
- Stimulating talk that helps to dispel sloth and torpor.
  The eight ways given to Maha Moggallana:
- Neglect the thought of drowsiness.
- Reflect on the Dhamma.
- Recite or repeat the Dhamma.
- Pull earlobes and massage or rub limbs with hands.
- Get up from sitting; wash and rub eyes with water; look into distance, sky and stars.
- Reflect on thought of light.
- Fix thought on ends of limbs, aware of controlling faculties, with the mind kept in.
- When all seven ways fail, sleep. Be conscious of the time of waking and on waking, get up quickly thinking that one will

not give oneself to the comforts of laying down, reclining and languor.

4 Restlessness and worry (*uddhacca kukkucha*) can be cast away by:
   - Knowledge of scriptures.
   - Questioning into the practice of the order.
   - Understanding the disciplinary rules.
   - Association with those more experienced and older than oneself in the practice of things like virtue.
   - Sympathetic and helpful companionship.
   - Stimulating talk that helps the rejection of restlessness and worry.

5 Sceptical doubts (*vicikiccha*) can be cast away by:
   - Being learned in the Buddha's teaching.
   - Inquiring about the Buddha, the teaching and the order of real saints (Noble Ones).
   - Understanding thoroughly the nature of the discipline.
   - Being decided (in ones' faith) about the truth of the Triple Gem.
   - Sympathetic talk and helpful companionship.
   - Stimulating talk that helps to dispel sceptical doubts.

In addition, the discourse on thought forms (*Vitakka Santhena Sutta*) mentions several ways to overcome impure and immoral thoughts.

   - By overcoming an immoral thought by moral thought. It is a process of replacement or substitution. This is efficiently done with a pure thought whose nature opposes the particular defilement.
   - By seeing the danger of the immoral thought; by contemplating on the dangers of such evil thoughts.
   - By ignoring those evil thoughts and through forgetfulness they will pass away.
   - By attending to the function and form of the thoughts.
   - By subduing and forcing them out through sheer will power.

Concept and Reality

It is important that the meditator understands the difference between "concept" and "ultimate realities," because it is the direction which he will have to lead his mind—from concepts to realities.

Concepts are those things or ideas thought out and conceived by the mind. They are built upon the ultimate realities. Concepts are only conventionally and subjectively true.

Ultimate realities, on the other hand, are those phenomena which can be directly perceived (thus ultimate) without going through the process of conceptual thinking, reasoning or imagination. These are truths not depending on conventional definitions. Ultimate realities, however, do not necessarily only mean the Absolute Reality which refers only to the unchanging, unconditioned state—"Nibbana."

Though conventional or conceptual realities are still a reality and we cannot really do away with them altogether, we will have to put them aside for periods of time during our meditation to allow us to really see and realise things as they really are.

Conceptualisation can occur in two ways:

i   **Active Thinking**
    Active thinking can occur as philosophising, scheming, planning or fantasising. It is obvious that when one does it

with lots of assumptions, preconceptions, ideas or hallu-cinations, then one cannot be, at the same time, experiencing nature directly. One has to put away all these before any insight can arise.

ii **'Unconscious' Thinking**

The second type of conceptualising is more subtle in that one is not actively "thinking" or at **least one is not conscious of it.**

These concepts are formed so habitually and are deeply embedded in the mind. These can also be part and parcel of the mental processes influenced by kamma and the results of kamma. Although one cannot abandon these altogether, it is still necessary to transcend these for periods of time (by means of highly concentrated bare mindfulness) to allow insight to arise.

Examples of concepts relevant to the meditator are:

1 **Word Concepts** (*Sadda Paññatti*)

Words are made up of many syllables or sounds that arise and pass away consecutively.

At one instant of time, the word does not exist, only the arising and passing away of sound, a vibrating form; materiality in nature.

Similarly a musical piece is made up of many "notes" of sound. These are words based upon the play of sound when we try to communicate our ideas and experiences with another. Now it is also visual as it has been put into writing.

Sound concepts (words) may be real if they refer directly to real phenomena that can be directly experienced. Unreal concepts are those that cannot refer directly to realities. They refer to other concepts and ideas which by themselves do not really exist.

As words combine with words, further concepts build up and can be the combination of real and unreal concepts. Example: The word "mind" is a real concept as it refers to mental phenomena that can be directly experienced without conceptualisation.

The word "man" is an unreal concept because it refers to something that cannot be directly experienced without conceptualisation. Some words may have both—eg patient who may refer to a sick person (unreal) or a tolerant mental state (real).

In meditation we use them (real concepts) as labels to help us recognise realities. Words and labels should not be grasped at in meditation. One should instead try to understand what is meant to be experienced.

2   **Form, shape and distance**
These concepts make up the two-dimensional and three-dimensional world.

If you study the television screen, the picture is made up of electron lights shooting at a great speed from the tube within. They arise and pass too fast for one to really know what is actually happening. What the mind grasps (too slowly) is a general play of colours which form shapes and so give us ideas. They occur so fast that they seem to occur at the same time.

3   **Directional Concepts** (*Disa Paññatti*)
These are concepts corresponding to directions, relationship of one thing to another eg east, west, right, left, above, below, inwards, outwards, sideways, upwards, and downwards.

4   **Time Concepts** (*Kala Paññatti*)
The Time concept is built upon ideas concerning the recurrent and consecutive occurrence of material and mental phenomena.

Materially, they involve light and darkness (as in day or night), physical state of body (as in old and young) and so on.

Mentally, they involve mental activities and functions such as sleeping time, working time, and so on.

Although we should have a general timetable or routine to guide our practice, we need not follow it blindly. Adjustments can be made if it is unsuitable. In groups, sometimes one's own welfare has to be sacrificed if benefit is meant for the welfare of the group.

5   **Collective Concepts** (*Samuha Paññatti*)
These correspond to groups or collections of things, eg a class, a race, a car, a city, group interviews, group meditation etc.

6   **Space Concepts** (*Akasa Paññatti*)
Space concepts are those that refer to open spaces—such as well, cave, hole and window.

7   **Sight Concepts** (*Nimitta Paññatti*)
These are visualised images such as the learner's sign and mirror image of tranquillity meditation. Many hallucinations and imageries also come under this category.

8   **Beings, Ego** (*Satta Paññatti*)
What people normally regard as "I," "you," "he," "she," "person," "dog" or "deva" are actually sets of ever-changing mental and material processes. These concepts of being, should be used as convenience in communication but when grasped upon as real, ultimate and absolute, one cannot help but fall into conflict and sooner or later fall to ruin.

The abandoning of this concept is of utmost importance to Vipassana meditation but upon the realisation that "All dhammas are not-self," one ought not to think "I" am walking but just be mindful eg the process of walking. Some may philosophise as they watch. This will, on the other hand, fall into another set of concepts.

There are still many more concepts such as of happiness, suffering, life and so on but we will not be dealing with them at the present. In order to have a better picture of the process of conceptualisation, it would be helpful to explain the thought processes.

A thought process can be defined as a series of consciousness arising in an order that makes up what we "see," "hear" and "think." These thought processes arise from the life continuum, a flow of consciousness in a deep sleep state following stimuli from an internal or external object.

There are six types depending on the "door" the object arises:

1 Thought processes that arise at the eye door.
2 Thought processes that arise at the ear door.
3 Thought processes that arise at the nose door.
4 Thought processes that arise at the tongue door.
5 Thought processes that arise at the body door.
6 Thought processes that arise at the mind door.

The first five are called "sense-door adverting thought processes" whilst the last is called "the mind-door adverting thought processes."

Within each process is a passive phase consisting of resultant consciousness (mental results of kamma) which receives its object (eg at eye door—the eye object ie colours) followed by a functional determining consciousness that determines an active phase which may be wholesome (good kamma) or unwholesome (evil kamma).

After the sense-door processes, the different types of mind-door processes arise building ideas and so on upon the object. These latter parts constitute conceptualisation. For example, in the case of the eye-door process, a typical order will be:

Five sense-door thought process: **b At bc bu pc v sp st vo J J J J J J J t t b**
Mind-door thought process: **b At bc bu M J J J J J J J t t b**

LEGEND:

At	past bhavanga
bc	vibrating bhavanga
bu	arresting bhavanga—when the life continuum stops.
pc	five sense-door apprehending—when the mind turns to receive the sense objects.
	The receiving of the sense objects
v	Five sense consciousness—eg seeing consciousness
sp	receiving consciousness (goes to receive the nature of object)
st	investigating consciousness (goes to bring out the nature of object)
vo	determining consciousness (determines course of action that follow)
J	(Javana) impulsion
t	retentive consciousness
M	mind door apprehending
b	bhavanga

Note: Bhavanga: the life continuum, a flow of consciousness when in deep sleep. It is the result of previous kamma and is responsible for maintaining the individual's existence and a condition for latent defilements to arise and kammic results to manifest. It is also regarded as the mind-door.

After this follows the mind-door processes, such as:

1   The first type of process is usually the compaction of past object process which is a carry over of the object from the sense doors (atitaghannavithi).

2   Following it is the amassing process, where the various eye objects are amassed into formation eg of shape concepts (samuhaghanavithi).

3   Next, ideas of what they are develop through the meaning or idea processes (atthaghanavithi).

4   Lastly, the names ascribed to it may be given mentally. This is through the naming process (namaghanavithi).

These may develop further into more abstract ideas especially when associated with other sense doors and ideas. But from here we may say that to note "seeing" without thinking would cut off a lot of concepts. It would also help to disregard the shape and forms as far as possible.

With the hearing process:

1   past process
2   amassing of sound forms
3   naming
4   meaning or ideas

Similarly, by just noting "hearing" we cut off concepts. It would also help to disregard the "words" if we are to arrive at the Vipassana object faster.

And again with smelling, tasting, and touching processes:

1   past
2   amassing
3   naming
4   meaning

Only by noting "smelling" merely as "smelling" etc, we cut off concepts. Idea of what is smelt, tasted or touched should also be disregarded.

The processes follow one another so quickly that they make what is complex seem solid and as a whole.

Four Kinds of Apparent Solidity (*Ghana paññatti*)

1 *Santati Ghana* (Compaction of continuity)
   The mental and material processes arise and cease so fast one after another that it seems as if they are one continuous unchanging occurrence.

2 *Samuha Ghana* (Compaction of mass)
   The mental and material processes are made up of so many characteristics or phenomena finely knitted by complex conditionings that they seem like one whole piece.

3 *Kicca Ghana* (Compaction of function)
   There are "different types of consciousness" each with their own specific functions eg seeing, hearing etc, which are very subtle and difficult to see. Hence one may mistake it for one working unit.

4 *Arammana Ghana* (Compaction of object)
   As the consciousness and process run very quickly by, so too the different objects that seem to appear together in one picture—giving rise to shapes, forms, etc.

Thus wrong perceptions and hallucinations arise. These hallucinations arises in ascending degree:

1 Hallucination of **perception**
   Wrong perception of an object eg one thinks one's own shadow as belonging to someone else.

2 Hallucination of **thought**
   Based on hallucination of perceptions, one develops wrong thoughts and reasoning, eg if one does not hear well, one may misunderstand other's intentions and implications.

3 Hallucination of **views**
   With many of the hallucination of thoughts, one may grasp at wrong views with regard to life such as holding firmly to the wrong view that the world is permanent, perfectly happy and belonging to an everlasting self.

From here we can clearly see that to break through all these concepts even for a while, to penetrate into realities, our mindfulness has to be:

i   agile and fast enough,

ii   thorough and continuous so that no stone is left unturned,

iii   very clear and concentrated to see through the complexity and perceive clearly the nature of the object.

As for Ultimate Realities (*Paramattha Dhamma*) the Abhidhamma classifies them into four main categories:

1   Consciousness (*Citta*)—eg wholesome or unwholesome consciousness.

2   Mental States (*Cetasika*)—eg greed, conceit.

3   Matter (*Rupa*)—eg the element of rigidity.

4   *Nibbana*—the unconditioned.

In short these (except for the last) are mental and material processes to be realised by the meditator as impermanent, unsatisfactory and non-self.

However, not all these can be noted by the beginner. For example, it is not possible to note the Jhanic (absorption) and Lokuttara (supramundane) consciousness for they do not arise in the meditator. Neutral feelings are also noted by more experienced meditators as these feelings are more subtle and need sharper and stronger mindfulness.

In fact, the beginners are not able to note without concepts because they have long been associated with them. So, to facilitate such situations, the beginners note using real concepts to help direct their mind to these realities. These are labels that will have to be increased when they are able to mindfully notice more phenomena. But Vipassana is not mere labelling or reciting, so one must not cling to them blindly. At times, it may be better to do without them. With progress, there will be so many of these phenomena arising and passing away at a great speed. Then, labelling must be abandoned or it will be an obstacle.

Of the idea-concepts, the concept of a being must be abandoned if one is to have any Vipassana insight at all. It is obvious that by being mindful of mind and matter, one will not find any being there at all, no matter how hard one tries. In the course of one's progress, when realities can be noted fairly well, one will have to abandon other concepts, like those of form, directions, shape, space and time. There are even finer concepts of happiness and reality which you will find out in due time. For example:

a   Walking Meditation
At first the meditators will do their walking meditation with the form of their legs still in their mind.

With constant help of labelling of the phases of steps like "lifting," "stepping," the meditators direct it to the various experiences. When they can experience clearly the movement, tension, pulling, heat and cold and so on, the form of legs will soon be abandoned. With increased mindfulness of the realities and their behaviour, even the labels will have to be abandoned. When concentration becomes deep, the meditators may even forget the time, direction or where they are for those moments.

b   Sitting Meditation
One first directs at the movements of the abdomen and other experiences labelled as "rising" and "falling."

When one can discern the "pulling," "pushing" movements and other experiences like pressure, hardness and so on, one may lose a sense of its directions and so noting it as it behaves rather than as "rising" or "falling." Here one may use another more suitable label or put it aside altogether.

At times when "rising" and "falling" is very clear and slow, more notings of "rising, rising, rising, rising..." will help the mind note moment to moment. If it can be perceived to be changing very fast from one moment after another, then, it will be difficult to put labels on the movement.

The meditators will have to sharpen their mindfulness by trying to experience moment to moment as many of these realities as they arise and pass away. To help the meditators see clearly, they are often asked to describe in their experience in their own words and make thorough reports. Technical terms like "Dukkha" are definitely to be avoided. Frequent usage may indicate that one's mind is still involved with theoretical thinking and concepts.

There is, however, a note of caution here. The abandoning of concepts would mean the disorientation of the conventional perception of the "person" and the "world" outside him. If one is not careful the mind may in a few cases lead to further disorientation and disorganisation. It is essential to understand that the presence of mindfulness and the understanding that the conceptual and conventional world, though not real in the ultimate sense, is built upon reality and has to be accepted and lived in.

For example, there are people who refuse to use the words "I" and "you" because they think that it will arouse the idea of self. This is impractical!

Dilemmas Along the Journey

I n the past few years, a fair number of Malaysians have taken up the
cultivation of insight meditation (*vipassana bhavana*) and from the
feedback received, we can make a list of the problems they encounter.
However, we shall deal only with the more common ones here.

WHY COMPLICATIONS ARISE

Mindfulness is the awareness of things as they really are. If we are
mindful, our minds will be very alert to the conditions within and
without us, whether they are profitable or otherwise and then act
accordingly.

The practice of vipassana bhavana involves cultivating intense and
uninterrupted mindfulness of any physical or mental process occurring
at every moment. This concentrated awareness, when sufficiently
powerful and rightly directed, is able to penetrate the thick veil of
delusions and liberate one from the defilements and suffering.

If this is so, how then, some meditators may ask, can complications
arise? The answer is simple—they are not mindful although they may
have tried to be. "Mindfulness is helpful everywhere." Without

mindfulness, you can expect trouble. I shall classify the dilemmas commonly faced by meditators:

1 Conflict of desires and values
2 Fears
3 Deficiencies

Conflict

The most common one is the conflict between material and spiritual aspirations. As the Dhammapada says:

"One way indeed, is to worldly gains
One way indeed, is to Nibbana."

I think that intrinsically most Buddhists know that spiritual happiness is superior and better than worldly happiness. After all, spiritual happiness is the only thing that really counts in the end. But it is also quickly agreed that spiritual happiness is far more difficult to attain than material possessions. As our surge of cravings is still very strong and our wisdom still superficial, most if not all of us, will remain as lay people throughout our mortal life. Some would strive to attain both their spiritual and worldly aspirations and find themselves torn apart. Others try to ignore one of them altogether but that will also not help to solve the problem.

Rightly, a Buddhist should, in his entire life, bear in mind the spiritual aim so that his life will have a spiritual blending to lift him and others above the mundane problems to supramundane liberation. Ignoring the cultivation of one's own innermost freedom will end one up in a pathetic condition.

In the Abhidhamma, it is explained that after emerging from the thought process of Path and Fruition (ie Enlightenment), the object of Nibbana is carried over to a mind-door process with a sensuous sphere consciousness, accompanied by wisdom running through the active phase (*javana*). This means that one clearly knows and perceives the Unconditioned Element, the Absolute Truth, that peaceful happiness, with one's mind. With that vision, one has completely abandoned forever:

- The wrong view of self (*sakkaya ditthi*).
- Doubts concerning the Triple Gem (*vicikiccha*).
- Taking practices other than the Noble Eightfold Path as a possible means out of samsara (*silabhata paramasa*).
- Sensual desires that can lead one to the woeful states (*apayagamaniya kamaraga*).
- Ill-will that can lead one to the woeful states (*apayagamaniya patigha*).

In the Commentaries, both avarice (*macchariya*) and jealousy (*issa*) have also been abandoned. One is said to have unshakeable faith in the Triple Gem and never again will transgress the Five Precepts.

As in the Scriptures, many have said,

> "*Wonderful, Venerable Gotama; Wonderful, Venerable Gotama! Just as one should turn up that which is upside down or lay bare that which is concealed, or tell the way to the one who has lost his way or to hold a lamp in the dark so that those with eyes might see things; the Dhamma has been revealed to me in more ways than one by the Venerable Gotama. We take refuge in the Buddha, Dhamma and Sangha. May the Venerable Gotama accept us as disciples from today onwards as long as our lives last.*"

If it has indeed happened, the Dhamma will live forever till that final cessation of the aggregates.

It may perhaps be better to ask:

"*Is there absolute truth?*"

The question can be further refined to:

"*Is there that that does not change?*"

In most instances, it is perhaps best to keep noble silence.

Then, what of the motivation?

"*Is not suffering enough motivation?*" is a counter question.

"Then, why not other ways and methods?"

A reply will be the Kalama Sutta where one is advised not to merely believe just because of hearsay, rumours, tradition, scriptures and etc.

If one practises, the faith will arise. So, maybe the best *answer* will be: *If you practise enough, things will be clear to you.*

Very often, I received this answer from my teacher to many of our questions and it is also a reply that I now often find most suitable to give to others.

It does not, however, mean that by having a lofty goal like the attainment of Nibbana, one must without fail, renounce all worldly pleasures and possessions. The attainment of Nibbana itself is an ultimate goal of all Buddhists but we have to recognise our shortcomings. One will, therefore, have to make subsidiary goals that will mean defining how much one wants to strive for spiritually or abandon materially, at least for a certain period of time. For example, we have to consider the kind of occupation we want to select. Whatever the decision may be, let it be firm, noble (bearing in mind the spiritual importance), realistic (taking into consideration the real situation—environmental and internal qualities—good and evil), and flexible (ie adaptable to the fast-changing world). When the decision has been made, that conflict should cease, or at least, be very much lessened.

May the movement of your subsidiary goals advance steadily towards the final one.

Another conflict we must not fail to mention is the choice between compassion and wisdom. Some fear to practise vipassana bhavana because the attainment of the Path will mean that they will no longer be able to take on the Bodhisatta vow to be a Samma Sambuddha. Actually, one has nothing to fear because if one has strongly vowed to become a Bodhisatta, one is unlikely to attain the supramundane state during meditation. However, one can still give up that aspiration to be a Buddha and opt for Arahantship when one reaches the threshold of the Path. Either Path is also very noble; one is pragmatic, the other idealistic.

Fears

a Fear of the unknown

This includes the fear of going mad. As a result of this fear, some people stop meditating, thus stalling their progress in meditation.

But this is by no means a groundless fear. People may "go off" for a variety of reasons. We may generalise them into two categories—abnormal behavioural tendencies and wrong practice.

i **Abnormal behavioural tendencies**

Deep within our mind lie hidden latent tendencies—both good and evil that may be accumulations of not only this present life but those from past lives. It is not unusual to find some very powerful ones surfacing in the course of one's meditation. If you cannot handle them, they will "handle" you. In some of us (luckily not too many), the tendency to break down is stronger than others. It usually occurs to people deeply troubled with neurotic problems, while others are due to genetic factors. If you happen to be one of them, you should be extremely cautious in your meditation. Intensive retreats, especially without guidance, are not recommended. It is therefore advisable to settle your worldly problems as best you can before meditation. It does not really disqualify one from taking up vipassana, only that it must be done under close supervision by an experienced teacher. One should seek counselling, inform one's teacher of one's nagging problems or previous breakdowns, if any.

ii **Wrong practice**

What is meant here is wrong concentration as compared to right concentration. The difference is the absence or presence of mindfulness. When mindfulness is absent, the mind will be unwholesome and so you will end up increasing the concentration of your greed, anger, and delusion. This means that when you are angry, your anger will be, say, ten times amplified; likewise when you are greedy or deluded. A mind of such nature is not too different from that of a madman's and it becomes more so if the meditator continues to exercise wrong concentration. What went wrong?

- It may be that the meditator started off on the wrong foot. People meditate for different reasons. If your motives are selfish, you will very likely end up more selfish and deluded. The aim of vipassana is to abandon the defilements (greed, anger, and delusion) by constant and uninterrupted mindfulness of mental and physical processes. If you meditate to become a millionaire, to communicate with unseen beings or read other people's minds, I suggest you stop meditating.

- The attitude is also another important factor to consider. Many people in this goal-orientated world are so hung up on set targets that they get terribly frustrated if things do not turn out according to their expectations. The result is that they either break down and cry, or they try to convince themselves and others they have what they do not have. There is a question often asked by meditators: How do we know when we are going mad? Answer: When you think you are an Arahant (or something like that), able to read others' minds, recollect your past lives, see and hear beings others cannot, then there is a likelihood that you are going mad. Nature will move at its own pace and it is no use being impatient. We must be especially mindful should we become obsessed with making progress.

- Handling objects in the wrong way. In the course of practice, the meditator may encounter unusual experiences that may be very fearful or blissful (such as visual images, voices or feelings). In vipassana, they are taken note of mindfully and they will eventually pass away. If they persist, the next step is to ignore them and watch another vipassana object (such as the "rising" and "falling"). If the object (fearful or blissful) continues to be dominant, one is advised to get up and do walking meditation.

The trouble is, meditators can become obsessively fearful or attached to these phenomena that they recur again and again; thus intensifying that unwholesome state of mind. When attachment or fear arises, they must (ignore the object and) note the mental state till it vanishes. Otherwise wrong concentration will result. If the unwanted objects are extremely powerful or persistent, it may be wise to stop meditation until you get the proper advice.

b   **Fear of pain and physical disability**

Pain is an inevitable occurrence in meditation as well as in life. But in meditation, we use it to train our mind to become strong and unaffected, and to penetrate into its (the pain's) true nature (of impermanence, suffering and non-self).

The new meditator will have to face the usual beginner's aches that will go away with just a little patience. Later, the pain may intensify owing to deepening concentration. After that one may come to experience its cessation. In more seasoned meditators, pain may actually be welcomed as it is a sharp object for the mind to hold on to, to build up concentration and mindfulness.

Fear also arises when one sees too much of pain. This is comparable to a child who could not take the medicine (although it is good for him/her) because it is bitter. More knowledge of the Dhamma can help to overcome this. One can also bear in mind that there are also a lot of joy and benefits in meditation. Besides, you can try to ignore the pain and watch another object. Please note the fear when it arises. If it does not work, frequent recollection of the Buddha will help overcome it.

Some people, while watching the pain, fear that they may suffer permanent disability or die. Here there are two cases: without actual ailments, and with real ailments, eg heart disorder, piles, asthma, high blood pressure, etc.

▪   **Without actual ailments**
In such cases, pain quickly disappears when they stop meditation. One must first note the intention before giving up. However, one should also try to note the fear until it goes away. The fear is actually groundless. People have sat for more than six hours without being crippled.

- **With real ailments**

  Medical aid in cases like this should be sought before coming for meditation. In vipassana, the pain and fear are first noted directly, but when that is not possible (because they are too strong and persistent), they will have to be ignored (by watching another object) until the mindfulness and concentration are powerful enough to tackle them again. Many illnesses deemed chronic and incurable had been overcome through vipassana but it needs a lot of effort and willpower. It is also considered to be very fortunate to be able to die during meditation.

Deficiency

a **Unsuitable place**

This is usually one of the worst excuses. If the place is noisy, "hearing" of "sound" can be your vipassana object. One can also note "heat" or "cold" accordingly. It is also not very difficult to find a cooler and quieter place.

b **Insufficient time**

The seemingly justifiable reason why people cannot find enough time to meditate is because of worldly commitments with regards to occupation and family. To have "no time" to meditate does not seem logical because one can surely make available some time (perhaps not quite enough, I agree) if we really want to—at least early in the morning or before sleep. Besides, we can practise mindfulness with regards to our daily activities by being fully alert and composed with whatever we are doing at that moment, be it driving, talking, walking, thinking, etc. We can also cultivate other virtues besides pure mindfulness such as the ten perfections of generosity, restraint, renunciation, wisdom, energy, patience, truthfulness, determination and loving-kindness.

c **Shortage of teachers**

There is a shortage of meditation teachers in this country. It is perhaps more correct to say that there is a shortage of qualified meditation teachers.

What qualifications? It is an undeniable fact that it is best for all concerned that a meditation teacher should really know how to meditate and is competent to show the way to others. To know how to meditate may be defined as having had thorough practice and thus, have clear understanding through one's own personal experience of the art of cultivating the mind. Also, a teacher's restraint can be noted from the observance of one's moral precepts. Tranquillity should be evident from the non-restless and unruffled state of mind oneself is in; and the strength of the defilements of greed, hatred, and delusion should be weak in oneself.

As for being competent to show the way, this may be defined as having a truly compassionate heart and endowed with sufficient knowledge of the Buddhist teaching as embodied in the Pali canon and its commentaries (eg the Satipatthana Sutta). The meditation teacher is also able to give precise instructions and timely encouragement so that meditators may progress quickly and surely along the path of purification.

Needless to say, effective communication between teacher and pupil is important and so is the necessity of sincerity and openness on the part of the latter. It is also sensible to choose a teacher whose temperament blends well with yours if you have several to choose from. Owing to the shortage of teachers, it may be wise to be on the lookout for retreats where you can spend days in intensive meditation, and where you will get a good idea of what meditation is and how it is to be done. After that, one may resort to regular correspondence as a means of communication to continue one's practice. Initial instructions are preferably given personally.

d **Deficiency in Concentration**

Another common reason why some people give up vipassana meditation is the extremely restless nature of their minds. Instead of getting peace, it would seem as if they are not only wasting their time but are also suffering unnecessarily more. Such persons should ask themselves:

- Did I keep my precepts well? How restrained have I been in my daily activities? If we have been strongly indulging in base actions, it is no wonder our minds are so distracted. Restraint from evil is the foundation of concentration, so it is clear that meditation should not be blamed. If they practise mindfulness in their daily activities thoroughly, they should be able to concentrate.

- How many hours a day do I meditate? Do I do it everyday – seriously? You cannot expect much if you did not really try. If you have been practising regularly, sincerely and enthusiastically, you will have no problem concentrating your mind.

- Did you obtain proper and complete instructions? Have you been having regular interviews? It is a wonder that you have not got worse if you have not had the proper instructions. This is usually acquired only after many sessions of interviews and discussions with the teacher (because we normally do not listen properly and tend to forget).

THE FOUR GUARDIAN MEDITATIONS

However, it is understandable that there are people who have powerful defilements that will make them give up pure vipassana without even giving it a fair trial. The four guardian meditations, therefore, help to give faith to people who are very much in need of some peace and joy before taking up the more arduous task of vipassana. Besides, we cannot deny that pure samatha meditation does help one to attain quick and strong concentration. It will also help us in our worldly enterprises if it is done properly.

Hence, the four guardian meditations are often recommended prior to the practice of vipassana. They are:

1   *Buddhanussati*
    recollection of one or more of the virtues of the Buddha
    (generates faith and energy).

2   *Mettabhavana*
    radiating loving-kindness to one or more beings (overcomes
    ill-will and dissatisfaction; instils amity).

3   *Asubha*
    contemplation of loathsomeness of the body, eg, the thirty-
    two parts separately (overcomes lust).

4   *Maranasati*
    contemplation on death (overcomes fear of death and instils a
    sense of urgency).

Burmese recommendation is two minutes for each of the guardian
meditations (making it eight minutes in all) before vipassana practice.

SUSTAINING PRACTICE

Another problem faced by vipassana meditators is the inability to
maintain zealous practice or at least regular sessions which is crucial
for progress. Practice, when we analyse it, is the effort made. This
faculty (effort) is very much dependent on faith/confidence. The
proximate cause of faith has been defined as the objects that inspire
faith (*saddhiya vatthu*).

The Triple Gem is what I have in mind now:

*   The Buddha—or symbols that represent the Teacher, eg images,
    footprint, Bodhi tree and relics.
*   The Dhamma—which may be represented by the Wheel of the
    Law, books, or it may be the actual teachings or practice one
    has come across or undertaken.
*   The Sangha—the community of enlightened disciples.

Therefore, it behoves us to be in constant communication with
spiritual objects, activities and people, and in particular, those directly
connected with vipassana. They will help to lift us up when our spirits
are low.

If we in turn consider the energy factor, we find that it can be stirred up by contemplation of the eight bases of urgency (*samvega vatthu*). These are: birth, old age, sickness, death, suffering in the woeful worlds, the round of suffering as rooted in the past, the round of suffering as rooted in the future, and the round of suffering in the search for food in the present.

One who does these contemplations will definitely stir up energy for striving towards the end of suffering.

May you strive on zealously and never stall in your effort until you reach that final emancipation, Nibbana.

Practical Vipassana Meditation Exercises

Mahasi Sayadaw

The following is a talk given by the Venerable Mahasi Sayadaw Agga Maha Pandita U Sobhana to his disciples on their induction into vipassana meditation at the Sasana Yeiktha Meditation Centre, Yangon, Myanmar. It was translated from the Burmese by U Nyi Nyi.

The practice of vipassana or insight meditation is the effort made by the meditators to understand correctly the nature of the psycho-physical phenomena taking place in their own bodies. Physical phenomena are the things or objects that one clearly perceives around one. The whole of one's body that one clearly perceives constitutes a group of material qualities (*rupa*). Physical or mental phenomena are acts of consciousness or awareness (*nama*). These (*nama-rupa*)—are clearly perceived to be happening whenever they are seen, heard, smelt, tasted, touched, or thought of. We must make ourselves aware of them by observing them and noting thus: "seeing, seeing," "hearing, hearing," "smelling, smelling," "tasting, tasting," "touching, touching" or "thinking, thinking."

Every time one sees, hears, smells, tastes, touches, or thinks, one should make a note of the fact. But in the beginning of one's practice, one cannot make a note of every one of these happenings. One should, therefore, begin with noting those happenings that are conspicuous and easily perceivable.

With every act of breathing, the abdomen rises and falls—that movement is always evident. This is the material quality known as *vayodhatu* (the element of motion). One should begin by noting this movement, which may be done by the mind intently observing the abdomen. You will find the abdomen rising when you breathe in, and falling when you breathe out. The rising should be noted mentally as "rising" and the falling as "falling." If the movement is not evident by just noting it mentally, keep touching the abdomen with the palm of your hand. Do not alter the manner of your breathing; neither slow it down nor make it faster. Do not breathe too vigorously either. You will tire if you change the manner of your breathing. Breathe steadily as usual and note the "rising" and "falling" of the abdomen as they occur. Note it mentally, not verbally.

In vipassana meditation, what you name or say does not matter. What really matters is to know or perceive. While noting the "rising" of the abdomen, do so from the beginning to the end of the movement just as if you are seeing it with your eyes. Do the same with the "falling" movement. Note the "rising" movement in such a way that your awareness of it is concurrent with the movement itself. The movement and the mental awareness of it should coincide in the same way as a stone that is thrown hits the target. Similarly, with the "falling" movement.

Your mind may wander elsewhere while you are noting the abdominal movement. This must be noted by mentally saying "wandering, wandering." When this has been noted once or twice, the mind stops wandering, in which case you go back to noting the "rising" and "falling" of the abdomen. If you imagine meeting somebody, note as "meeting, meeting." Then go back to the "rising" and "falling" of the abdomen. If you imagine meeting and talking to somebody, note as "talking, talking."

In short, whatever thoughts or reflections occur, they should be noted. If you imagine, note as "imagining." If you think, note as "thinking." If you perceive, "perceiving." If you reflect, "reflecting." If you feel happy, "happy." If you feel bored, "bored." If you feel glad,

"glad." If you feel disheartened, "disheartened." Noting all these acts of consciousness is called cittanupassana.

If we fail to note these acts of consciousness, we tend to identify them with a person or individual. We tend to think that it is "I" who is imagining, thinking, planning, knowing (or perceiving). We think that there is a person who, from childhood onwards, has been living and thinking. Actually, no such person exists. There are instead only these continuing and successive acts of consciousness. That is why we have to note these acts of consciousness and know them for what they are. That is why we have to note each and every act of consciousness as it arises. When so noted, it tends to disappear. We then go back to noting the "rising" and "falling" of the abdomen.

When you have sat meditating for some time, sensations of stiffness and heat will arise in your body. These are to be noted carefully too. Similarly, with sensations of pain and tiredness. All of these sensations are *dukkhavedana* (feelings of unsatisfactoriness) and noting them is vedananupassana. Failure or omission to note these sensations will make you think, "I am stiff, I am feeling hot, I am in pain, I was alright a moment ago. Now, I am uneasy with these unpleasant sensations." The identification of these sensations with the ego is a mistake. There is really no "I" involved, only a succession of one new unpleasant sensation after another.

It is just like a continuous succession of new electrical impulses that light up the lamps. Every time unpleasant contacts are encountered in the body, unpleasant sensations arise one after another. These sensations should be carefully and intently noted, whether they are sensations of stiffness, heat or pain. In the beginning of the meditators' practice, these sensations may tend to increase and lead to desire to change their posture. The desire should be noted, after which the meditators should go back to noting the sensations of stiffness, heat, etc.

"Patience leads to Nibbana," as the saying goes. This saying is most relevant in the effort to meditate. One must be patient in meditation. If one shifts or changes one's posture too often—because one cannot be patient with the sensation of stiffness or heat that arises—*samadhi* (good concentration) cannot develop.

If samadhi cannot develop, insight cannot result and there cannot be attainment of Magga (the path that leads to Nibbana), Phala (the fruit of that path) and Nibbana. That is why patience is needed in meditation. It is mostly being patient with unpleasant sensations in the body like stiffness, sensations of heat and pain, and other sensations that are hard to bear. One should not immediately give up one's meditation on the appearance of such sensations and change one's meditation posture. One should go on patiently, just noting "stiffness, stiffness" or "hot, hot." Moderate sensation of these kinds will disappear if one goes on noting them patiently. When concentration is good and strong, even intense sensation tends to disappear. One then reverts to noting the "rising" and "falling" of the abdomen.

One will, of course, have to change one's posture if the sensations do not disappear even after one has noted them for a long time, and if on the other hand, they become unbearable. One should then begin noting as "wishing to change, wishing to change." If the arm rises, note as "rising, rising." If it moves, note as "moving, moving." This change should be made gently and noted as "rising, rising" "moving, moving" and "touching, touching."

If the body sways, "swaying, swaying." If the foot rises, "rising, rising." If it moves, "moving, moving." If it drops, "dropping, dropping." If there is no change, but only static rest, go back to noting the "rising" and "falling" of the abdomen. There must be no intermission in between, only continuity between a preceding act of noting and a succeeding one, between a preceding samadhi (state of concentration) and a succeeding one, between a preceding act of intelligence and a succeeding one. Only then will there be successive and ascending stages of maturity in the meditator's state of intelligence. *Magga* and *Phala ñana* (knowledge of the path and its fruition) are attained only when there is this kind of gathering momentum. The meditative process is like that of producing fire by energetically and unremittingly rubbing two sticks of wood together so as to attain the necessary intensity of heat for the flame to arise.

In the same way, the noting in vipassana meditation should be continual and unremitting, without any resting interval between acts of noting whatever phenomena may arise. For instance, if a sensation of itchiness intervenes and the meditator desires to scratch because it is hard to bear, both the sensation and the desire to get rid of it should be noted, without immediately getting rid of the sensation by scratching.

If one goes on perseveringly noting thus, the itchiness generally disappears, in which case one reverts to noting the "rising" and "falling" of the abdomen. If the itchiness does not in fact disappear, one has, of course, to eliminate it by scratching. But first, the desire to do so should be noted. All the movements involved in the process of eliminating this sensation should be noted, especially the touching, pulling and pushing, and scratching movements, with an eventual reversion to noting the "rising" and "falling" of the abdomen.

Every time you make a change of posture, you begin with noting your intention or desire to make the change, and go on noting every movement closely. For example, rising from the sitting posture, raising the arm, moving and stretching it. You should make the changes at the same time as noting the movements involved. As your body sways forward, note it. As you rise, the body becomes light and rises. Concentrating your mind on this, you should gently note "rising, rising."

The meditators should behave as if they were weak invalids. People in normal health rise easily and quickly or abruptly. Not so with feeble invalids, who do so slowly and gently. The same is the case with people suffering from backache who rise gently lest the back hurts and cause pain.

So also, with meditators. They have to make their changes of posture gradually and gently; only then will mindfulness, concentration and insight become good. Begin, therefore, with gentle and gradual movements. When rising, the meditator must do so gently like an invalid and at the same time noting "rising, rising." Not only this; though the eyes see, the meditators must act as if they do not see. Similarly when the ears hear. While meditating, the meditators' only concern is to note. What they see and hear is not their concern. So, whatever strange or striking things they may see or hear, they must behave as if they do not see or hear them, merely noting carefully.

When making bodily movements, the meditators should do so gradually as if they were weak invalids, gently moving the arms and legs, bending or stretching them, bending down the head and bringing it up. All these movements should be made gently. When rising from the sitting posture, one should do so gradually, noting as "rising, rising." When straightening up and standing, note as "standing, standing." When looking here and there, note as "looking, seeing." When walking, note the steps, whether they are taken with the right or left foot. You must be aware of all the successive movements involved, from the raising of the foot to the dropping of it. Note each step taken, whether with the right foot or the left foot. This is the manner of noting when one walks fast.

It will be enough if you note thus when walking fast and walking some distance. When walking slowly or doing the cankama walk (walking up and down), three movements should be noted in each step; when the foot is raised, when it is pushed forward, and when it is dropped. Begin with noting the raising and dropping movements. One must be properly aware of the raising of the foot. Similarly, when the foot is dropped, one should be properly aware of the "heavy" falling of the foot.

One must walk, noting as "raising, dropping" with each step. This noting will become easier after about two days. Then go on noting the three movements as described above, as "raising, pushing forward, dropping." In the beginning, it will suffice to note one or two movements only, thus "right step, left step" when walking fast and "raising, dropping" when walking slowly. If when walking thus, you want to sit down, note as "wanting to sit down, wanting to sit down." When actually sitting down, note in full concentration the "heavy" falling of the body.

When you are seated, note the movements involved in arranging your legs and arms. When there are no such movements, but just a kind of stillness (static rest) of the body, note the "rising" and "falling" of the abdomen. If while noting thus, stiffness of your limbs and sensations of heat in any part of your body arise, go on to note them. Then back to "rising, falling." If while noting thus, a desire to lie down arises, note it and also the movements of your legs and arms as you lie down. The raising of the arm, the moving of it, the resting of the elbow on the floor, the swaying of the body, the stretching of legs, the listing of the body as one slowly prepares to lie down—all these movements should be noted.

To note as you lie down thus is important. In the course of this lying down movement, you can gain distinctive knowledge (that is Magga ñana and Phala ñana—the knowledge of the path and its fruition). When samadhi (concentration) and ñana (insight) are strong, the distinctive knowledge can come at any moment. It can come in a single "bend" of the arm or in a single "stretch" of the arm. Thus, it was that that the Venerable Ananda became an Arahant.

The Venerable Ananda was trying strenuously to attain Arahantship overnight, on the eve of the first Buddhist council. He was practising the whole night the form of vipassana meditation known as kayagatasati, noting his steps, right and left, raising, pushing forward and dropping of the feet; noting happening by happening the mental desire to walk and the physical movement involved in walking. Although this went on till nearly dawn, he had not yet succeeded in attaining Arahantship. Realising that he had practised the walking meditation to excess and that, in order to balance samadhi (concentration) and viriya (effort), he should practise meditation in the lying posture for a while, he entered his chamber. He sat on the couch and lay himself down. While doing so and noting "lying, lying," he attained Arahantship in an instant.

Prior to that time, Venerable Ananda was only a Sotapanna (that is, a stream-winner or one who has attained the first stage on the path to Nibbana), before he thus lay himself down. From sotapannahood, he reached Sakadagamihood (that is, the condition of the once-returner or one who has attained the second stage on the path), Anagamihood (that is, the state of the non-returner or one who has attained the third stage on the path) and finally, Arahantship (that is, the condition of the noble one who has attained the last stage on the path). Reaching these three successive stages of the higher path took only a little while. Just think of this example of the Venerable Ananda's attainment of Arahantship. Such attainment can come at any moment and need not take long.

That is why meditators should note with diligence all the time. They should not relax in their noting, thinking "this little lapse should not matter much." All movements involved in lying down and arranging the arms and legs should be carefully and unremittingly noted. If there is no movement, but only stillness (of the body), go back to noting the "rising" and of the abdomen. Even when it is getting late and time for sleep, the meditators should not go to sleep yet, dropping their noting. A really serious and energetic meditator should practise mindfulness as if one were foregoing one's sleep altogether. He should go on meditating till he falls asleep. If the meditation is good and has the upper hand, he will not fall asleep. If, on the other hand, drowsiness has the upper hand, he will fall asleep. When one feels sleepy, one should note "sleepy, sleepy;" if one's eyelids droop, "drooping;" if they become heavy or leaden, "heavy;" if the eyes become smarting, "smarting." Noting thus, the drowsiness may pass and the eyes become "clear" again.

The meditator should then note as "clear, clear" and go on to note the "rising" and "falling" of the abdomen. However, the meditator may perseveringly go on meditating. If real drowsiness intervenes, he does fall asleep. It is not difficult to fall asleep; in fact it is easy. If you meditate in the lying posture, you gradually become drowsy and eventually fall asleep. That is why the beginners in meditation should not meditate too much in the lying posture. They should meditate much more in the sitting and walking postures of the body. But, as it grows late and becomes time for sleep, they should meditate in the lying position, noting the "rising" and "falling" of the abdomen. They will naturally fall asleep.

The time one is asleep is the resting time for the meditator. But for the really serious meditators, they should limit their sleeping time to about four hours. This is the "midnight time" permitted by the

Buddha. Four hours of sleep is quite enough. If the beginners in meditation think that four hours' sleep is not enough for health, they may extend it to five or six hours. Six hours' sleep is clearly enough for health.

When the meditators awaken, they should at once resume noting. The meditators who are really bent on attaining *Magga* and *Phala ñana*, should rest from their noting effort only when they are asleep. At other times in their waking moments, they should be noting continually and without rest. That is why, as soon as they awake, they should note the awakening state of their mind as "awakening, awakening." If they cannot yet make themselves be aware of this, they should begin noting the "rising" and "falling" of the abdomen.

If they intend to get up from bed, they should note as "intending to get up, intending to get up." They should then go on to note the changing movements they make as they arrange their arms and legs. When they raise their heads and rise, the meditators should note "rising, rising." When they are sitting, note as "sitting, sitting." If they make any changing movements as they arrange their arms and legs, all of these movements should also be noted. If there are no such changes, but only sitting quietly, the meditators should revert to noting the "rising" and "falling" movements of the abdomen.

One should also note when one washes one's face and when one takes a bath. As the moments involved in these acts are rather quick, as many of them should be noted as possible. There are then acts of dressing, of tidying up the bed, of opening and closing the door; all these should be noted as closely as possible.

When the meditators have their meal and look at the table, they should note as "looking, seeing, looking, seeing." When they extend their arms towards the food, touch it, collect and arrange it, handle it and bring it to their mouth, bend their head and put the morsel of food into their mouth, drop their arm and raise their head again, all these movements should be duly noted. (This way of noting is in accordance with the Burmese way of taking a meal. Those who use fork and spoon or chopsticks should note the movements in an appropriate manner).

When they chew the food, they should note "chewing, chewing." When they come to know the tastes of the food, they should note "knowing, knowing." As they relish the food and swallow it, as the food goes down their throats, they should note all these happenings. This is how the meditators should note as they take one morsel after another of their food. As they take soup, all the movements involved such as extending of the arm, handling of the spoon and scooping with it and so on, all these should be noted. To note thus at meal times is rather difficult as there are so many things to observe and note. The beginning meditators are likely to miss several things that they should note, but they should resolve to note all. They cannot, of course, help it if they overlook and miss some, but as their samadhi (concentration) become strong, they will be able to note closely all these happenings.

Well, I have mentioned so many things for the meditators to note. To summarise, there are only a few things to note. When walking fast, note "right step," "left step," and "raising, dropping" when walking slowly. When sitting quietly, just note the "rising" and "falling" of the abdomen. Note the same thing when you are lying down, if there is nothing particular to note. While noting thus and if the mind wanders, note the acts of consciousness that arise. Then back to the "rising" and "falling" of the abdomen. Note also the sensations of stiffness, pain and aches and itchiness as they arise. Then back to the "rising" and "falling" of the abdomen. Note also, as they arise, the bending, stretching and moving of the limbs, bending and raising of the head, swaying and straightening of the body. Then back to the "rising" and "falling" of the abdomen.

As the meditators go on noting thus, they will be able to note more and more of these happenings. In the beginning, as their minds wander here and there, the meditators may miss noting many things. But they should not be disheartened. Every beginner in the meditation encounters the same difficulty, but as one becomes more practised, one becomes aware of every act of mind wandering till eventually the mind does not wander any more. The mind is then riveted on the object of its attention, the act of mindfulness becoming almost simultaneous with the object of its attention such as "rising" and "falling" of the abdomen. (In other words, the "rising" of the abdomen becomes concurrent with the act of noting it, and similarly with the "falling" of the abdomen).

The physical object of attention and the mental act of noting are occurring as a pair. In this occurrence, there is no person or individual involved, only this physical object of attention and the mental act of noting occurring as a pair. The meditators will, in time, actually and personally experience these occurrences. While noting the "rising" and "falling" of the abdomen they will come to distinguish the "rising" of the abdomen as physical phenomenon and the mental acts of noting it as mental phenomenon; similarly, with the "falling" of the abdomen. Thus the meditators will distinctly come to realise the simultaneous occurrence in pair of these psycho-physical phenomena.

Thus, with every act of noting, the meditators will come to know for themselves clearly that there is only this material quality which is the object of awareness or attention and the mental quality that makes a note of it. This discriminating knowledge is called *namarupa-pariccheda-ñana*, the beginning of the *vipassana-ñana*. It is important to gain this knowledge correctly. This will be succeeded, as the meditator goes on, by the knowledge that distinguishes between the cause and its effect, the knowledge which is called *paccaya-pariggaha-ñana*.

As the meditators go on noting, they will see for themselves that what arises passes away after a short while. Ordinary people assume that both the material and mental phenomena go on lasting throughout life, that is, from youth to adulthood. In fact, that is not so. There is no phenomenon that lasts forever. All phenomena arise and pass away so rapidly that they do not last even for the twinkling of an eye. The meditators will come to know this for themselves as they go on noting. They will then become convinced of the uncertainty of all such phenomena. Such conviction is called *aniccanupassana-ñana*.

This knowledge will be succeeded by *dukkhanupasana-ñana*, which realises that all this impermanence is suffering. The meditators are also likely to encounter all kinds of hardship in their bodies, which is just an aggregate of suffering. This is also *dukkhanupassana-ñana*.

Next, the meditators will become convinced that these psycho-physical phenomena are occurring of their own accord, following nobody's will and subject to nobody's control. They constitute no individual or ego-entity. This realisation is *anattanupassana-ñana*.

When, as they go on meditating, the meditators will come to realise firmly that all these phenomena are anicca, dukkha and anatta, they will attain Nibbana. All the former Buddhas, Arahants and Ariyas realised Nibbana following this very path. All meditators should recognise that they themselves are now on this Satipatthana path, in fulfilment of their wish for attainment of *Magga ñana* (knowledge of the path), *Phala ñana* (knowledge of the fruition of the path) and Nibbana-dhamma and following the ripening of their parami (perfection of virtue). They should feel glad at this and at the prospect of experiencing the noble kind of samadhi (tranquillity of mind brought about by concentration) and *ñana* (supramundane knowledge or wisdom) experienced by the Buddhas, Arahants and Ariyas and which they themselves have never experienced before.

It will not be long before they will experience for themselves the *Magga ñana*, *Phala ñana* and Nibbana-dhamma experienced by the Buddhas, Arahants and Ariyas. As a matter of fact, these may be experienced in the space of a month or of twenty or fifteen days of their meditational practice. Those whose parami is exceptional may experience these dhammas even within seven days.

The meditators should therefore rest content in the faith that they will attain these dhammas in the time specified above, that they will be freed of *sakkaya-ditthi* (ego-belief) and *vicikiccha* (doubt or uncertainty) and be saved from the danger of rebirth in the nether worlds. They should go on with their meditational practice in this faith.

May you all be able to practise meditation well and quickly attain that Nibbana which the Buddhas, Arahants and Ariyas have experienced.

Sadhu! Sadhu! Sadhu!

The Foundations of Mindfulness

Translated by Nyanasatta Thera

Thus have I heard. At one time the Blessed One was living among the Kurus, at Kammasadamma, a market town of the Kuru people. There the Blessed One addressed the bhikkhus thus: "Monks," and they replied to him, "Venerable Sir." The Blessed One spoke as follows:

This is the only way, monks, for the purification of beings, for the overcoming of sorrow and lamentation, for the destruction of suffering and grief, for reaching the right path, for the attainment of Nibbana. namely the four Foundations of Mindfulness. What are the four?

Herein (in this teaching) a monk lives contemplating the body in the body,[1] ardent, clearly comprehending and mindful, having overcome, in this world, covetousness and grief; he lives contemplating feelings in feelings, ardent, clearly comprehending and mindful, having overcome, in this world, covetousness and grief; he lives contemplating consciousness in consciousness,[2] ardent, clearly comprehending and mindful, having overcome, in this world, covetousness and grief; he lives contemplating mental objects in mental objects,[2] ardent, clearly comprehending, having overcome, in this world, covetousness and grief.

THE CONTEMPLATION OF THE BODY

1 **Mindfulness of Breathing**

And how does a monk live contemplating the body in the body?

Herein, monks, a monk having gone to the forest, to the foot of a tree or to an empty place, sits down, with his legs crossed, keeps his body erect and his mindfulness alert.[3]

Ever mindful he breathes in, and mindful he breathes out. Breathing in a long breath, he knows "I am breathing in a long breath;" breathing out a long breath, he knows "I am breathing out a long breath;" breathing in a short breath, he knows "I am breathing in a short breath;" breathing out a short breath, he knows "I am breathing out a short breath."

"Experiencing the whole (breath-) body, I shall breathe in," thus he trains himself. "Experiencing the whole (breath-) body, I shall breathe out," thus he trains himself. "Calming the activity of the (breath-) body, I shall breathe in," thus he trains himself. "Calming the activity of the (breath-) body, I shall breathe out," thus he trains himself.

Just as a skilful turner or turner's apprentice, making a long turn, knows "I am making a long turn," or making a short turn, knows "I am making a short turn," just so the monk, breathing in a long breath, knows "I am breathing in a long breath;" breathing out a long breath, knows "I am breathing out a long breath;" breathing in a short breath, knows "I am breathing in a short breath;" breathing out a short breath, knows "I am breathing out a short breath." "Experiencing the whole (breath-) body, I shall breath in," thus he trains himself. "Experiencing the whole (breath) body, I shall breathe out," thus he trains himself. "Calming the activity of the (breath-) body, I shall breathe in," thus he trains himself. "Calming the activity of the (breath-) body, I shall breathe out," thus he trains himself.

Thus he lives contemplating the body in the body internally, or he lives contemplating the body in the body externally, or he lives contemplating the body in the body internally and externally.[4] He lives contemplating originations-factors[5] in the body, or he lives contemplating dissolution-factors in the body,[6] or he lives contemplating origination-and-dissolution factors[7] in the body. Or his mindfulness is established with the thought: "The body exists,"[8] to the extent necessary just for knowledge and mindfulness, and he lives detached,[9] and clings to naught in the world. Thus also, monks, a monk lives contemplating the body in the body.

2 The Postures of the Body

And further, monks, a monk knows when he is going "I am going;" he knows when he is standing "I am standing;" he knows when he is sitting "I am sitting;" he knows when he is lying down "I am lying down;" or just as his body is disposed so he knows it.

§ Thus he lives contemplating the body in the body internally, or he lives contemplating the body in the body externally, or he lives contemplating the body in the body internally and externally. He lives contemplating origination-factors in the body, or he lives contemplating dissolution-factors in the body, or he lives contemplating origination-and-dissolution-factors in the body.[10] Or his mindfulness is established with the thought: "The body exists," to the extent necessary just for knowledge and mindfulness, and he lives detached, and clings to naught in the world. Thus also, monks, a monk lives contemplating the body in the body. §

3 Mindfulness with Clear Comprehension

And further, monks, a monk, in going forward and back, applies clear cpmprehension; in looking straight on and looking away, he applies clear comprehension; in bending and in stretching, he applies clear comprehension; in wearing robes and carrying the bowl he applies clear comprehension; in eating, drinking, chewing and savouring, he applies clear comprehension; in attending to the calls of nature, he applies clear comprehension; in walking, in standing, in sitting, in falling asleep, in walking, in speaking and in keeping silence, he applies clear comprehension.

§ Thus he lives contemplating the body in the body...

4 The Reflection on the Repulsives of the Body

And further, monks, a monk reflects on this very body enveloped by the skin and full of manifold impurity, from the soles, up, and from the top of the head-hair down, thinking thus: "There are in this body, hair of the head, hair of the body, nails, teeth, skin, flesh, sinews, bones, marrow, kidney, heart, liver, midriff, spleen, lungs, intestines, mesentery, gorge, faeces, bile, phlegm, pus, blood, sweat, fat, tears, grease, saliva, nasal mucus, synovial fluid, urine."

Just as if there were a double mouthed provision bag full of various kinds of grain such as hill paddy, paddy, green gram, cowpeas, sesamum, and husked rice, and a man with sound eyes, having opened that bag, were to take stock of the contents thus: This is hill paddy, this is paddy, this green gram, this is cowpea, this is sesamum, this is husked rice. Just so monks, a monk reflects on this very body enveloped by the skin and full of manifold impurity, from the soles up, and from the top of the head-hair down, thinking thus: There are in this body, hair of the head, hair of the body, nails, teeth, skin, flesh, sinews, bones, marrow, kidney, heart, liver, midfriff, spleen, lungs, intestines, mesentery, gorge, faeces, bile, phlegm, pus, blood, sweat, fat, tears, grease, saliva, nasal mucus, synovial fluid, urine.

§ Thus he lives contemplating the body in the body...

5 The Reflection on the Material Elements

And further, monks, a monk reflects on this very body, however it be placed or disposed, by way of the material elements: "There are in this body the element of earth, the element of water, the element of fire, the element of wind."[11]

Just as if, monks, a clever cow-butcher or his apprentice, having slaughtered a cow and divided it into portions, should be sitting at the junction of four high road, in the same way, a monk reflects on this very body, as it is placed or disposed, by way of the material elements: "There are in this body the elements of earth, water, fire and wind."

§ Thus he lives contemplating the body in the body...

6 The Nine Cemetery Contemplations

1   And further, monks, as if a monk sees a body dead one, two, or three days, swollen, blue and festering, thrown in the charnel ground, he then applies this perception to his own body thus: "Verily, also my own body is of the same nature; such it will become and will not escape it."

Thus he lives contemplating the body in the body internally, or lives comtemplating the body in the body externally or lives contemplating the body in the body internally and externally. He lives contemplating origination-factors in the body, or he lives contemplating dissolution-factors in the body, or he lives contemplating origination-and-dissolution-factors in the body. Or his mindfulness is established with the thought: "The body exists," to the extent necessary just for knowledge and mindfulness, and he lives independent, and clings to naught in the world. Thus also, monks, a monk lives contemplating the body in the body.

2   And further, monks, as if a monk sees a body thrown in the charnel ground, being eaten by crows, hawks, vultures, dogs, jackals or by different kinds of worms, he then applies this perception to his own body thus: "Verily, also my own body is of the same nature; such it will become and will not escape it."

§ Thus he lives contemplating the body in the body...

3   And further, monks, as if a monk sees a body thrown in the charnel ground and reduced to a skeleton with some flesh and blood attached to it, held together by the tendons, he then applies this perception to his own body thus: "Verily, also my own body is of the same nature; such it will become and will not escape it."

§ Thus he lives contemplating the body in the body...

4   And further, monks, as if a monk sees a body thrown in the charnel ground and reduced to a skeleton, blood-be-smeared and without flesh, held together by the tendons, he then

applies this perception to his own body thus: "Verily, also my own body is of the same nature; such it will become and will not escape it."

§ Thus he lives contemplating the body in the body...

5 And further, monks, as if a monk sees a body thrown in the charnel ground and reduced to a skeleton without flesh and blood, held together by the tendons, he then applies this perception to his own body thus: "Verily, also my own body is of the same nature; such it will become and will not escape it."

§ Thus he lives contemplating the body in the body...

6 And further, monks, as if a monk sees a body thrown in the charnel ground and reduced to disconnected bones, scattered in all directions—here a bone of the hand, there a bone of the foot, a shin bone, a thigh bone, the pelvis, spine and skull, he then applies this perception to his own body thus: "Verily, also my own body is of the same nature; such it will become and will not escape it."

§ Thus he lives contemplating the body in the body...

7 And further, monks, as if a monk sees a body thrown in the charnel ground, reduced to bleached bones of conch-like colour, he then applies this perception to his own body thus: "Verily, also my own body is of the same nature; such it will become and will not escape it."

§ Thus he lives contemplating the body in the body...

8 And further, monks, as if a monk sees a body thrown in the charnel ground, reduced to bones, more than a year-old, lying in a heap, he then applies this perception to his own body thus: "Verily, also my own body is of the same nature; such it will become and will not escape it."

§ Thus he lives contemplating the body in the body...

9 And further, monks, as if a monk sees a body thrown in the charnel ground, reduced to bones gone rotten and become dust, he then applies this perception to his own body thus:

"Verily, also my own body is of the same nature; such it will become and will not escape it."

Thus he lives contemplating the body in the body internally, or he lives contemplating the body in the body externally, or he lives contemplating the body in the body internally and externally. He lives contemplating origination-factors in the body, or he lives contemplating dissolution-factors in the body, or he lives contemplating origination-dissolution-factors in the body. Or his mindfulness is established with the thought: "The body exists," to the extent necessary just for knowledge and mindfulness, and he lives detached, and clings to naught in the world. Thus also, monks, a monk lives contemplating the body in the body.

THE CONTEMPLATION OF FEELING

And how, monks, does a monk live contemplating feelings in feelings?

Herein, monks, a monk when experiencing a pleasant feeling knows "I experience a pleasant feeling;" when experiencing a painful feeling, he knows "I experience a painful feeling;" when experiencing a neither-pleasant-nor-painful feeling, he knows "I experience a neither-pleasant-nor-painful feeling." When experiencing a pleasant worldly feeling, he knows "I experience a pleasant worldly feeling;" when experiencing a pleasant spiritual feeling, he knows "I experience a pleasant spiritual feeling;" when experiencing a painful worldly feeling, he knows "I experience a painful worldly feeling;" when experiencing a painful spiritual feeling, he knows "I experience a painful spiritual feeling;" when experiencing a neither-pleasant-nor-painful worldly feeling, he knows "I experience a neither-pleasant-nor-painful worldly feeling," when experiencing a neither-pleasant-nor-painful spiritual feeling, he knows "I experience a neither pleasant nor painful spiritual feeling."

Thus he lives contemplating feelings in feelings internally, or he lives contemplating feelings in feelings externally, or he lives contemplating feelings in feelings internally and externally. He lives contemplating origination-factors in feelings, or he lives contemplating dissolution-factors in feelings, or he lives contemplating origination-and-dissolution factors in feelings.[12] Or his mindfulness is established with the thought, "Feeling exists," to the extent necessary just for knowledge and mindfulness, and he lives detached, and clings to naught in the world. Thus, monks, a monk lives contemplating feelings in feelings.

THE CONTEMPLATION OF CONSCIOUSNESS

And how, monks, does a monk lives contemplating consciousness in consciousness?

Herein, monks, a monk knows the consciousness with lust, as with lust; the consciousness without lust, as without lust; the consciousness with hate, as with hate; the consciousness without hate, as without hate; the consciousness with ignorance, as with ignorance; the consciousness without ignorance, as without ignorance; the shrunken state of consciousness as the shrunken state;[13] the distracted state of consciousness as the distracted state;[14] the developed state of consciousness, as the developed state;[15] the undeveloped state of consciousness as the undeveloped state;[16] the state of consciousness with some other mental state superior to it, as the state with something mentally higher;[17] the state of consciousness with no other mental state superior to it, as the state with nothing mentally higher;[18] the concentrated state of consciousness as the concentrated state; the unconcentrated state of consciousness as the unconcentrated state; the freed state of consciousness as the freed state;[19] and the unfreed state of consciousness as the unfreed.

Thus he lives contemplating consciousness in consciousness internally, or he lives contemplating consciousness in consciousness externally, or he lives contemplating consciousness in consciousness internally and externally. He lives contemplating origination-factors in consciousness, or he lives contemplating dissolution-factors in consciousness, or he lives contemplating origination-and-dissolution factors in consciousness.[20] Or his mindfulness is established with the thought, "Consciousness exists," to the extent necessary just for knowledge and mindfulness, and he lives detached, and clings to naught in the world. Thus, monks, a monk lives contemplating consciousness in consciousness.

THE CONTEMPLATION OF MENTAL OBJECTS

1 The Five Hindrances

And how, monks, does a monk live contemplating mental objects in mental objects?

Herein, monks, a monk lives contemplating mental objects in the mental objects of the five hindrances.

How monks, does a monk live contemplating mental objects in the mental objects of the five hindrances?

Herein, monks, when sense-desire is present, a monk knows "There is sense-desire in me" or when sense-desire is not present, he knows "There is no sense-desire in me." He knows how the arising of the non-arisen sense-desire comes to be; he knows how the abandoning of the arisen sense-desire comes to be; and he knows how the non-arising in the future of the abandoned sense-desire comes to be.

When anger is present, he knows "There is anger in me" or when anger is not present, he knows "There is no anger in me." He knows how the arising of the non-arisen anger comes to be; he knows how the abandoning of the arisen anger comes to be; and he knows how the non-arising in the future of the abandoned anger comes to be.

When sloth and torpor are present, he knows "There are sloth and torpor in me," or when sloth and torpor are not present, he knows "There are no sloth and torpor in me." He knows how the arising of the non-arisen sloth and torpor comes to be; he knows how the abandoning of the arisen sloth and torpor comes to be; and he knows how the non-arising in the future of the abandoned sloth and torpor comes to be.

When agitation and scruples are present, he knows "There are agitation and scruples in me" or when agitation and scruples are not present, he knows "There are no agitation and scruples in me." He knows how the arising of the non-arisen agitation and scruples comes to be; he knows how the abandoning of the arisen agitation and scruples comes to be; and he knows how the non-arising in the future of the abandoned agitation and scruples comes to be.

When doubt is present, he knows "There is doubt in me," or when doubt is not present, he knows "There is no doubt in me." He knows how the arising of the non-risen doubt comes to be; and he knows how the non-rising in the future of the abandoned doubt comes to be.

Thus he lives contemplating mental objects in mental objects internally, or he lives contemplating mental objects in mental objects externally, or he lives contemplating mental objects in mental objects internally and externally. He lives contemplating origination-factors in mental objects, or he lives contemplating dissolution factors in mental objects, or he lives contemplating origination-and-dissolution factors in mental objects.[21] Or his mindfulness is established with the thought, "Mental objects exist," to the extent necessary just for knowledge and mindfulness, and he lives detached, and clings to naught in the world. Thus also, monks, a monk lives contemplating mental objects in the mental objects of the five hindrances.

2 The Five Aggregates of Clinging

And further, monks, a monk lives contemplating mental objects in the mental objects of the five aggregates of clinging.[22]

How, monks, does a monk live contemplating mental objects in the mental objects of the five aggregates of clinging?

Herein, monks, a monk thinks "Thus is material form; thus is the arising of material form; and thus is the disappearance of material form. Thus is feeling; thus is the arising of feeling; and thus is the disappearance of feeling. Thus is perception; thus is the arising of perception; and thus is the disappearance of perception. Thus are formations; thus is the arising of formations; and thus is the disappearance of formations. Thus is consciousness; thus is the arising of consciousness; and thus is the disappearance of consciousness."

Thus he lives contemplating mental objects in mental objects internally, or he lives contemplating mental objects in mental objects externally, or he lives contemplating mental objects in mental objects internally and externally. He lives contemplating origination-factors in mental objects, or he lives contemplating dissolution-factors in mental objects, or he lives contemplating origination-and-dissolution factors in mental objects.[23] Or his mindfulness is established with the thought, "Mental objects exist," to the extent necessary just for knowledge and mindfulness, and he lives detached, and clings to naught in the world. Thus also, monks, a monk lives contemplating mental objects in the mental objects of the five aggregates of clinging.

3 The Six Internal and the Six External Sense Bases

And further, monks, a monk lives contemplating mental objects in the mental objects of the six internal and the six external sense-bases.

How, monks, does a monk live contemplating mental objects in the mental objects of the six internal and the six external sense-bases?

Herein, monks, a monk knows, the *eye* and *visual forms* and the fetter that arises dependent on both (the eye and forms);[24] he knows how the arising of the non-arisen fetter comes to be; he knows how the abandoning of the arisen fetter comes to be; and he knows how the non-arising in the future of the abandoned fetter comes to be.

He knows the *ear* and *sounds*... the *nose* and *smells*... the *tongue* and *flavours*... the *body* and *tactile objects*... the *mind* and *mental objects*, and the fetter that arises dependent on both; he knows how the arising of the non-arisen fetter comes to be; he knows how the abandoning of the arisen fetter comes to be; and he knows how the non-arising in the future of the abandoned fetter comes to be.

Thus monks, a monk lives contemplating mental objects in mental objects internally, or he lives contemplating mental objects in mental objects externally, or he lives contemplating mental objects in mental objects internally and externally. He lives contemplating origination-factors in mental objects, or he lives contemplating dissolution-factors in mental objects, or he lives contemplating origination-and-dissolution factors in mental objects.[25] Or his mindfulness is established with the thought, "Mental objects exist," to the extent necessary just for knowledge and mindfulness, and he lives detached, and clings to naught in the world. Thus, monks, a monk lives contemplating mental objects in the mental objects of the six internal and the six external sense-bases.

4 The Seven Factors of Enlightenment

And further, monks, a monk lives contemplating mental objects in the mental objects of the seven factors of englightenment.

How monks, does a monk live contemplating mental objects in the mental objects of the seven factors of englightenment?

Herein, monks, when the enlightenment-factor of mindfulness is present, the monk knows "The enlightenment-factor of mindfulness is in me," or when the enlightenment-factor of mindfulness is absent, he knows "The enlightenment-factor of mindfulness is not in me;" and he knows how the arising of the non-arisen enlightenment-factor of mindfulness comes to be; and how perfection in the development of the arisen enlightenment-factor of mindfulness comes to be.

When the enlightenment-factor of the investigation of mental objects is present, the monk knows "The enlightenment-factor of the investigation of mental objects is in me;" when the enlightenmentfactor of the investigation of mental objects is absent, he knows "The enlightenment-factor of the investigation of mental objects is not in me;" and he knows how the arising of the non-arisen enlightenment-factor of the investigation of mental objects comes to be; and how perfection in the development of the arisen enlightenment-factor of the investigation of mental objects comes to be.

When the enlightenment factor of energy is present, he knows "The enlightenment-factor of energy is in me;" when the enlightenment-factor of energy is absent, he knows "The enlightenment-factor of energy is not in me;" and he knows how the arising of the non-arisen enlightenment-factor of energy comes to be; and how perfection in the development of the arisen enlightenment-factor of energy comes to be.

When the enlightenment-factor of joy is present, he knows "The enlightenment-factor of joy is in me;" when the enlightenment-factor of joy is absent, he knows "The enlightenment-factor of joy is not in me;" and he knows how the arising of the non-arisen enlightenment-factor of joy comes to be, and how perfection in the development of the arisen enlightenment-factor of joy comes to be.

When the enlightenment-factor of tranquillity is present, he knows "The enlightenment-factor of tranquillity is in me;" when the enlightenment-factor of tranquillity is absent, he knows "The enlightenment-factor of tranquillity is not in me;" and he knows how the arising of the non-arisen enlightenmentfactor of tranquillity comes to be, and how perfection in the development of the arisen enlightenmentfactor of tranquillty comes to be.

When the enlightenment-factor of concentration is present, he knows "The enlightenment-factor of concentration is in me;" when the enlightenment-factor of concentration is absent, he knows "The enlightenment-factor of concentration is not in me;" and he knows how the arising of the non-arisen enlightenment-factor of concentration comes to be, and how perfection in the development of the arisen enlightenment-factor of concentration comes to be.

When the enlightenment-factor of equanimity is present, he knows "The enlightenment-factor of equanimity is in me;" when the enlightenment-factor of equanimity is absent, he knows "The enlightenment-factor of equanimity is not in me;" and he knows how the arising of the non-arisen elightenment-factor of equanimity comes to be, and how perfection in the development of the arisen enlightenment-factor of equanimity comes to be.

Thus he lives contemplating mental objects in mental objects internally, or he lives contemplating mental objects in mental objects externally, or he lives contemplating mental objects in mental objects internally and externally. He lives contemplating origination-factors in mental objects, or he lives contemplating dissolution factors in mental objects, or he lives contemplating origination-and-dissolution factors in mental objects.[26] Or his mindfulness is established with the thought, "Mental objects exist," to the extent necessary just for knowledge and mindfulness, and he lives detached, and clings to naught in the world. Thus, monks, a monk lives contemplating mental objects in the mental objects of the seven factors of enlightenment.

5 The Four Noble Truths

And further, monks, a monk lives contemplating mental objects in the mental objects of the four noble truths.

How, monks, does a monk live contemplating mental objects in the mental objects of the four noble truths?

Herein, monks, a monk knows, "This is suffering," according to reality; he knows "This is the origin of suffering," according to reality; he knows, "This is the cessation of suffering," according to reality; he knows, "This is the road leading to the cessation of suffering," according to reality.

Thus he lives contemplating mental objects in mental objects internally, or he lives contemplating metal objects in mental objects externally, or he lives contemplating mental objects in mental objects internally and externally. He lives contemplating origination-factors in mental objects, or he lives contemplating dissolution factors in mental objects, or he lives contemplating origination-and-dissolution factors in mental objects.[27] Or his mindfulness is established with the thought, "Mental objects exist," to the extent necessary just for knowledge and mindfulness, and he lives detached, and clings to naught in the world. Thus monks, a monk lives contemplating mental objects in the mental objects of the four noble truths.

Verily, monks, whosoever practises these Four Foundations of Mindfulness in this manner for seven years, then one of these two fruits may be expected by him: Highest Knowledge (Arahantship), here and now, or if some remainder of clinging is yet present, the state of Non-returning.[28]

O monks, let alone seven years. Should any person practise these Four Foundations of Mindfulness in this manner for six years... five years... four years... three years... two years... one year, then one of these two fruits may be expected by him: Highest Knowledge, here and now, or if some remainder of clinging is yet present, the state of Non-returning.

O monks, let alone a year. Should any person practise these Four Foundations of Mindfulness in this manner for seven months... six months... five months... four months... three months... two months... a month... half a month, then one of these two fruits may be expected by him: Highest Knowledge, here and now, or if some remainder of clinging is yet present, the state of Non-returning.

O monks, let alone half a month. Should any person practise these Four Foundations of Mindfulness in this manner for a week, then one of these two fruits may be expected by him: Highest Knowledge, here and now, or if some remainder of clinging is yet present, the state of Non-returning.

Because of this was it said: "This is the only way, monks, for the purification of beings, for the overcoming of sorrow and lamentation, for the destruction of suffering and grief, for reaching the right path, for the attainment of Nibbana, namely the Four Foundations of Mindfulness."

Thus spoke the Blessed One. Satisfied, the monks approved of his words.

Satipatthana Sutta,
Majjhima Nikaya, Sutta No. 10.

Notes

1 The repetition of the phrases "contemplating the body in the body," "feelings in feelings," etc is meant to impress upon the meditator the importance of remaining aware whether, in the sustained attention directed upon a single chosen object, one is still keeping to it, and has not strayed into the field of another contemplation. For instance, when contemplating any bodily

process, a meditator may unwittingly be side-tracked into a consideration of his feelings connected with that bodily process. He should then be clearly aware that he has left his original subject, and is engaged in the Contemplation of Feelings.

2 Mind (Pali citta, also consciousness or viññana) in this connection are states of mind or units in the stream of mind of momentary duration. Mental objects, dhamma, are the mental contents or factors of consciousness making up the single states of mind.

3 Literally, "setting up mindfulness in front."

4 "Internally:" contemplating his own breathing; "externally," contemplating another's breathing; "internally and externally;" comtemplating one's own and another's breathing, alternately, with uninterrupted attention. In the beginning one pays attention to one's own breathing only, and it is only in advanced stagges that for the sake of practising insight, one by inference pays attention also to another person's process of breathing.

5 The origination-factors (samudaya-dhamma), that is, the conditions of the origination of the breathbody; these are the body in its entirety, nasal aperture and mind.

6 The conditions of the dissolution of the breath-body are: the destruction of the body and of the nasal aperture, and the ceasing of mental activity.

7 The contemplation of both, alternately.

8 That is, only impersonal bodily processes exist, without a self, soul, spirit or abiding essence or substance. The corresponding pharase in the following Contemplations should be understood accordingly.

9 Detached from craving and wrong view.

10 All Contemplations of the Body, excepting the preceding one, have as factors of origination: ignorance, craving, kamma, food, and the general characteristic of originating; the factors of dissolution are: disappearance of ignorance, craving, karnma, food, and the general characteristic of dissolving.

11 The so-called "elements" are the primary qualities of matter, explained by Buddhist tradition as solidity (earth), adhesion (water), caloricity (fire) and motion (wind or air).

12 The factors of origination are here: ignorance, craving, kamma, and sense-impression, and the general characteristic of originating; the factors of dissolution are: the disappearance of the four, and the general characteristic of dissolving.

13 This refers to a rigid and indolent state of mind.

14 This refers to a restless mind.

15 The consciousness of the meditative absorptions of the fine corporeal and uncorporeal sphere (*rupa-arupa-jhana*).

16 The ordinary consciousness of the sensuous state of existence (*kamavacara*).

17 The consciousness of the sensuous state of existence, having other mental states superior to it.

18 The consciousness of the fine corporeal and the uncorporeal spheres, having no mundane mental state superior to it.

19 Temporarily freed from the defilements either through the methodical practice of Insight (vipassana) freeing from single evil states by force of their opposites, or through the meditative absorptions (*jhana*).

20 The factors of origination consist here of ignorance, craving, kamma, body-and-mind (*nama-rupa*), and of the general characteristic of originating; the factors of dissolution are: the disappearance of ignorance, etc., and the general characteristic of dissolving.

21 The factors of origination are here the conditions which produce the hindrances, as wrong reflection, etc; the factors of dissolution are the conditions which remove the hindrances eg right reflection.

22 These five groups or aggregates constitute the so-called personality. By making them objects of clinging, existence, in form of repeated births and deaths, is perpetuated.

23 The origination-and-dissolution factors of the five Aggregates: for Material Form, the same as for the Postures (Note 10); for Feeling, the same as for the Contemplation of Feeling (Note 12); for Perception and Formations, the same as for Feeling (Note 12); for Consciousness, the same as for the Contemplation of Consciousness (Note 20).

24 The usual enumeration of the ten principal Fetters (*samyojana*), as given in the Discourse Collection (Sutta Pitaka), is as follows: 1 self-illusion, 2 scepticism, 3 attachment to rules and rituals, 4 sensual lust, 5 ill-will, 6 craving for fine corporeal existence, 7 craving for uncorporeal existence, 8 conceit, 9 restlessness, 10 ignorance.

25 Origination-factors of the ten physical sense-bases are ignorance, craving, kamma, food, and the general characteristic of originating; dissolution-factors: the general characteristic of dissolving and the disappearance of ignorance, etc. The origination-and-dissolution factors of the mind-base are the same as those of feeling (Note 12).

26 Just the conditions conducive to the origination and dissolution of the Factors of Englightenment comprise the origination-and-dissolution factors here.

27 The origination-and-dissolution factors of the Truths should be understood as the arising and passing of Suffering, Craving, and the Path; the Truth of Cessation is not to be included in this contemplation since it has neither the origination nor dissolution.

28 That is the non-returning to the world of sensuality. This is the last stage before the attainment of the final goal of Saintship or Arahantship.

Recommended reading

1 The Heart of Buddhist Meditation—*Ñyanaponika Thera* (BPS)
2 The Power of Mindfulness—*Ñyanaponika Thera* (BPS)
3 The Satipatthana Vipassana Meditation—*Mahasi Sayadaw* (BPS)
4 The Progress of Insight—*Mahasi Sayadaw* (BPS)
5 The Way of Mindfulness—*Soma Thera* (BPS)
6 The Seven Stages of Purification—*Ñanarama* (BPS)
6 Seven Contemplation of Insight—*Ñanarama* (BPS)
7 Path to Deliverance—*Ñyanatiloka* (BPS)
8 Living Dharma (formerly known as Living Buddhist Masters)—*Jack Kornfield* (Shambala)
9 The Basic Principles of Satipatthana Vipassana Practice and Other Lectures—*Sayadaw U Pandita* (free publication)
10 In This Very Life—*Sayadaw U Panditabhivamsa* (BPS)
11 Vipassana Meditation Guidelines—*U Janakabhivamsa* (free publication)
12 The Path of Purification—*Buddhagosha* (translated by *Ñanamoli*) (BPS)
13 The Four Foundations of Mindfulness—*Venerable U Silananda* (Wisdom)

Books by the same author

1 Stilling of the Volcanoes *(English & Chinese)*
2 Divine Abodes *(English & Chinese)*
3 Walking Iris *(poems)*
4 The Door *(poems)*
5 Wind in the Forest *(poems)*
6 Funny Monks Tales

Website to Theravada Buddhism/Vipassana

Access to Insight
  http://www.accesstoinsight.org/
  The best Theravada websites containing lots of Dhamma text.

Sadhu! The Theravada Buddhism Web Directory
  http://www.quantrum.com.my/sadhu/
  The best and most comprehensive index to Theravada websites.

Dhamma discussion
  http://www.egroups.com/list/dhamma-list/
  Reputed to be one of the most active and useful discussion group on Theravada Buddhism. Started by members of the Malaysian Buddhist community.

myVipassana
  http://www.egroups.com/list/myvipassana/
  An announcement list for Vipassana meditation retreats in Malaysia.

INSIGHT MEDITATION CENTRES IN MALAYSIA & SINGAPORE

Buddhist Wisdom Centre
> 5, Jalan 16/3, 46350 Petaling Jaya, Selangor.
> ▪ Tel: 03-7568019 ▪ Email: bwc@quantrum.com.my ▪ Web Site: www.quantrum.com.my/bwc/>

Bodhirama Estate (Kuala Kubu Bharu Meditation Centre)
> ▪ Tel 03-3415605 (person-to-contact: Dr Wong/Flora)

Kota Tinggi Buddhist Society (Santisukharama)
> 3, Jalan Bayam 3, Taman Sri Lallang, 81900 Kota Tinggi, Johor.
> ▪ Tel: 07-8838569 ▪ Fax: 07-8836857 ▪ Email: ktba@tm.net.my

Cittasukha Meditation Centre
> 12, Jalan Undan 5, Taman Perling, 81200 Johor Bahru, Johor.
> ▪ Tel: 07-2391540/019-7606727 (person-to-contact: Mr Lim Bon Cheng)

Malacca Buddhassananuggaha Society
> 795–K, Jalan Mas 8, Taman Kerjasama, Bukit Beruang, 75450 Melaka.
> ▪ Tel: 06-2325346 (person-to-contact: Mr Ong) ▪ Email: sassana@pd.jaring.my

Malaysian Buddhist Meditation Centre
> 355, Jalan Mesjid Negeri, 11600 Penang.
> ▪ Tel/Fax: 03-2822534 ▪ Email: mbmc@tm.net.my ▪ Web Site: www.karensoft.net.my/mbmc

Selangor Buddhist Vipassana Centre
> 29B, Jalan 17/45, 46400 Petaling Jaya, Selangor.
> ▪ Tel: 03-7550596

Taiping Insight Meditation Centre
> 96, Lorong 4, Taman Bersatu, Kampung Boyan, 34000 Taiping, Perak.
> ▪ Tel: 05-8052977/05-8084128 (person-to-contact: Ms Lim Lay Hoon) ▪ Email: agganani@tm.net.my

Sabah Vipassana Meditation Centre
> 1st Floor, Lot 30-32, Kian Yap Industrial Estate, Mile 5.5 off Jalan Tuaran, 88803 Kota Kinabalu, Sabah.
> ▪ Tel: 088-427589

Vipassana Meditation Centre (Singapore)
> 5C-5D, Jalan Haji Salam, Singapore 468748.
> ▪ Tel: 02-4453984

ASSOCIATIONS CONDUCTING REGULAR VIPASSANA RETREATS

Subang Jaya Buddhist Association
> Lot 12593, Jalan Kewajipan, SS13 Subang Jaya, 47500 Petaling Jaya, Selangor.
> ▪ Tel: 03-7348181 ▪ Fax: 03-7315262 ▪ Email: sjba@po.jaring.my

Buddha Dhamma Fellowship Association
> 82, 2nd Floor, Jalan Pending, 93450 Kuching, Sarawak.
> ▪ Tel/Fax: 082-333232 / 010-8867299 ▪ Email: m0060@tm.net.my

Website: http://www.egroups.com/list/myvipassana/
An announcement list for Vipassana meditation retreats in Malaysia.

Venerable Sujiva

is a well-known Buddhist Theravadin monk who has devoted his early years to the teaching of *vipassana* meditation in Malaysia. He is also very well-respected by his students for his compassion, skilful guidance and deep understanding of the Buddha's teaching. The Venerable has conducted countless vipassana retreats at the Santisukharama hermitage in Kota Tinggi, Johor, Malaysia since 1982.

Another milestone in the development of his teaching of vipassana meditation occurred in 1996 when he began conducting retreats abroad, particularly in Australia. Since then he has held numerous retreats in Hong Kong, New Zealand, Republic of Czech, Republic of Slovakia, Sweden, Italy and the United States. He has also conducted meditation workshops and discussions during a brief stay in Switzerland in 1999. An Abhidhamma course was also held that year in the United States and Hong Kong.

The Venerable donned the robes shortly after graduating from the University of Malaya with an honours degree in Agricultural Science in 1975. During his monastic training, he practised under several distinguished meditation masters, notably Ovadacariya Sayadaw U Pandita of Burma.

He has authored a number of books on Vipassana Meditation and Buddhist poetry.

*P*rogress in Insight Meditation, ie, the progress of penetration into the three universal characteristic (impermanence, unsatisfactoriness and non-self) is like a growing tree. When a tree grows, it must first gain firm and strong roots. If the root system is not strong, then it cannot support the growth of a tall tree. The roots represent the entire good kamma and morality, etc. Once the tree grows, it does so according to certain levels. The first branches grow, then as it puts out branches at the next higher level, the lower level must expand, and the roots must expand further. When these two levels are more established, then a third level grows. When the third levels grows, the lower two levels must grow further. This means that a proper base of the lower experiences must be developed further before the higher levels can grow. For example, your concentration must last longer and deeper, before you are able to watch more phenomena.

Therefore, when you watch a certain new experience, you have to watch it longer and clearer before you can watch the deeper ones. For the third level to become stronger, the first and second level must become stronger too. You do not forget the lower levels. This means that there will be a constant repetition of the earlier experiences for some time, before a new experience comes. The lesson to be learned is that you must have patience.

DEDICATION OF MERIT

May the merit and virtue
accrued from this work
adorn Amitabha Buddha's Pure Land,
repay the four great kindnesses above,
and relieve the suffering of
those on the three paths below.

May those who see or hear of these efforts
generate Bodhi-mind,
spend their lives devoted to the Buddha Dharma,
and finally be reborn together in
the Land of Ultimate Bliss.
Homage to Amita Buddha!

NAMO AMITABHA
南無阿彌陀佛

財團法人佛陀教育基金會 印贈
台北市杭州南路一段五十五號十一樓
Printed and donated for free distribution by
The Corporate Body of the Buddha Educational Foundation
11F., 55 Hang Chow South Road Sec 1, Taipei, Taiwan, R.O.C.
Tel: 886-2-23951198 , Fax: 886-2-23913415
Email: overseas@budaedu.org
Website:http://www.budaedu.org
This book is strictly for free distribution, it is not for sale.
Printed in Taiwan
20,000 copies; Jan 2004
EN154-3588